MW01627199

KNOWING THE UNKNOWABLE

PUTTING PSI TO WORK

KNOWING THE UNKNOWABLE

PUTTING PSI TO WORK

Damien Broderick, PhD.

Tables and graphs by George Papadakis,
Gary W. Livick and Gavin L. O'Keefe

Surinam Turtle Press
2015

Surinam Turtle Press
an imprint of
Ramble House
10329 Sheephead Drive
Vancleave MS 39565
USA

First American paperback edition

Copyright © 2015 Damien Broderick
Cover art © 2015 Anders Sandberg

ISBN-13: 978-1-60543-861-0

Surinam Turtle Press #57

KNOWING THE UNKNOWABLE

Table of Contents

To the memory of James B. Reswick (1922-2013)
and Lojze Vodovnik (1933-2000)
whom I never met,
but who got me launched on this long, strange trip

Special thanks to Gary W. Livick,
for technical suggestions
that saved my bacon a few times
and some slick Excel work

Introduction

> We need mathematical constructs to understand any aspect of our world... And those figures and equations are beautiful. Like a musical composition, they give life meaning and us the possibility of knowing the unknowable.
>
> *Bones*, season 4, episode 6, by Karinia Csolty (2008)

> He felt as though he were suffering from a negative hallucination, where instead of seeing something that didn't exist, he was failing to see something that did... Whenever he tried to follow the evidence to its logical conclusion, he found many of his long-established beliefs being threatened... It occurred to him that this same situation arose at any time when old beliefs were challenged or negated by new discoveries. That was why old errors died so hard, why new concepts had to beg so long for acceptance. Men would rather destroy their bodies than alter the pattern of their thoughts.
>
> *Occam's Razor*, by David Duncan (1957, p. 149)

This book is a study in one branch of what could be called *fringe science.* Or call it "protoscience," as the open-minded skeptical sociologist Marcello Truzzi proposed.

What's "fringe science"? I mean *the disciplined, scientific acquisition of knowledge at the edge of the unknown*, sometimes even science *over* the edge—learning how to know what is unknown and, allegedly, unknowable. For example, using paranormal forecasting to learn (if only with a certain probability greater than chance, greater than informed expert inference) which stocks will rise or fall next week. Or where and when the next major natural disaster will strike. Fringe science of this kind probes the boundary zone where apparently crazy ideas roam and do battle with established theories. We'll look at some of these just barely thinkable ideas, and their upstart champions.

What I *don't* mean is "folk science"—folk physics, folk medicine, folk psychology, the sorts of unsophisticated models we possess, almost from infancy, concerning the shape of our world and how it works. Superstitions, to use another, less neutral word.

Folk physics thinks that heavy objects fall faster than light ones. (Wrong, unless air resistance slows the lighter ones.) It tells us that if we fire a projectile straight ahead, it will hit the ground *after* another object that's dropped straight down from the same place at the same time. (Also wrong: both fall under the same force of gravity, however far they travel, and hence land at the same instant. And yes, that can be hard to believe, it's so counterintuitive.)

Folk medicine warns us that an expectant mother terrified by a bear is likely to have a child who resembles a bear. Folk psychology imputes agency and intention to the mindless workings of natural forces, so that every hurricane is regarded as proof that supernatural beings are wreaking vengeance for our sins, or that the benefits of ample wealth prove that the rich are virtuous and blessed by heaven.

That sort of thing, though, is not what we'll be discussing.

Admittedly, the zaniest ideas from fringe science are often just as mistaken and ridiculous as folk science. With considerable justice, they tend to be ignored or derided, except by cultish devotees. But some wild ideas, venturing well beyond the current precincts of accepted or canonized knowledge, turn out to form the next great tipping points in our understanding of ourselves and the universe.

Plate tectonics is a classic example: the idea formerly mocked under the names "continental drift" or "floating continents," until it turned out to be the literal truth of our planet's geological history and future. Another is the discovery that most ulcers are not caused by stress and worry but by a bacterium (*Helicobacter pylori* by name) that infects the gut and can be cured quickly by a course of antibiotics. That seemed entirely crazy when first suggested, but in 2005 won its discoverers a Nobel Prize (after they infected and then cured themselves).

Only in hindsight can we be sure that such ideas and phenomena were valuable *fringe* science rather than *pseudo*-science or bogus nonsense—that they are the real deal. Often they start out half-cooked or half-cocked, but eventually prove to be the key to a larger or deeper understanding of the world.

§

Perhaps the fringe science that has proved most prevalent and enduring, perched out there on the rim of accepted reality, is the quest for psychic or paranormal abilities, known collectively as *psi*. Those (if they exist, which most scientists deny, despite the evidence[1]) are capacities to know and do things that orthodox physics declares to be impossible except with the aid of mechanical or electronic aids, or just plain old-fashioned hand-is-quicker-than-the-eye trickery. In this book we shall ask how much sense can be made of psi's outrageous claims, and whether this corner-post of fringe science might be tamed, turned to our advantage, as a reliable and controlled technology.

During recent decades, as trillions of dollars were squandered, as blood poured into the sands of Iraq and the rocky soil of Afghanistan, and global climate change continued its long blight of the world as we know it, and conspiracy theorists with an eye on the Internet teased out baroque hopes of salvation from Illuminati Secrets and extraterrestrial abductors, a handful of fringe scientists closed in on doing for psychic phenomena what Von Braun did for space travel, and Marconi for radio.

By curious irony, the continuing surge of credulous enthusiasm for the occult made this assertion appear at once banal and unbelievable. When the skies allegedly swarmed with rectal-probing UFO Grays and Reptilians, when popular television and radio programs presented mediums and ghost whisperers in a sort of high-tech rerun of the start of the 20th century, there was a tendency to yawn and turn to the sports pages.

If you make a practice of believing six impossible things before breakfast—in line with the White Queen's parodic advice to Alice—paying avid attention to Bigfoot, Mothman, astrology, numerology, Illuminati conspiracies, Satanic black-eyed children, zombies, the latest in apocalypse warnings, and alien abductions, you will end up with an extraordinary quantity of nonsense in your head. It is necessary to constrain our wistful or horrified dreams with skepticism.

Where does this crazy stuff come from? Well, we've evolved as pattern-makers and pattern-seekers. It's the human specialty, stamped into the folds of our brains. And, of course, in an important sense none of us *really* knows what's truly impossible and what merely seems highly unlikely.

---

1. See Broderick and Goertzel, eds., *Evidence for Psi*, 2015.

Our understanding of the world, particularly when it is codified as science, advances by revolutionary lurches. Each dislocation of thought is followed by lengthy, painful consolidation. Eventually, inevitably, a time always comes when some rogue implications of the old, together with an urgent need to account for new wild data, give birth to the unexpected, in drastic, dramatic upheavals.

The hard part in grasping this for most of us is identifying the real paradigm changes and sorting them from the gibberish. And the reason this is hard is because the best tools we have are the global as well as the specialized bodies of knowledge, of evidence-supported theory, accumulated and tested by science—and science is rarely easy, intuitive, or conveyed quickly in any depth by the mass media.

§

Psi, as it happens, is not *new,* not in the way that cosmology's dark matter and dark energy and the accelerating expansion of the cosmos (known for only about a decade and still not understood) are genuinely new and utterly surprising. But unlike those revolutionary concepts, which were swiftly accepted by orthodoxy, fringe science phenomena and theories such as psi remain on the margins to haunt and provoke us.

So how can we tell the difference between fringe science and, say, those brushfire rumors that appear and then evaporate about apocalyptic doom, like the one that was alleged to be forecast by the Mayan calendar for 2012, already largely forgotten? Or an invisible planet that is still supposedly rushing toward the solar system (undetected by astronomers, but named Nibiru by credulous believers), bringing our doom or transfiguration? Here's one good test: *unexplanation,* and the need to avoid it.

Isaac Asimov once drew an astute but amusing distinction between genuine paradigm changing theories and sloppy-minded crackpot silliness. Fruitful new ideas not only explain and even predict the previously unexpected, he pointed out. They also refuse to *unexplain* what is already known. If we find a tree split in half, he noted, we can explain it as due to a flying elephant that must have set down briefly in the upper branches. "Unfortunately, in the process, it *unexplains* everything you previously knew about elephants. So, in seeking an explanation for some phenomenon you should be careful that, in doing so, you don't *unexplain* everything else."[2]

---

2. Cited by Robyn Williams, "Remembering Asimov," *the Skeptic*, Vol. 12, No. 2, 1992, p. 11.

The key question about the propositions of fringe science is whether they are more akin to an invisible flying elephant or to the radioactivity that solved Lord Kelvin's bafflement over the immense outpouring of the Sun's light despite our star's great age. Models of nuclear reactions did more than explain such puzzles; they opened up fresh avenues of investigation, new and sometimes terrifying technologie—and did so without *unexplaining* anything already considered well-established.

Well, that's not *quite* true. Powerful, evidence-supported theories of species evolution by random mutation and natural selection of the survivors certainly *un*explained, with a tremendous echoing clang, the simple scriptural doctrines that humankind was hand-made by divine creation only a few thousand years ago. It also accounted for the frighteningly rapid modification of disease-causing bacteria and viruses. So old mysteries and new were genuinely explained by evolution—not "explained away"—and without the need to *un*explain anything already understood by science, if not by "ancient wisdom.".

So: can the puzzling data accumulated by the fringe science of the paranormal also be explained without unexplaining everything else science has established (in its always provisional way)? This could be done either by demonstrating that these are just ordinary phenomena willfully misunderstood by ardent believers, or by providing a commanding new theory that authentically and satisfactorily explains these oddities while adding to the corpus of what is already understood about the universe.

§

The exercise of science, according to the conventional wisdom famously propounded by Austrian philosopher of science Sir Karl Popper, always begins with a problem, or a puzzle. You respond to the problem by telling yourself a story; that is, by inventing a simplified narrative (or hypothesis) that includes the problem and those bits of reality that seem to impinge directly on the problem area.

Next, on the basis of the story (which probably contains compressed subsidiary stories written in numbers and other efficient symbols), you deduce as many logically consistent consequences as you can. Finally, you return to the world of reality and measurement, and physically test those speculative consequences. If it turns out that your measured results disagree severely with the outcome anticipated by your story, you modify or abandon your invented story and repeat the procedure, until you find a story that matches reality reasonably well—or give it up as hopeless, for now.

How severe must the disagreement be, before you tear up your hypothesis? That's a matter for negotiation. You might feel that any story is better than none. But then stories that are freely invented are easily come by, and usually there will be more than one in competition. In that case, you might wish to stick to the one that fails the fewest tests.

There again, if you are very stringent, you will set rather savage standards up front. If *all* of your invented stories, or hypotheses, fail to meet those standards, you will conclude that your initial problem simply can't be solved *in a scientific way* at this stage. One day, someone might come along with a new slant, and the question can be re-opened in the scientific arena. Until that day, science is obliged to abstain from advancing solutions that are known to be erroneous for that particular problem.

It is a stern prescription, and I'm not sure how many breakthrough discoveries have been made by sticking to it. Of course, it does save people an awful lot of time that might otherwise be wasted on ridiculous ideas. Surprisingly, though, ridiculous ideas can be very entertaining, and have even been known to lead to insights that otherwise might have been ignored, or never discovered.

§

When I was ten years old, I took a book about satellites and space travel to school with me. Caught during a history lesson poring over its illustrations of moon rockets and orbital space stations, I was treated to an outpouring of scorn from my crusty fifth-grade teacher. And this was a school run by Jesuits, famed for their dedication to logic and science.

Spaceships were utterly impossible, he told me angrily.

Rockets would never get beyond the earth's atmosphere, let alone to the Moon or planets. Any scientific credentials the book's authors possessed carried no weight. No, it was all lies and childish foolishness. Science had proved that rockets in space was idiotic fantasy.

Three years later, Sputnik, the first artificial satellite, was beeping overhead.

Within 15 years, two men were stamping their fat serrated footprints in the Moon's dust, and the entire world watched it live on grainy television.

Today we are perhaps less dogmatic. Too many impossibilities have clamored from the front pages of our newspapers. Test-tube babies and cloned animals and synthetic genomes compiled in the lab; word-processing and spreadsheet computer programs that threw trained white-collar workers on the trash heap of redundancy; computers that control automated laboratories on the red surface of Mars, looking for alien life.

Most bizarre of all, maybe, secret multi-million dollar government programs in the USA and Russia that with a surprising measure of success investigated, developed and utilized remote viewing by trained military psychics.[3] (And were then shut down in the US for the most unconvincing reasons.)

Yet some ideas remain absolutely unthinkable, except as science fiction. They might titillate us on the computer monitor or the Imax, but surely no-one takes them seriously. Time travel, for example. We have become accustomed to voyages in space, and find it hard to believe how ridiculous that proposition seemed only half a century ago (except for the gullible naysayers who just know their bones that it's all a giant hoax perpetrated by the Illuminati). But despite *The Terminator* and *The Time Traveler's Wife* and all the other movies, we *know* that nothing can pass backward through time. Hasn't science proved that time travel is childish fantasy?

Well, not quite. On the contrary—grotesque as it might seem—the movement of particles and energy backwards as well as forwards in time is consistent with the basic symmetries of modern physics. What's more, it might prove to be the key to quantum entanglement.[4]

By harnessing such forces—proposed not by occultists, but by orthodox scientists—a technology of the future might well find that time-bending forces have been tapped already, by psychics present and past.

---

3. See Edwin May, et al., *ESP WARS: East and West*, 2014.
4. See the excellently clear and accessible discussion of this approach to time in "The Quantum Mechanics of Fate," by George Musser (Jan 2014) at http://nautil.us/issue/9/time/the-quantum-mechanics-of-fate. Musser notes: "Physicists as renowned as John Wheeler, Richard Feynman, Dennis Sciama, and Yakir Aharonov have speculated that causality is a two-headed arrow and the future might influence the past. Today, the leading advocate of this position is Huw Price, a University of Cambridge philosopher who specializes in the physics of time. 'The answer to the question, "Could the world be such that we do have a limited amount of control over the past," ' Price says, 'is yes.' What's more, Price and others argue that the evidence for such control has been staring at us for more than half a century." Musser and Price are referring to entanglement, but the evidence is even stronger from laboratory parapsychology.

In presenting this speculation, we will look at the cogent evidence from current scientific theories and ESP research. As noted, there is a mandate in modern physics for the idea of time reversal, of matter or energy travelling into the past, or at least of a more abstract kind of retrocausality embodied in quantum entanglement. According to the deepest current understanding of the cosmological universe provided by science in the 20th and 21st centuries, begun by Albert Einstein and his colleagues, space and time are bonded together. (The great 17th century genius Sir Isaac Newton held that they were altogether different, time proceeding uniformly everywhere in the universe. He was wrong.) Time and space are not entirely separate categories, but form one unity: spacetime.

By the standards of our common experience, this is a truly shocking discovery. We take it for granted that the physical length of a road is quite a different sort of measurement from the length of time it takes to drive along it. True, we use the same word "length" to denote intervals of both space and time, but this hardly causes us to confuse the two.

Pre-mechanical societies might find the link between space and time less peculiar than we do, though they would be unable to cope with the advanced principles of special and general Relativity theory. People lacking motor vehicles—or even carts and horses—find nothing strange in describing a distant place as "five days' march from here." Without a standardized system for measuring distance, it's simpler to specify an interval in space by translating it into a period of time: the time it takes a healthy person on foot to cover that distance. Granted, that is a psychological observation, not one guided by physics. Yet the theory of Relativity insists that time and space vary under acceleration—not as a metaphor, but actually and measurably. And Relativity is the intellectual framework of our age (alongside quantum theory, with which, embarrassingly, it doesn't quite fit).

§

To summarize our starting point:

Paranormal phenomena such as telepathy ("mind-reading"), clairvoyance (knowing intuitively about distant events), precognition (accurate knowledge of otherwise unpredictable future events), and psychokinesis ("mind over matter") are dubbed, collectively, *psi.* Most scientists still refuse to accept its reality, often without investigating the abundant evidence. At the same time, frustratingly, all too many non-scientists eagerly embrace some extravagant claims of the paranormal even when there's no good evidence for them.

There was a tremendous vogue for such alleged mental or spiritual skills at the end of the 19th century and the early years of the 20th, which fell away with the emergence of the very weird but distinctly *not* fringe sciences of relativity, electronics, nuclear physics and quantum theory. Vacuum tubes, transistors and large scale integrated circuits replaced dreams of mental contact, ectoplasm, Ouija boards and table-rapping by the spirits of the dearly departed.

A surge in mysticism-lite in the second half of last century brought the topics back, often helped along by a whiff of marijuana or a tab of acid, and was lucratively transformed into new age teachings that assured troubled seekers for truth and prosperity that all minds are One Mind, that there was a Secret or two you could use to gain the whole world and improve your soul at the same time, and that you'd better look sharp because the Apocalypse was on its way (again), maybe any year now if those ancient Mayans knew what they were talking about, and who could doubt it?

Not all uses of techniques that were once dismissed as "occult" are worthless. Joseph McMoneagle, first and perhaps premier remote viewer of the long-classified US military Star Gate program, recently described what he had learned about engaging with psi (which I cite with his permission):

> There is a war going on in the mind which involves the Ego which feels it must be in control. When it comes to something apparently paranormal, like Remote Viewing, the Ego will try to take control, and the effort during RV is to challenge that control and deny the Ego.
>
> I meditate with a process called ZaZen—or empty mind meditation. I've been doing it for years. I was filmed for one of the Japanese television programs at a brain and neurological study lab within Nihon University in Tokyo. A professor, Dr. Akio Mori, a physiologist who founded the Japanese Society of Health and Behavior Sciences and has studied meditators for over 30 years, agreed to test my ability to empty my mind prior to a remote viewing. At the time, his lab was one of two in the world with a 122 channel bilateral EEG system. I was placed inside a shielded

room and would respond with numbers one through four when I was entering a specific phase of my viewing process. At (1), I would begin to control my breathing and preparing to meditate; at (2), I would enter my meditation and mind clearing prep for remote viewing; at (3), with an empty mind, I would open to the target—whatever it might be; and at (4) I'd conclude my remote viewing with drawings. All of this was shown on a huge flatscreen TV through the computer system monitoring my 122 channel EEG. The presentation was very cool, since all the different frequencies were in a multitude of different colors. You could see all the different colors and shades going off and on inside my brain.

Right after I said two, the playback of my mind clearing showed all these different frequencies quickly dying out and disappearing from the large screen, to the point that the screen went completely black. I do not think anyone in the room was prepared for that. My wife said many in the room were shocked by it. Of course there was probably lots of activity going on down in the brain stem area or in areas the different channels might not have had the depth to reach; but he said in more than 30 years of studying professional meditators, Mori had never seen that happen with his equipment. This out there on one of the programs which you might be able to find at an Asian store. I have a copy which I've asked permission to extract still pictures from. Professor Akio Mori was impressed enough to take two very rare prints by a very famous Japanese wood cut artist off his wall, that he then gave me.

I can attest that being able to empty one's mind of all the garbage can help significantly when it comes to collecting data; but it takes considerable effort over 30+ years to develop the ability. So, going out and hunting for special people is most appropriate, rather than using for study just anyone volunteering from the street. (email, April 14/15, 2015)

§

So, for a number of decades, a small number of parapsychologists around the world have worried at the psi topic. They used both distinctly conventional tools of science—formidable statistics, laboratory investigations of hypotheses, computerized tests—as well as meditation and directed-intention skills. Sometimes, especially in the USA and the former USSR, they did this with multi-million dollar funding from secretive government agencies. I described much of this still-fringe scientific work in my book *Outside the Gates of Science,* and a technical compendium, *Evidence for Psi*, co-edited with Dr. Ben Goertzel.

But there was another approach to the disciplined search for command of psi, one that was more or less abandoned in the 1970s with the development of espionage-targeted remote viewing of the kind McMoneagle helped fine-tune.

That path was not taken very far until quite recently, as I shall describe in some detail in this book. Or rather, it was repeatedly taken but then abandoned too quickly. Even so, it is possible that, done right, with 21st century tools, this approach to psychic applications (technically, repeated guessing trials with majority vote statistical averaging) might yield abundant rewards without requiring heroic battles with the Ego and the noise of the brain. Ubiquitous cheap computers and the global Internet have provided a foundation for its realization.

But this will not be your father's or your grandfather's ESP, even though these ideas were first explored a lifetime ago and many of its pioneers are already dead or very old.

One: Psi

The method explored in this book is summarized quite neatly in a 1957 paper published by G.W. Fisk and Dr. D.J. West, two notable psi researchers of the mid 20th century. In "Toward Accurate Predictions from ESP Data," they wrote:

> In some previously reported mass ESP experiments... we found that better scores than usual were obtained by taking the majority opinion of a large number of guessers who were all aiming at the same targets. Assuming the majority opinion of a group to be more reliable than the guesses of individual subjects, we thought it might be possible to make use of this principle to increase ESP efficiency. (Fisk and West, 1957, p. 157)

This was not an altogether new approach to using mass efforts at psi winnowed by taking majority votes on the result, but it was very different from the more classical forecast offered in Aldous Huxley's 1923 novel *Antic Hay.* Huxley's Mr. Gumbril mused, viewing his starlings,

> "If we knew a good method of educating and drawing out the latent faculty, most of us could make ourselves moderately efficient telepaths; just as most of us can make ourselves into moderate musicians, chess players and mathematicians... Look at the general development of the mathematical and musical faculties only within the last 200 years. By the 21st century, I believe, we shall all be telepaths. Meanwhile, these delightful birds have forestalled us."

Just four years later, something like Mr. Gumbril's vision was attempted, but it had less resemblance to the "education of a latent faculty" than to the design specifications of a radio telescope. More than 15,000 British men and women jointly tried to identify by telepathy two randomly selected playing cards, during a brief ESP experiment broadcast in 1927 by the British Broadcasting Corporation, under the auspices of the physicist Sir Oliver Lodge, as we'll see in detail in Chapter 4.

This experiment produced 38,877 guesses, massively contaminated by biases. Because the appropriate tools of interpretation had not yet been developed, the experiment was mistakenly written off as worthless. It would languish as such for nearly half a century, until I went back and re-analyzed the data in a small exercise in fringe science.

The ideas I was using had emerged, bit by bit, and in various countries. In 1962, for example, in Czechoslovakia, an attested psychic sensitive named Pavel Stepanek paranormally identified five coded numbers, each of three digits, with perfect accuracy, under the scientific direction of Dr. Milan Rýzl.

It took them 50 hours and 19,350 guesses, as we'll see in detail in Chapter 7.

This is very different indeed from the dreamy, yet controlled, intuition summoned up by the careful protocols of remote viewers, military or otherwise. You can see why this method was abandoned. 38,877 guesses to get misleading answers! 19,350 guesses by one man! It sounds excruciatingly boring, and surely was. Worse, it seems the final brutal encroachment of the machine into the shyest, most guarded recesses of dream.

But sometimes dreams require the machine to bring them into reality. The most surprising feature is that we're surprised. I would not be shocked if commanding the secrets of time turns out to require the latest in technological prowess.

§

It might be no accident that H.G. Wells did not write about a time dream or time viewer, but a time *machine*. Consider again the exploration of space—the wildest of fringe science in its day, as my recollection of early schooldays half a century ago should convince even those of you for whom trips to the moon had already been mothballed before you were born.

Thirty-eight years after Giordano Bruno was put to the torch for his opinions on the plurality of worlds, and other heresies, a certain Bishop John Wilkins published *A Discourse Concerning a New World and Another Planet.* The impetuous ecclesiastic confessed that "I do seriously, and upon good Grounds, affirm it possible to make a Flying Chariot, in which a man may sit, and give such motion unto it, as shall convey him through the Air...'tis likely enough, that there may be Means invented of Journeying to the Moone."

As the centuries ticked by, and experts supposedly established beyond doubt the absurdity of this wistful forecast, there were always a few rogues sufficiently shameless to beguile the public with mad dreams of lunar voyage. Today these scoundrels are hailed as prophets—quite erroneously.

Nearly all of them had missed the point.

Anyone with an ounce of imagination could see the charm in wafting to the moon. Virtually no one appreciated what a stupendous, treasure-devouring, and specialist-intensive job it would be, getting that Flying Chariot one centimeter off the ground.

"The real story of Apollo," NASA's publicists for the Apollo mission proclaimed with perfect justice, "is people. There were 350,000 of them, inventing, fabricating, and testing the hardware, manning the complicated systems..." More than a billion dollars, and that was before a billion dollars became just loose change. Five million working parts. Just to *launch* the Saturn V spacecraft took 550 control-room specialists, backed by 5000 technicians.

Four years later, in 1973, in Australia, 603 women and 353 men jointly identified a coded message not to be created until *one week in their future*. They did it by paranormal means—or maybe by a fluke, nothing better than the long arm of coincidence. There was nothing mystical about this prophecy: the message specified the winners of two horse races run some days after the respondents had completed their guesses. I extracted the forecast from 17,208 consolidated guesses.

Using precognitive extrasensory perception by this means, on demand and reliably, will take the same tiresome, hard-headed technical application as flying to the moon, another ambition that the poets had to pass over to the engineers. Consider this single scarifying detail from Peter Ryan's *The Invasion of the Moon*:

> On 21 May the Apollo 11 Saturn was ready for the first part of its journey to the moon: just over three miles along the 131-foot-wide crawlerway roadbed to Launch Pad 39A... This short piece of highway cost NASA over $24 million, or $1500 a foot. As the crawler carried its precious load with its two 2750-horsepower diesel engines, the roadbed sank several inches of its tracks.

Such gargantuan statistics are often considered distasteful, unseemly. The function they convey might be necessary to lofty human goals, as sewers are, but decorum decrees that they should be buried decently out of sight. Yet without this astonishing complexity, the Flying Chariot could never have attained her Columbian glory.

Similarly, one of the key scientific breakthroughs of the early 21st century was CERN's discovery of the (or a) Higg's particle, the last missing ingredient of what's called the standard model of elementary particles. CERN's immensely expensive and delicate Large Hadron Collider, a 27-kilometer underground ring of superconducting magnets chilled to minus 271 degrees Celsius, accelerates high-energy particle beams close to the speed of light before smashing them together in a blaze of barely detectable shrapnel. CERN's website spells out some of the appalling complexity of that project:

> Thousands of magnets of different varieties and sizes are used to direct the beams around the accelerator. These include 1232 dipole magnets 15 meters in length which bend the beams, and 392 quadrupole magnets, each 5–7 meters long, which focus the beams. Just prior to collision, another type of magnet is used to "squeeze" the particles closer together to increase the chances of collisions. The particles are so tiny that the task of making them collide is akin to firing two needles 10 kilometers apart with such precision that they meet halfway.[5]

This international teamwork cost more than $6 billion to build and $30 million a year in electricity to run the immense device. That's what it takes to track down a Nobel-winning and highly skittish subatomic particle these days.

I suspect that it might turn out to be somewhat the same—although, thankfully, on a vastly more manageable scale—with psi science. Perhaps we are on the edge of just such a revolution. It is possible that the psi analyses documented in the following pages could shift some of the boundaries between fringe science and accepted science.

§

Parapsychology, then, is an interface between psychology and superstition, until now at the extreme fringes of science, but one that is shifting nearer to the realm of technological application. Isaac Asimov, hardly an unimaginative pedant, termed it "a field that is usually the

5. http://home.web.cern.ch/topics/large-hadron-collider

domain of quacks." As yet, it's true, parapsychologists still have not developed a thorough-going science, with a sound theoretical base and a mature body of laws, or codified regularities.

What we do possess are at least two techniques for *using* paranormal capabilities at the modest level of reliability found in many other techniques of applied social science. One of these, increasingly fashionable in the domain of fringe science, is remote viewing, a formalized protocol for getting "unknowable" information via what used to be called clairvoyance, and, later, Ganzfeld or sense exclusion. Since I have discussed the genesis and development of this method in *Outside the Gates of Science*, I will emphasize here a different process—as far as I know, for the first time outside of specialist journals. I'll sketch how it has developed from the early confused hunches of pioneer researchers to a specific set of practical routines.

I will attempt to unfold both a general perspective and step-by-step techniques, directing my discussion to the ordinary non-specialist reader—but I'm not offering a titillating romp through mysteryland. So parts of the book will take moderately concentrated effort and attention. That's what you pay out; what you get is a technique for utilizing human psychic capabilities.

On the other hand, I am not trying to *prove* anything here. I assume that the reality of some psi phenomena is sufficiently well established, and does not benefit by endless further piling-up of data for the sake of convincing skeptics who refuse to look at the mountain of data already gathered. So I will not burden the discussion with calculus or more than a minimum of statistics. All that can be found in the detailed specialist studies in *Evidence for Psi*.

Rather, my approach to readers will be this: Just look these unexpected facts in the eye, in rather the same startled way you would if a potato jumped out of the pot and ran yelping around the kitchen floor.

Leave the detailed scientific analysis to the experts, and meanwhile let's see what practical benefits might arise from this overlooked but still provocative material.

A warning, though (of a gentle kind):

You *will* find some numbers in this book. Tables of them in many chapters. Decimals that are added and changed into percentages and subtracted and turned on their heads. Don't be alarmed. As I just promised, there will be no calculus or anything resembling advanced mathematics, or even strict statistics.

My purpose here is to tell the story of one way in which psi can be used to bring about interesting and even rewarding results in the real world. I want you to read this book for the fun of it, not as a slog through grade-school math.

If your head *does* start to spin, take a break, watch some Netflix, hit Facebook for some laughs and gossip, and come back refreshed for another look. That's the way I cope with this stuff. And if I were writing the book on a blog, I'd add a big jolly emoji face here to reassure you.

§

Some scientists will be offended, no doubt, that such research should be presented to the general public. There are cautionary tales. In 1971, Dr. John Gribbin, then of the Institute of Theoretical Astronomy, Cambridge, England, announced in the scientific press his hypothesis that sunspot activity and the rotation of the earth are linked with the triggering of devastating earthquakes. He received absolutely no response. Yet, if he were right, Los Angeles might have been due for seismic disaster within a few years. (It wasn't, as things turned out.)

The possibility seemed to him worthy of public discussion, so Dr. Gribbin finally co-authored a popular book on the topic. Five years later, he reported: "The *existence* of such odd theories didn't seem to worry the scientists who didn't subscribe to them; what they object to (at least, what a vociferous minority of them object to) is that the ideas should be made available to nonscientists."

The instant his book appeared, there was what he called an almost frenzied response. Yet I believe that Gribbin was right in presenting these fringe science ideas in the public arena. I prefer to take my cue from him than from his hostile critics. The late Nobel laureate Doris Lessing once wrote of parapsychology that "perhaps books on the subject should be got out fast, like dispatches from the battlefield."

Are the implications of psi technologies like remote viewing, and the methods discussed in this book, so disquieting that a profound case can be made for secrecy? Maybe, if that were possible. It is not. The cat has escaped from the bag, especially since declassification of the Star Gate program and the ongoing publication by its scientific director Dr. Edwin May, and his associates, of the research funded by the US government.

But ethicists do have grounds for concern. If the method described in this book were adopted by militaries, intelligence spooks, or activist groups, the impact could be powerful and even horrifying use of psi, conducted by means derived from repeated psychic efforts winnowed by a majority consensus. Here are four such imaginary scenarios. I don't put them forward as realistic or imminent, but neither are they necessarily entirely absurd.

§

On the third floor of the "Citadel," South Carolina headquarters of the new National Security Force's classified Bio-Surveillance Unit, two thousand trained witches lie relaxed and alert on comfortable couches. The vast honeycomb auditorium housing them hums gently with bland Muzak, and the strobes flickering at nine cycles per second make even the nurses drowsy. Beside each couch, electronic equipment monitors the subtle fluctuations in each witch's bio-fields, transmitting data to the adiabatic quantum computer buried 15 floors below.

In Mission Control on the fifth floor, NSF experts watch meters and cut closed-circuit hologram images from one section of the auditorium to another, waiting for the optimum moment to start the search for Thomas Jefferson Chandler, son of the Republican Party's Presidential front-runner.

Operatives from the FBI, CIA and NSA look on with interest. If their own Psi Corps have obtained a lead on the terrorist they are not saying: the politics of empire-building has not changed.

Now a clear tone draws their attention to the display map of the USA. The pursuit program has been initiated.

For each of the witches, deep in alpha tranquility, nothing is real but the sensory bombardment that has begun. Screens flicker with symbols at the edge of visibility. Beyond the Muzak, bursts of sound tantalize the ears. The computer is asking them a question.

With instant reflex, conditioned by months of stinging pain during training sessions, their fingers begin a spastic dance on keyboards placed at their sides. Field-detectors register their EEG, pulse, respiration, the constriction of their bowels. They are hunting Thomas Jefferson Chandler, the adolescent rebel who has deserted his parents' class and speaks now for the urban guerrilla group, We The People.

There has been nothing like this since the protracted hunt in the mid-1970s for Patty Hearst. The stakes are similar: the enemy has been nurtured within the bosom of the ruling elite. He has posted videos on the internet, declaring his apostasy, identifying himself with crippling raids on Google, major media, three financial conglomerates and two nuclear power utilities.

The videos have been yanked and suppressed, but rumors are rife. They must be stopped. His father's hopes of the White House, spearhead of the dreams of millions of conservatives, hang in the balance. Printers and screens blaze with activity. The witches are on the scent.

Mission Control shows a GPS map alive with fleeting dots of light. They come and go randomly for a moment, and then stabilize. A cloud of brilliant points contracts around Colorado, shrinks to Denver. The map's perspective changes, enlarging to show only that single city halfway across the continent. In their honeycomb, the witches view a meaningless pattern of new instructions from the computer, interpreting them below the level of conscious awareness.

The map shifts again, picks out a suburb, a street, a house. The dwelling is shown at good resolution, images borrowed from Google World maps. The computer displays the address on the big screen, and on monitors hundreds of kilometers away. Already, in that distant city, vehicles crammed with armed men are whining toward the house. They will only have to mop up. By the time they get there, Thomas Jefferson Chandler will be dead.

The witches wait in ignorance. From Mission Control, an executive decision is shot to the computers. Lights flicker on screens. The pulse of the strobes changes, slurs, beats at five cycles a second. Captive to the imposed rhythm, the mood of the witches changes. They grow wrathful, knowing nothing of the reason. Their anger is a boiling, impalpable cloud in the huge auditorium. The individual screens flash a final message. That monstrous, mobilized hatred lances like lightning.

At the breakfast table of his Denver refuge, interrupted in the midst of his meal by the angel of death, Thomas Jefferson Chandler stares at his friends in utter surprise as his heart bursts. When he slides from his chair, a moment later, the guerrillas are incredulous. He has always possessed perfect health. They do not yet know about the clotted ruin inside his chest.

In South Carolina, the strobes are flashing now on a beta rhythm, purging the artificial anger, wakening the witches to brisk good cheer. They climb from their couches, chat pleasantly to their support staff, move with disciplined ease into the corridors leading out of the air-conditioned nest. They have reason to be pleased; their program, whatever it was, is reportedly successful.

They will get a week's vacation, with a bonus. And the snows are still fine for skiing.

§

The enormous cobalt expanse of Central Australia's desert sky has darkened, and shadows dance outward from the fire across the barren sand hills. Burly young aboriginal men, faces and bodies scarred by proud rite-of-passage incisions, crouch beside white-haired elders. Only a few years earlier these oldsters were generally to be found slumped outside country pubs in demoralized stupor. Now the old men chant joyfully in the ancient, almost forgotten tribal tongue. They chew a quid of beeswax impregnated with pituri, passing it around the circle.

Now the long, hand-hewn didgeridoos are groaning, their bass tones droning down into a realm of subliminal vibration. The corroboree begins. Its ritual stems from no pure tradition, for the white men destroyed that as thoughtlessly as they broke up the sacred tribal lands. The ceremony is a synthesis from tribal cultures worldwide, constructed lovingly by young black anthropologists, who do not hesitate to incorporate, among other things, elements from Yaqui and other American Indian cultures.

In far off Canberra, the white bureaucrats have acquiesced to the muscle of a gigantic multinational corporation, used a loophole in the Federal legislation that supposedly forbids alienation of tribal territories. The payment they have negotiated for this land is trifling, an insult, but that is beside the point. These lands—stark, denuded of their old ecology—are rich with power and symbolism to the tribe. They are rich, unfortunately, in other ways as well, harboring tremendous lodes of valuable ore.

A German firm has located the deposits by means of a wild statistical anomaly their computers have revealed: that traditional sacred grounds frequently coincide with buried minerals. It did not occur to them that the "power sources" of the aboriginals' Paleolithic magic might be directly related to that fact...

The hallucinogenic pituri has triggered gusts of neurotransmitters coursing now through the brains of young men and old. Dancing begins. Stiff, mimetic movements: the tribe's animal totems gravely telling the cycles of sun, wind, water. Gradually, random movements superimpose themselves on the pattern. Voices cry and mutter in the dark. An old man reads the shifting, subtle oracle, interprets it; a black psychologist stoops, records the dreamy words on a digital recorder. Others graph the prophetic utterances on screen. The fire dies, the dancers slump exhausted, kind hands help the old man to his sleeping place.

In a nearby caravan, several men work with laptop computers to reduce the oracle to precise, quantified instructions. When the sun rises again, they will have a list of stock market maneuvers to send tonight on the shortwave link. The fluctuating fortunes over the next two months of several key stocks have been forecast tonight by the tribe with better than 90 percent accuracy. The aboriginal physicist in charge of the sacred project confidently expects to bring about the ruinous crash of their conglomerate enemy within 10 months...

§

Synchronous weather satellites report an immense flare erupting from the sun's chromosphere. Within hours, gales of electrified particles in the solar wind will be lashing earth's magnetic environment. A military jet rushes a skilled operative from the A. S. Popov group to the Parapsychological Defense laboratories on the Dnieper River in Russianized Kiev. Computer disks, programmed with medical histories, spin. Conditions for psychic sabotage have seldom been more auspicious.

In his great marble mansion in Islamabad, the mad president of Pakistan tosses restlessly in the night. Food riots in Bangladesh enabled the general to engineer his *coup d'état* late in 2019, but the pressures of office and war have somehow interrupted his personal revelations from Allah. He rubs the long wound over his chest, and peevishly demands instruction from God.

He does not know it, but his guardian angels are going into trance in Kiev. Magnetic fields pulse from the generators surrounding the operatives' supine bodies, matching their biorhythms to the known circadian cycle of the general. That data has been ordered carefully since the Pakistani received emergency cardiac surgery six years earlier. The solar storm floods invisibly across the world. Brainwaves continents apart fall into step... and the operatives begin to impose a tailored fantasy on the tired mind of the general.

For the president, the moment comes as a benediction. Willingly, he gives himself up to the revelation. His paranoiac fears and ambitions surge in sympathy with the vision. Enemies may whisper that he invents these disclosures from Allah, and compare him satirically with Idi Amin and Robert Magabi. He has heard these rumors, and they infuriate him; he knows they are not true.

When Allah's messengers depart from his spirit, he rises from the bed in excitement. Now it is all plain. He must send his crack troops across the border, strike at once into the northern provinces of India. He gives no thought to the flimsy, delicate balance of international power, to the hundreds of thousands, perhaps millions who will perish. If he is lighting a powder keg, it is on the instructions of Allah Himself.

The masters of the former Soviet Union, when reports reach them from Kiev, wait with some anticipation for the blow-up. Their games theoreticians claim that China will almost certainly become embroiled in an extended skirmish, easing the pressure on the Mongolian border. A decoration is dispatched to the operatives, and additional funds become available to the Popov group for their important Research & Development program...

§

Locked securely and incommunicado in an Osaka prison for political detainees, a key Japanese women's brigade activist pursues an apparently senseless discipline. For hours after lights-out she remains awake, keeping time by the regular activities of the guards. At one a.m. daily, she clenches first one fist then the other, tightly enough to make blood flow when they puncture flesh. There is pattern in her self-inflicted pain, as though she considers her body a telegraph through which she is transmitting a coded message.

At the same hour, in Tokyo, Sendai, Sapporo, Fukuoka and a dozen lesser cities, close to 12,000 women are throwing coins and matching the random patterns with runes in a modified edition of the *I Ching*. Within minutes, disposable cell phones are ringing in the homes of cell leaders. Information trickles, gushes, becomes a flood as it rises through the levels of organization. Finally a definitive pattern emerges. It is identical with that scored on the prisoner's nervous system by the clenching of her fists.

An ultimatum is sent to Tokyo, commanding the woman's release. It is taken seriously; Cabinet debate the proposal for hours, frightened of the possible repercussions, angered by the presumption of the illegal group. They reject the demand. Four days later, as the prime minister inspects a reinstated US military base, an impossible sequence of short-circuits activates two armed low kiloton nuclear missiles. Detonating to stellar incandescence, the warheads volatilize the Prime Minister, his staff, and most of the military personnel in the area.

Twelve thousand women, sick with anguish and fierce headaches, seek out aspirin and tea before turning to their TV sets and computers to hear the government's reaction to their reprisal...

§

Are these scenarios totally a product of fantasy? I am afraid something like them might prove not be. It is conceivable that the breakthrough to a reliable working psi technology of this kind has already occurred, possibly the hidden offspring of official psi research programs of the USA and the former Soviet Union, or even in some form developed in the enormous, shambling international Internet communities devoted to remote viewing and related topics. The shapes in which it manifests itself probably won't be much like those I have sketched above. But they might not be entirely different, combining collective mass effort with the meditative and remote viewing techniques now so fashionable.

§

More happily, controlled psi techniques also promise unprecedented benefits, handled responsibly.

Many of the world's key ideologies pay token service to the proposition that, in the last analysis, the crucial policies that shape our future are to be adjudicated by the citizenry at large. In practice, those judgments and decisions are reached in private by a small number of extraordinarily wealthy and powerful elites. Our concurrence is generally insured either by restricting our grasp of the options or, more simply, by refusing point-blank to inform us of them.

Has this already happened with some major psi breakthrough? If it has, the world of the future may be far stranger than the global electronic concentration camp envisaged by George Orwell and now coming into existence with computerized surveillance of email, smartphone messages, Google and other searches. But psychic methods of knowing the unknowable might allow us to do the previously unthinkable: run our own lives, and do so cooperatively.

Two: Research

LET US ACCEPT, then (if only for the sake of seeing whether this takes us), that the evidence is sound, that some psychic abilities really do exist. How could they be brought under control, and put to use for human benefit? One place to start, as McMoneagle indicated, is with the obstacles our mental mechanisms place in the way of psi.

Information mediated by psi turns out to be often adulterated with messy personal associations from the unconscious, as well as misleading trains of rush-to-judgment thought and conscious interpretations. Remote viewers have to learn not to be distracted by this mental machinery, but it's not easy. Dr. J.B. Rhine's original purpose in devising the standard ESP deck of 25 symbolic cards (square, circle, cross, waves, star) was to avoid the emotional biases all too evident in experiments using conventional playing cards (King, Queen, Jack, hearts, diamonds, etc).

For many people, the ace of clubs is unlucky, as is the nine of diamonds, and everyone has his or her own select preconceptions about other numbers. No doubt the ESP pack contains its own loaded symbols, and has gathered extra loading during the decades, but it is more neutral than many other sets of symbols or icons.

It's still desirable, though, to further reduce the degree of bias or "noise" wherever possible. One way is to use autonomic reactions, those we are not usually in control of. Currently, good results are coming in from an on-going series of experiments (by Drs. Dean Radin, Edwin May, Dick Bierman, Julia Mossbridge, and others) in what is dubbed *presentiment.* This is a search for *pre-stimulus* activity in the nervous system that's apparently reacting *in advance* to bland versus emotionally loaded targets randomly selected and displayed a few seconds *after* the measurement is taken.

Earlier, the use of EEGs pioneered by Russell Targ and Dr. Hal Puthoff and some Soviets attempted to signal psi-mediated data by monitoring signals in the autonomic nervous system. Another was the discovery of Dr. Stepan Figar of Prague, later elaborated by chemist and parapsychologist E. Douglas Dean (1916-2001), that blood pressure can be altered at a distance by psi intention.

The plethysmograph is a device for registering changes in blood volume as it pulses through a blood vessel. A variety of emotional reactions, such as fear or love, affect systolic blood pressure. If a series of words is presented to a subject, and she reacts strongly to one or two of them, her blood volume will indicate those reactions. The changes are very small, and must be interpreted carefully by an expert, but if a participant is cooperative these autonomic responses can give a fair clue to her subjective reactions.

Mr. Dean, a former president of the Parapsychological Association, based a telepathic monitoring system on this phenomenon. A sender, provided with a list of words known from previous tests to cause strong reactions in the percipient, uses the loaded stimuli to transmit a Morse-coded message. A plethysmograph records the subject's blood volume fluctuations, which are (it was hoped) changes being metered.

It's worth noting that Dean announced his early findings some half century ago, at the First Space Conference of the Canaveral Council of Technological Societies in 1964. If his claims of success for this system had been tested and confirmed that long ago by military or NASA laboratories, those organizations would already have a functioning, reliable psi program. However, psi specialists from the long-secret Star Gate program in the USA tell me they know of no such venture, other than their own, now abandoned by Congress.

§

One more series of experiments from the 1960s must be mentioned, for it attracted the enthusiasm of psychologists generally to a degree not seen since the balmy days of Rhine's early announcements. In 1962, the respected Maimonides Mental Health Center in the USA opened a laboratory for dream research under psychoanalyst Montague Ullman. Two years later, psychologist Stanley Krippner joined the team, and later became director of the project. One of their concerns was to establish whether, as Freud and Jung had asserted, psi can influence dreams. Using EEGs, Rapid Eye Movement monitors and a battery of electronic recording equipment, they found solid evidence that it does.

In their classic book *Dream Telepathy* (1975) which looks closely into the relations between psi data and psychoanalytic factors in dreaming, they concluded: "Our main surmise is that the psyche of man possesses a latent ESP-talent that is most likely to be deployed during sleep, in the dreaming phase. Psi is no longer the exclusive gift of rare beings known as 'psychic sensitives,' but is a normal part of human experience, capable of being experienced by nearly everyone under the right conditions."

Without wishing to detract from their stimulating achievement, it must be pointed out that this avowal went rather in advance of the evidence presented by the team (now long disbanded). They admitted as much themselves in a pre-emptive segment at the close of the volume: "What the experts say." In a useful innovation, the authors circulated the manuscript widely before publication. They cited, without any attempt at refutation, the laconic comment of Dr. D.J. West: "The dream techniques for eliciting ESP produce results which, on statistical standards, are about the same level as the traditional card calling tests."

That is, the team had undeniably shown that psi has its impact on dreams... but not to any greater extent than under waking conditions.

This criticism was actually spelled out by another expert: "Dreaming may well be a favorable factor for extrasensory effects, but it would seem that a clear proof that it is so must await a series of comparative experiments with a waking and a dreaming studies."

§

Paradoxically, the psi approach I'll consider in some detail in this book was the child not of elaborated sleep laboratory studies, or lavish computerized and instrumented projects—provocative and valuable as those have been, and continue to be—but of the classic techniques developed by parapsychology pioneers J.B. Rhine, J.G. Pratt, S.G. Soal and their colleagues on both sides of the Atlantic. Much of our insight into reliable psi application is built on those dogged—and, it must be confessed, often dull—researches. Let us now consider those central findings.

A valuable, authoritative summary was provided decades ago by the late Dr. Robert H. Thouless's survey *From Anecdote to Experiment in Psychical Research* (1972). I shall adopt Thouless (1894-1984) as our guide for the remainder of this chapter, bolstering his cautious resume with more radical assertions, when they seem well-founded, from other sources.

More than forty years ago, Dr. Thouless—Reader Emeritus in Educational Psychology at Cambridge University—was one of the grand old men of parapsychology. A past president of the Society for Psychical

Research, he was involved in psi investigation for many decades, and had close links with J.B. and Louisa Rhine. It was Thouless, in fact, who proposed the neutral term "psi" for the entire realm of paranormal capacities.

From quantitative experiments of the kind he favored, certain distinct psi characteristics emerged to be mapped. They form an interesting and consistent pattern.

From the earliest ESP experiments—mostly card-guessing tests, generally using the Duke laboratory's decks of 25 Zener cards showing a square, a circle, a cross, a star and wavy lines—two "decline effects" were evident. These were instantly fascinating, since they showed that psi responses were subject to regular "cycles," not a feature of random coincidence.

Less happily, they were to prove the major bane of parapsychology, since they operated to the detriment of useful application.

The first is *episodic decline*. During any given structured psi task—such as guessing through one deck of 25 cards—subjects tend to be significantly right (or wrong) more often at the beginning and end of their stint than in the middle. It is usually a temporary effect. When a fresh start is made—if, say, a new deck is produced after a brief rest—performance is almost completely recovered.

In time, however, a second downward slide sets in. "An experimental subject, who showed promising ESP results in his early experiments," Thouless states, "very commonly shows declining scores, which may reach chance levels within a period of months."

Again, this can be no result of sheer coincidence. True, probability theory predicts clumps of high and low scores over a long period, but these are as likely at the end and middle as at the beginning. *Long period decline* manifests itself as a definite downhill trend, as though the psi capacity involved in a given task is gradually being snuffed out. (Psychologist Charles Tart, as we'll see later, offers a learning theory explanation for this effect: the "extinction paradigm.") Eventually success usually recovers, but not on any reliable schedule.

Here, at once, is a principal reason why psi findings have not leapt into practical application. Humans would hardly have reached the moon if it were a feature of rocket ballistics that a given propellant became less and less effective as time went on.

This is not an absurd analogy. Many chemicals, particularly complex synthetic ones, have a short shelf life: they deteriorate if stored. If all rocket fuels decayed so rapidly that the time necessary to test and use a batch was longer than the period it remained stable, no astronaut would trust his or her life to a spacecraft.

To make the analogy more exact, suppose the materials from which any given fuel was made were very rare. In psi research, the "fuel" is each individual's capacity to score with significant variation from mean chance expectation. Once his or her capacity is diminished by long-period decline—at least, in relation to a certain task—it is either gone for good or returns slowly and unpredictably. Indeed, for a long time that was regarded as one of the most suspicious aspects of the claims of continued success by supposed psychic superstars like Uri Geller. On the other hand, certified remote viewers such as Joseph McMoneagle of the CIA's now-disbanded Star Gate project claim not to experience any decline, and the public evidence of their continued success supports them.

Decline is a most deplorable characteristic. It is not unique, however, to parapsychology. The repetition of a task usually leads to learning (which is why children and soldiers are "drilled"—but if the task is unpleasant, what is learned may be the trick of avoiding it in the future.

So why do psi capacities decline? Episodic decline, as Thouless and others pointed out, resembles the U-shaped curve found in rote memory tasks. Try memorizing a long, boring column of numbers or words. You will best remember the beginning, tend to forget the middle, and recall the end moderately well. This comparison is in no way an explanation, since most quantified ESP tasks are done bit by bit and resemble on-going perception more than memory. Or perhaps they resemble attempts to remember a perception, bearing in mind that a memory is always a construction, not a Xeroxed or photographic copy. It is a minor comfort, though, to find that psi is not totally unlike other psychological characteristics.

Long period decline can more clearly be likened to fatigue and boredom, particularly since it was observed mainly during dreary, years-long guessing sessions with few variables to enchant the mind. (The advent of Ganzfeld and remote viewing protocols altered that pattern very significantly, but most of the foundational work in parapsychology continued the original paradigm, including the many years of data gathering by the Princeton Engineering Anomalies Research group before it was disbanded in 2007 with its director's retirement.) By switching from one task to another, though, a promising subject was quite often able to revive high-scoring.

This fact would suggest that the brain (if indeed the brain is a critical part of the psi process, and not merely a neutral decoder for information handled elsewhere) is not literally being damaged or degraded by using psi. If, for example, neurological damage was brought about by psi akin to the havoc wrought by chronic alcoholism, one would expect all psi capacities to be inhibited at the same rate. This, it seems, does not happen.

Still, long term deterioration of psi functioning *in a given test regime* does usually appear to be inevitable, except perhaps for superstars. A technology of psi, reliable and repeatable, will have to be based on some method of avoiding or circumventing this effect. We do not yet know for certain how to prevent decline. But there are ways to cut around it, and the long-overlooked psi method we'll discuss below might prove to be one of these side-roads.

In support of the view that decline is a form of psychological inhibition, another interesting discovery was made early by Rhine. If a subject has been scoring positively (guessing correctly above mean chance expectation), then in time drops to chance, she'll sometimes begin scoring *negatively* to a statistically significant extent if pressed to continue. That is, she will guess incorrectly more often than one would predict on the basis of only chance responses.

To do this, she clearly needs to know (unconsciously) what the right answer is, so she can avoid it. This effect, called "psi-missing," will reappear later in another important form. It is not the case, alas, that subjects goaded beyond endurance will eventually miss all their targets; if they did, one could usefully keep them at it, merely reversing their answers to discover the true message!

§

Intrigued by these recurring trends, parapsychologists looked for other *position effects*. In general, such an effect is defined by Thouless as the systematic and predictable tendency for a successful psi subject "to score [positively] in some parts of every experimental occasion while he may show chance results or even negative scoring in other parts of his session."

There is an eerie tendency to score more highly at the end of a run of 25 cards than in the middle. This has come to be called "terminal salience," and an index of its presence, called the "salience ratio," can be calculated.

If a particular subject consistently obeys such regularities within his guesses, this is obviously good news to the would-be psi technologist. By concentrating one's attention on the most effective parts of a session, perhaps the reliability of interpretation can be enhanced (at the cost of throwing out a lot of data).

The discovery of regular internal variations in scoring led to a search for other useful contrasts. "It was fairly late in the history of experimental work in psychical research (from about 1950)," Thouless notes, "that experimenters began to find that if subjects were given *two contrasting operations* to perform it was very likely that they would score positively on one of them and negatively on the other, and that the difference between the two sets of scores might prove to be statistically significant" (my italics). What are these "differential effects" and what possible mental specialties might underlie them? As a first cut at the problem, we can distinguish a persistent tendency to score some kinds of target correctly (to *psi-hit* such targets) from a tendency to score other kinds of target incorrectly (to *psi-miss* those target). Call these examples of a conjectured *psi mode*, to which we shall turn a little later.

Three: Repeat

> ...we found that better scores than usual were all obtained by taking the majority opinion of a large number of guessers who were all aiming at the same targets. Assuming the majority opinion of the group to be more reliable than the guesses of individual subjects, we thought it might be possible to make use of this principle to increase ESP efficiency. By arranging a group test and deciding in advance to count only those trials on which a substantial majority of subjects made the same guess we hoped to produce an accurate forecast of at least some of the target cards.
>
> G.W. Fisk and D.J. West,
> "Towards Accurate Predictions from ESP Data" (1957)

WHAT MAKES PSI difficult to apply with any reliability is the massed background of typical responses—typical, that is, in regard to popular and disliked targets, psychological patterns and "order effects." On top of that disruptive "noise," psychic responses or perceptions simply don't pop up predictably each time a given individual attempts to perceive a given image or word or number by paranormal means. That was one of the key findings of Star Gate, the US government program, even with its selected psi-proficient remote viewers operating with stringent protocols.

Consequently, neither you nor I can *know* when our choices are being influenced by psi. Indeed, all we know from the parapsychological evidence is that it's going to happen quite rarely. Psi can be found reliably only in the collective behavior of a large number of people, preferably an enormously large number. (Alternatively, of course, it can become statistically visible in the droningly repeated guesses of a single person, which is the classic—and utterly boring—method used until recent decades by most academic parapsychologists.)

The principal finding from nearly a century and a half of psychical research is that psi phenomena are sporadic, low in efficiency, and resistant to normal teaching or reinforcement techniques. While some researchers claim to have uncovered certain psi-conducive states, their results always remain at the margins of visibility.

With psi, it is background *regularities* that must be identified and smoothed out, their lock-step noise edited from the data base of results, in order to detect any paranormal component that is hidden behind them.

§

One method for defanging biases and prejudices was developed by Professor Robert Jahn's engineering-inflected team at Princeton university, now disbanded with Jahn's retirement. Jahn's principal colleague, psychologist Brenda Dunne, had been involved in remote perception experiments before Jahn set up his Princeton Engineering Anomalies Research program, and she brought with her a body of informed knowledge on techniques ironed out in the 1970s. As a result, PEAR's remote perception protocol attempted to guard against familiar, well-grounded criticism by making all its remote data amenable to explicit computerized statistical assessment.

As well as providing impressionistic reports, the percipient filled out a checklist of 30 binary descriptors. Questions include the following: Is the central focus of the scene predominantly natural, that is, not man-made? Is the scene predominantly dark: for example, poorly lighted indoors or nighttime outside? Are steps or stairs prominent (excluding curbs)?

Targets are chosen in two ways. In the first, a randomizer selects from a large pool of prepared locations. Alternatively, an agent is permitted to visit some distant place (typically thousands of miles away, perhaps in another country) and choose from the unpredictable options available there.

This second approach undoubtedly raises some analytical difficulties, which have been seized on quite properly by critics. Since those involved in PEAR's perception experiments usually know each other, they can estimate (if only unconsciously) what features of the landscape are likely to attract their friend's notice. Dunne disputes the weight of this objection; her statistical analysis shows no difference in the levels of significance obtained under the two alternative conditions. Still, it must be granted as the most obvious point of potential weakness in all the PEAR remote viewing experiments.

Estimating the degree of success or failure is not merely made easier by forcing results into computerized binary form. It is also made more precise, and protected from certain bias hazards. For instance, a computer search of the prepared target pool shows that more than half the available locations are outdoors. So the probability of getting a positive result by guessing at an indoor setting is less than one in two—to be precise, it is 39.7 percent. There are trees in 64.5 percent of locations, glass or windows in more than 70 percent, but only 15.4 percent scenes are judged "oppressively confined." A quick computer evaluation can rescale or "normalize" each 30-point report to take into account this set of biases, and assign a clear probability-rating to its degree of match or mismatch.

What's more, an empirical control can be generated in the same way for the whole aggregated series of remote events. Using 334 scores, PEAR's computer deliberately mismatched calls and targets, deriving 42,000 control scores. Graphed, these "false" results show a very impressive correlation with chance expectation.

By contrast, the number of correct bits of information garnered by PEAR's operators exceeded the normalized chance result by some 15 percent. This is spectacular in terms of laboratory psychic success (which, when it shows up at all, tends to be between one and 0.02 of a percent above or below chance), and Jahn estimated the probability of its occurring by accident at about one in 50,000,000,000.

§

Can this result be taken seriously? If it is not a fairly pointless and silly fraud, might it be a colossal fluke? In any case, can statistics tell us anything about the real world? Haven't we been warned often enough about "lies, damned lies, and statistics"? Certainly the accumulated research findings still have not converted the die-hard skeptics.

Curiously, those top ranking scientists who bothered to look at the Princeton figures were by no means unanimous in either applauding or decrying Jahn's work. "We have had commentary on our program from no less than six Nobel laureates," Jahn told a gathering of parapsychologists at Fairleigh-Dickinson University in 1983, "two of whom categorically rejected the topic, two of whom encouraged us to push on, and two of whom were evasively equivocal."

Why do skeptics continue to resist this evidence? In part, no doubt, because the accumulated database is indigestibly vast. In a 1991 paper, Jahn, Dunne and York Dobyns note: "Unfortunately, given the highly stochastic nature of the process, the marginal scale of the anomalous effects, and the number of parameters that can influence operator performance, monumental amounts of data must be accumulated before any credible systematic trends in the individual count populations can be identified, and it is only relatively recently that our total data base has reached adequate dimensions to support such an effort. To date, the microelectronic random event generator (REG) ensemble of experiments has compounded some six million trials, encompassing 108 operators, three machines, and three major protocol variations."

In short: only with such large amounts of data was the search for fine-grained patterns becoming feasible.

§

So psi has been recorded and calibrated in the laboratory—but the interpretation, alas, remains obscure. Still, this needn't prevent us from considering how psi might be put to work. Since we know that an extraordinarily feeble electronic signal from deep space can be amplified by suitable instruments and decoded into a set of photographs of planets and moons at the edge of the solar system, might it not be possible to do something similar with psi data almost buried in the random hiss of response-preferences and other still-unknown noise factors?

To understand how that works, consider the hazards that afflicted early long-distance methods of communication—the old-fashioned electrical telegraph, for instance, for the start of the 19th century.

Sending messages down the line with any degree of efficiency meant that telegraph engineers needed to develop a *code* in which dots and dashes could be exchanged for the units—words or letters, say—of a natural language like English. (Samuel Morse patented his famous method, devised in fact by his assistant Alfred Vail, in 1837.) Now it turns out that English uses the various letters of the alphabet in strikingly different ways. The vowel E is very common, while consonants Z, Q, and X hardly ever show up. So there are a number of canny ways to compress any message and send it more swiftly down the line.

Claude Shannon, one of the founders of information theory, found that English is about 50 percent redundant, taken eight letters at a time. We can throw out the vowels, for example, and still have a pretty good chance of understanding a sentence. I said, w cn thrw t th vwls nd stll hv prtt gd chnc f ndrstndng sntnc.

That is, you can leave out a quarter of the letters and still retrieve the meaning. For longer sequences, the redundancy climbs to 75 percent. Whether we realize it or not, we all have learned the statistical character of our ordinary speech, and use it to fill in the blanks, hesitations, coughs and other interference that cloud daily communication.

Since E is the most common letter, Morse code assigned it the shortest, simplest unit—a dot. Less frequently used letters were given longer strings. International Morse gives Z as dash-dash-dot-dot, Q as dash-dash-dot-dash.

Suppose the message PSYCHIC is transmitted in Morse by ordinary electric telegraph. If some sporadic interference blocks parts of the message (we can use the asterisk * to denote a confusing blurt of noise), it might be received as, say, *SY*H**, or P**C*I*.

Even if attempts to clear the line fail, the message can still be received correctly if it is repeated a number of times. This is the factor of *redundancy*, a key to psi application. So we might get:

*	**S**	**Y**	*	**H**	**I**	*
P	*	*	**C**	*	*	**C**
P	**S**	*	**C**	*	**I**	*
*	*	**Y**	*	**H**	*	**C**
P	*	**Y**	*	*	**I**	**C**

It's not difficult to see that the common factor coming through in the first position is a P, in the second an S, and the last a C. The word PSYCHIC is readily retrieved, though the number of repetitions needed to assure clarity depends on the noise in the channel. The more blurts of static, the greater the number of repeat transmissions needed.

Then again, a worse case, it might simply *alter* the message, by turning a dot into a dash, or shortening a dash into a dot.

.—. ... -.— -.-. .... .. -.-. in International Morse is

P/S/Y/C/H/I/C

..-. ... -.— -.-. ..-. .. -.-. is, however, the meaningless or at least rather confusing

F/S/Y/C/F/I/C.

To make the operator's job easier, let us imagine he knows how many letters are going to be sent per block of data and that each letter is coded by a combination of exactly five binary digits—dots and dashes, ones and zeroes, or pluses and minuses. Since the noise is actually altering or mutating the letters, a number of genuine but wrong words might be created by accident. Fortunately, our redundancy protocol means that the operator is not looking for one particular clear transmission of the message.

The computer on the Voyager 2 mission, for instance, sent back pictures of Saturn's rings with a 100 percent redundancy—one extra check digit for each data digit. The Hubbard Space Telescope protected its blurry early images (the $5 billion mirror was incorrectly ground, you'll recall, one of the greatest embarrassments in the history of Big Science) with three redundant digits for each data bit.

In our imaginary protocol, each letter is coded by five binary digits. This choice permits 32 permutations, rather as the DNA nucleotide code—used by all living things to create and control tissue—is coded into amino acids by 64 permutations of a protocol using four rather than two fundamental units taken three at a time.

Using such a code, the operator will expect noise to deform the message in quite predictable ways. Since we know that the letters of the alphabet do not appear with equal frequency in English sentences, we don't expect each letter to appear on average one time in 26. On the contrary, E should appear much more often, Z and Q very rarely. It doesn't matter, though. Redundancy—repeating the message several times—ensures that the *right* letter will get through *more often* at the same position in the line than will any other mutant alternative.

§

To make matters nastier, though, let's suppose the operator at the receiving post has an unreasonable devotion to the letter "A" (it's the first letter in "anchovy," a fish he adores). Try as he might, his unconscious fixation on this letter will betray him time and again.

Whenever static clouds the clarity of transmission, this besotted fool shows an unnerving tendency to read the incoming 5-bit letter as "A." If it happens often enough, and the channel is sufficiently noisy, his decoded version of the message "PSYCH" will read "AAAAA."

Don't despair.

If the message has got through to any extent at all, the letter "P" will be recorded *more often* than any other letter *except* "A" in the first five-letter block. Similarly, the letter "S" will follow "A" as favorite in the second slot. "Y" will score well in the third slot. Short of sacking this lunatic for gross incompetence (boss's son, you know), it may be feasible to screen out the unwanted A's by establishing in advance that this bias exists.

If the operator possesses more than one of these disturbing propensities, it'll be necessary to measure the strength and regularity of each one before allowing him near the machine. Once that's done, though, we can compensate for them all during decoding. It makes life harder, but then it's an imperfect world.

Alas, our man may be afflicted by a still more galling penchant. As the series of repeated messages continues to come in, he may slowly develop an unconscious loathing for the letter "P." It appears in the word PSYCHIC but isn't pronounced, and this infuriates him. Now we find him failing to recognize "P" when it comes through the machine. He changes it to some other letter or letters.

Alternatively, he may unconsciously warm to it (he's always wanted to be psychic) and start to interpolate it here and there without rhyme or reason.

These hazards are also a form of noise, but they are much harder to combat. A complex preliminary analysis of the operator's behavior might reveal this tendency, so we could allow for it by analyzing the changing frequency with which he reports each letter. A computer program can do it in real-time, and for the sorts of noise-reduction required for psi applications a specialized program is almost essential, for precisely this kind of reason. That may well be why large-scale psi applications were not thick on the ground until fairly recently—though they have an honorable history, as the next chapter shall detail. The presence everywhere today of inexpensive yet powerful home computers, tablets and smartphones, and widespread "computer literacy," has at last remedied this lack (for good or ill).

§

Finally we can apply these considerations directly to a psi application program.

In 1967, a Soviet experiment was conducted by the engineer I. M. Kogan, chairman of the Bioinformation Section of the Moscow Board of the Popov Society. As described in Dr. Thelma Moss's *The Probability of the Impossible*, the actor Karl Nikolaiev in Leningrad detected a coded series of emotional jolts aimed at him by biophysicist Uri Kamensky in Moscow.

Many observers have surmised that the boring, dehumanized aspect of card-guessing or random event generator (REG) parapsychology tests hamper the exercise of a capacity more often associated with raw emotion. These Soviet experiments used feelings rather than conceptual symbols—but arranged them in a coded format that remained amenable to crisp statistical evaluation.

Kamensky concentrated, in bursts, on a fantasy of physically thumping his distant partner. A 45 second burst stood for a Morse code dash, while a 15 second effort stood for a dot. Kogan monitored Nikolaiev's EEG in the hope that it would register any psychic response. Each element or "bit" of the coded message was sent 15 times, and a majority vote was taken on the results. That is, if 8, 9 or more of the 15 repetitions were received as a "dash," say, rather than a "dot," this majority out of 15 was accepted as the true signal.

In the first experiment, the four-letter Russian name "IVAN" was received correctly using this redundant coded procedure.

By Western standards of the time, the duration allotted to each information bit was unusually long. Nor was this merely due to the difference between emotional and cognitive images, though clearly it's quicker to shift your attention between shapes or symbols than to modify your whole emotional state. Reportedly, though, the experimenter Dr. Pavlova found rapid-fire Western lab methods too swift for optimal psi results. "If different telepathic bits come too rapidly, the changes in the brain associated with telepathy begin to blur and finally disappear."

This was confirmed by Dr. Vladimir Fidelman, an engineer who used simultaneous visual and auditory inundation as stimuli. He found that each target or information bit had to be presented to the sender for between 10 and 90 seconds. Of 135 numbers transmitted across a distance of three kilometers, he claimed that 100 were received correctly in this fashion—an extraordinary degree of success if true.

In part, it was claims of this kind that encouraged Western development of remote viewing, dream report and Ganzfeld techniques during the 1970s and 1980s. Nevertheless, the subsequent marginal but impressively consistent success of Jahn's Princeton methods confirmed the value of "repeated guessing"—just so long as it is scrupulously monitored, electronically recorded, and computer-analyzed.

On the evidence, the true psi breakthrough might yet come from these forays into coded, high-redundancy experiments.

§

Repetitive psi screened by majority vote *has* been used quite regularly by parapsychologists. The earliest attempt I know of to use a coded version was a test with Native American children carried out in 1943 by A.A. Foster. The children were given decks of red and black cards, sealed in opaque envelopes, and asked to sort them into two piles. A question had been formulated before the test began. The answer "Yes" would be indicated by finding the black cards (psychically, of course) and sorting them into a particular pile. In those early days of psi research, nobody took the possibility of psi-missing into account, but in any event there was no significant deviation from chance in this experiment: no psi.

Similar approaches were tried out in the mid-1950s by British researchers G.W. Fisk, D.J. West and Donald Michie. During the 1960s and 1970s, theoretical and practical contributions were published in the literature by Dr. J.B. Rhine himself, Dr. Remy Cadoret in France, Dr. Robert Thouless in Britain (he dubbed the procedure the "repeated guessing technique"), by Dr. Lozanov, a Bulgarian, and Dr. Rýzl, a Czechoslovakian, by Drs. Reswick and Vodovnik at Case University in the USA, by Dr. Bob Brier and Walter Tyminski (who applied it successfully to gambling), by William Cox, Dr. James Carpenter, Stanford Research Institute investigators Russell Targ and Dr. Hal Puthoff, Dr. Helmut Schmidt, Dr. G.L. Heseltine, Dr. J.E. Kennedy, Dr. Robert Taetzsch, JoMarie Haight and Debra H. Weiner then at Rhine's Institute for Parapsychology (now the Rhine Research Center), Denise McCain, and others.

Not all the experiments described in their reports paid off—a risk one runs when exploring the paranormal. Alternative methods such as the psi Ganzfeld and remote viewing became the favored methods of choice in subsequent decades. Majority-votes taken on repeated trials cannot concentrate psychic impressions that aren't there, and Ganzfeld remains an effective psi-conducive state, so the two methods are not mutually exclusive. An obvious way to run them in parallel is to give a number of Ganzfeld percipients the same target (differently encoded in each case, of course), and take a majority vote on *those* aggregated results. Targ and Puthoff's *Mind-Reach* (a somewhat unreliable source, alas) noted of remote-viewing tests: "In general, it appears that use of multiple-subject responses to a single target provide better results than target identification by a single individual."

In short, the elements of this method have been in the public domain for years. Masses of suitable test data have gathered dust, unanalyzed on library shelves. Nor are the statistical steps required particularly arcane. They have been the commonplace of demography, epidemiology, sociological surveys and public opinion polls since those arts first emerged.

For a time, the method went into eclipse because many parapsychologists doubted its experimental value. In his 1964 Presidential Address to the British Society for Psychical Research, Dr. D.J. West gave a gloomy appraisal. (West had himself been a pioneer of this approach in the 1950s, before concentrating on his distinguished career as a psychiatric criminologist).

"Attempts to extract significance from the guesses of large numbers of subjects, by making a majority vote or most popular guess, have not proved fruitful," he declared with some disappointment. "The process of dividing a mass audience into sheep and goats, and then taking two separate votes, has yet to be tried, but does not seem all that promising in the light of so many failures in the past."

When I came to read this dismissive summary many years later, I thought it unduly pessimistic. Piqued by Dr. West's loss of faith in his own methodology, I hunted out his "failed" experiments. Surprise, surprise! Some of them, including the most important, proved far from deficient in psi. Examined by only slightly more complex majority vote methods than West had to hand, the data disclosed suggestive support for the very hypothesis he thought they falsified.

West's typical error was failing to take account of response bias, which skewed his subjects' guesses away from pure chance expectation. We shall consider these experiments in a later chapter. It was an encouraging finding.

West's negative assessment was presumably based as well on such mass experiments as a radio broadcast test conducted in 1927 by Dr. V.J. Woolley and Sir Oliver Lodge through the British Broadcasting Corporation, a German radio experiment the following year with 12,552 trials from 2092 subjects, reported by Dr. Alexander Herzberg, and a series of tests run in the USA between September, 1937, and January,

1938, by the Zenith radio network. The Woolley experiment failed to evoke any significant deviation, though re-analysis using better methods also suggests that the Woolley test shows us some critical factors to take into account with multiple guessing aimed at single targets.

The Zenith tests, by contrast, are extremely provocative. At first, in the early flush of excitement at Dr. Rhine's announcement of what he dubbed "Extra-Sensory Perception," these tests seemed to give such an overwhelming positive deviation that all America thrilled to the news that scientists had proved ESP once and for all. Skeptical psychologists swiftly dispelled that hope by showing convincingly that audience preferences, coupled with stereotyped guessing patterns and some inadvertent cues, accounted for this remarkable "success." Dr. J.G. Pratt, Rhine's associate, also concluded that "both positive and negative results are to be accounted for in large part by means of public preference for certain patterns of guesses. Whether any positive effects not so explicable, and therefore possibly telepathic remain, is impossible to state from the data at hand" (Pratt, typescript, 1938, "Analysis of the Data from the Zenith Radio Experiments...").

And yet... Here, too, a belated look at the original data reveals that there *is* powerful evidence in the Zenith tests for the influence of ESP. It's just that everyone—parapsychologists and skeptics alike—were looking in the wrong place for it. Initially, everyone expected the right answer to poke up cheekily above *mean* chance expectation. In fact, the kinds of targets the Zenith audience were sent—Light versus Dark, most conspicuously—attract very different bias-perturbed votes. Even so, as Pratt noted, far too much uncontrolled "noise" remains in the experiment for it to be a truly satisfactory test-case for the alleged merits of the majority vote method.

In order to minimize the distorting impact of all the multitude of forces promoting error in a repeated-guessing or pooled multiple-agent application, psi programs have to be highly devious. Instead of posing an emotionally-charged question outright, and thus tripping off all manner of distractions and wishful thinking, an exhaustive list (or matrix) of its possible answers must be coded into a series of choices between innocuous symbols (or those with an established bias weighting).

It should go without saying that neither experimenter nor subject/s know what the real targets are: a double-blind condition.

When West declared the method a failure, he was presumably unaware of an elegant theoretical elaboration of this method described by Dr. Robert Taetzsch in his “Design of a Psi Communication System.” This harnessed signal detection theory and computer processing of data in a well-nigh perfect exposition of the approach... as early as 1962.

Equally impressive was “A Model of Parapsychological Communication’, published in Czech in 1962 by Dr. Milan Rýzl, then a chemist with the Institute of Biology of the Czechoslovakian Academy of Science. Rýzl’s paper was translated into English four years later.

§

I shall return to these advanced discussions. Let us go immediately to the method investigated in this book. Its slow development, like a detective story, will follow in subsequent chapters. But like a sneak preview, I will set out the line of thought with which these investigations concluded.

The Parapsychology Association fired a counterblast at a US Army report disparaging the usefulness of psi (Palmer, Honorton, and Utts, 1989):

“Since the NRC [National Research Council] report was explicitly funded by the Army to assess potential applications, the Committee has been remiss in ignoring controlled psi studies directed toward eventual applications,” Palmer and his colleagues declared. Examples cited included a 1966 paper by Milan Rýzl, a 1975 report by James Carpenter, and a 1985 paper by Harold Puthoff. They went on:

> These experiments all used statistical averaging techniques based on information theory to enhance accuracy... Carpenter’s experiment resulted in the successful identification of the binary (Morse) code equivalent of the word “PEACE”. A successful effort to improve the accuracy of detection of random binary sequences generated by hidden roulette-wheel spins (red/black) and coin tosses (heads/tails) was reported by Puthoff...

The PA did not rush headlong into claims of general success. But they concluded their summary on a positive note:

> While no responsible parapsychologist would claim that legitimate practical applications of psi abilities have yet been achieved, more intensive applications-oriented basic research is clearly justified by the success of these and other similar efforts.

The paper by Dr. Harold Puthoff which they referenced was rather more enthusiastic:

> When one considers the application of psi in such practical tasks as message transmission or outcome prediction, one is led naturally to the use of redundancy in one form or another (e.g., repetitive calling, multiple response) in order to combine small statistical advantages into an overall higher-accuracy result. Such techniques can range from the use of simple majority vote procedures to the application of sophisticated error-correcting codes of the type specified in communication theory texts. These approaches are in keeping with the precepts of information theory by which, at least in principle, it is possible to approach error-free transmission in an arbitrarily high-noise channel provided appropriate statistical averaging techniques are used.

§

Let's examine a highly simplified version of psi communication in action.

The phones are out. Mail's on strike. The net has been burned by hackers. How can you let your friend in a distant city know whether or not you're coming to visit next week?

Well, by a piece of good preparation, you have arranged this protocol in advance. At the stroke of midnight, you take out two cards—one yellow, one purple—and consult the protocol. In this case, *purple* encodes the decision to go, while *yellow* means you're staying home. As you've decided not to go, you retain the yellow card and put the purple card away.

Hundreds of kilometers away, starting at five minutes after 12, your friend writes down 100 guesses at the color of the card you are holding. Leaving color preference aside, the laws of probability tell us she has only one chance in 20 of matching the target color 60 or more times out of 100 guesses. By chance, since there are only two colors, she ought to get roughly half her guesses right. But suppose she chooses "yellow" 65 times and "purple" only 35 times. This exceeds by a small amount the irregularity in calls she would expect by chance alone, and so she accepts the "majority vote" on these calls as pin-pointing the yellow card. You won't be coming to town.

Badly false as it is to reality, this crude example of statistical averaging demonstrates how majority vote on a string of guesses can improve the reliability of purported psi communication. On the basis of only 65 percent of correct guesses, your friend is almost 100 percent confident that she has received your message accurately. Already, then, we can see the basis for a workable psi technology.

What's awry in that example is its absurd simplicity. The statistical assumption needed to reach a majority vote was that the individual guesses made by your friend were *independent* of each other—and nothing could be further from the case. Anyone faced with such a blatant "yellow or purple" choice, especially knowing that the same card is presented in every call, falls prey to well-established tricks of the mind.

A coarse way to compensate might be to divide your 100 guesses into four blocks of 25. If Purple signifies your intention to visit in the first 25 "transmissions," its value is reversed in the second set. Now Yellow becomes the target. The alternation continues. If your percipient has a consistent bias in favor of Yellow, say, it will influence her votes equally in all four blocks. And if psi-hitting is going on throughout her responses, she will guess Yellow *even more often* than usual when it is target, and less often when it's not.

§

An even more damnable problem arises in the context of one of parapsychology's special banes: the possibility of *psi-missing*, mentioned previously

Even if all the biases could be eliminated, even if one were certain that psi is operating, there's no way to know if your friend is in "hitting" or "missing" mode. A significant tendency to choose yellow might actually be due to suppression of paranormal information transfer of the fact that the card is really purple. This is the sort of thing that makes hostile opponents of the psi hypothesis gnash their teeth in fury, but statistically significant psi-missing is a recurrent feature of all parapsychological experiments, including the Princeton data, and it simply has to be taken into account.

There is a way to circumvent it. There's always a way. Well, usually.

We need to stop the percipient from creating her own disruptive bias patterns, which at the very least means she has to be kept in the dark about the code until *all* her guessing is completed. Despite this carefully imposed ignorance, she needs to be given a definite and exclusive range of possible targets—in this case, yellow versus purple. And an important additional factor is required: some element that will allow the analyst to discern if her guesses (supposing that they show a significant shift from chance expectation) are directed toward hitting or missing.

The simplest method that occurs to me would use a computer program containing a list of several hundred thousand randomly shuffled yellows and purples, 50 of each for every sequence of 100. (Actually, the complete list would not be stored—just a set of heterogeneous "seed numbers" and a brief random-number generating program to produce the full list when that seed number is called for.) Inside the program, safe from ordinary human knowledge, a selection drawn from these lists could be allocated years in advance to certain future calendar dates. Both percipient and transmitter could hold copies of this program, and could call it up on their computer screens whenever they wished to run a psi-application. Each would then know that the same decoding protocol was in force for both of them, and yet be quite blind to the contents of the coded sequence.

I'll explain. You decide to visit your friend. The machine tells you that on this particular day the protocol for "Yes, I'm coming', is List A, while the protocol for "Sorry, can't make it', is List B. You enter "A', and the program starts presenting a series of brightly colored words: PURPLE, YELLOW, YELLOW, YELLOW, PURPLE, YELLOW, PURPLE, YELLOW, YELLOW..., accompanied each time by the instruction "Acknowledge TARGET by Pressing Y or P, then ENTER." It does this for 100 cycles, and turns itself off.

Your friend, who knows you're going to try to send her your answer through the psi channel, has also turned on her machine at the same time. But in her case, the screen shows both bright graphic options: PURPLE or YELLOW. She enters "P" or "Y', the screen blanks out briefly, and the option is presented a second time (maybe with the choices transposed just to help overcome any bias she has for choosing the left or right option).

This tedious procedure continues for as long as it take to get through 100 answers. At the end, your friend's computer calculates whether her pattern of guesses is closer to List A or List B, thanks her for participating, and reveals whether the vote for the selected configuration differs from its alternative to a statistically significant extent. In this case, say, she's chosen the List A sequence 68 times out of 100. So, although she has not been aware of the way List A is coded, the machine tells her the message: "I'm on my way."

Simple when you know how.

§

Still just that one persistent problem, though. Is your friend psi-hitting or psi-missing? There's no way to tell from these data.

The answer is to include a separate "index" sample of another 50 or 100 guesses, preferably folded through the rest of the guesses so that it is a representative sample of the percipient's general psychic state (hit, miss, or out to lunch). This sample can be decoded ahead of the main message, which can then be interpreted with some confidence.

There's an obvious drawback to this repeated trials method. Demanding 100, 150 or 200 guesses to code up just one prediction seems far too inefficient. Can't we cut the number down?

Alas, no. Quite the reverse.

A single *standard deviation* from the mean, in statistics, marks out the range within which you can confidently expect about 34 percent of experimental results to be clustered. Toss a coin 100 times. How many heads? 52 (let's say). Toss it another 100 times. 47 heads. Another 100. 49 heads. Keep it up for a few months, and you'll find that 34 percent of your combined results are in the range 50 to 55 (because the mean is 50, and a single standard deviation in such a case is 5). Another 34 percent will be in the range 45 to 50. Two-tailed, as they say, the range between 45 and 55 covers just over 68 percent of all such experimental runs of 100 throws.

If we mark off *two* standard deviations either side of the mean, we encompass 95.4 percent of all random results. In other words, in fewer than 5 percent of cases can we expect results to exceed 60 (50 plus 5 plus 5) or be fewer than 40 (50 minus 5 minus 5).

But parapsychology experiments suggest that psi only functions effectively on some one percent (at the most, usually) of random guesses. By throwing the coin only 100 times—making only 100 binary choices—any noticeable impact from psi is virtually written off in advance. It might well be there, but it'll be hidden from sight behind the random swings.

The human brain has trouble coping with this proposition, which is why so many people lose their shirt every week at the race track or the roulette table.

There's a way around it..

More guesses. Many more guesses. Many, many more guesses.

Look at it this way. If a coin turns up heads 7 throws out of 10, nobody is startled. But if it's thrown 100 times in succession and comes up heads 70 times, you'll start scratching your own head. Throw it 1000 times and see it fall heads 700 times, and if you've been betting on what you thought was a fair coin you'll be after someone's blood.

Yet in each case, the proportion of that excess—2 heads, 20, 200—is exactly the same: 20 percent of the total throws.

The longer such a stochastic (or random) process continues, the more likely it is that the actual score will tighten up around the theoretical average. As the number of events increases, so too the degree of variation from the mean falls off drastically.

Suppose we toss the coin 10,000 times instead of 100. The standard deviation grows in one sense (it's now 50, rather than 5 as it was in the case of 100 throws), but in another sense it plummets fabulously. 50 is only half a percent of 10,000, while 5 is (of course) 5 percent of 100. Two standard deviations either way of the mean of 5,000 brings the likely range down to between 4,900 and 5,100 heads.

So that's the answer to psi application. Simple. Just repeat each binary choice in your coded message 10,000 times, and look for any psychic excess to peek over the small chance variations.

What? *What?*

Ten thousand calls at each Morse dot or dash?

§

It's worse than that, actually. Sorry.

I just said that the likely range with 10,000 heads-or-tails guesses is 4,900 to 5,100. Which implies that at least half the time you try this trick the aggregated guesses will fall in the range 4,900 to 5000. Even if psi-hitting is tossing in an extra one percent... *half the time it's going to be masked by this low but absolutely inevitable effect.*

Then there's the need for index calls, to check for the direction of psi. We're looking at *hundreds of thousands* of calls here, maybe millions, just to be absolutely sure of getting the equivalent of a simple email through.

Luckily, and coincidentally, the internet will come to the rescue.

Now that we know how averaged repeated guessing can help extract the signal of psi from the surrounding tumult of noise (so to speak, although psi is unlikely to be much like a familiar electronic signal), we can look back at the way the evidence for this approach slowly emerged from bold experiments in ESP that nobody, for decades, properly understood.

Four: Woolley

Some five decades ago, a notable critic of parapsychology, Dr. C.E.M. Hansel, explained why it is so difficult to discuss the topic of fraud in any science, even one regarded by most as dubious. His 1966 book *ESP: A Scientific Evaluation* was revised as *ESP & Parapsychology* (1981) and again as *The Search for Psychic Power* in 1989. One of his analogies in 1966 was disquietingly prescient (almost psychic):

> It is often difficult to discuss the possibility of cheating objectively. Parapsychologists tended to present their critics with a "fait accompli." A similar situation will arise in orthodox science if a notable chemist reported an experimental result that contradicted all the previous research findings and theories of his fellow chemists, together with the statement "Either this finding must be accepted as valid or else you must accuse me of being a cheat and a liar..." In such circumstances, orthodox chemists might feel diffident about openly expressing their doubts. They might, however, repeat the experiment to see whether they got the same result.

Hansel's example had an unexpected sting buried in it. In the same year his third revision was published, the chemists Martin Fleischmann and Stanley Pons announced at a press conference held by the University of Utah that their experiments had discovered a previously unknown chemical process they called "cold fusion."

After a brief flurry of extreme media excitement, the community of chemists and physicists, contrary to Hansel's expectation, fell upon them with denunciation and scorn.

Part of this was due to the unorthodox way Pons and Fleischmann had revealed their discovery—not after the customary process of peer review and solemn journal publication, but directly to the public. Then most attempts to replicate the results failed, adding to the derision, although the chemists claimed that these failures were caused by inadequacies in replicating their precise methods (hardly helped by the scant details they had provided).

In the quarter century since, most scientists with a stake in the matter, or indeed simply as onlookers, have assumed that the whole cold fusion fuss was due to sloppy carelessness at best, and to flagrant fraud at worst. And yet the controversy continues, bubbling below the surface. Hundreds of successful or partial replications have been claimed by accredited scientists in several nations, notably Japan, but these claims (and others such as "bubble fusion" or sonofusion) have rarely been published by the establishment scientific press. Indeed, in 2006, Nobel physicist and psi proponent Professor Brian Josephson raged against what he saw as a disgraceful persecution of physicist Rusi Taleyarkhan by the scientific journal *Nature*. But there it was, Hansel's unlikely analogy had come true, and the reaction of the chemists' peer group was more venomous than he had anticipated.

§

The situation for parapsychology was, inevitably, even more fraught. Some 60 years ago, at a CIBA Foundation symposium on extrasensory perception, the psi-friendly researcher and psychiatrist Dr. D.J. West stated baldly: "The field of extrasensory research remains in no man's land between the lunatic fringe on the one hand and the academically unorthodox on the other... all the serious work is done by a handful of people who could easily be swamped by cranks. Indeed, the field is so small that any fool can make a name for himself in it" (p. 21). He said that in 1956; it remains true today.

It's as well to bear that caution in mind. Despite the dignified roll call of a small scientific cadre whose reputations continue to adorn the field, psychic research has never lacked for more than its fair share of liars, psychotics, the befuddled and cranks. How can the claims of the scoundrels and the inept be separated out and discarded?

"Knowing these facts only too well," West added all those years ago, "parapsychologists tend to look upon each other with a distrust far exceeding the distrust of scientists in general. I have been present on occasions when persons who have worked in the field for years have seriously discussed whether the whole of the evidence for extrasensory perception might not be worthless conglomeration of fraud and fallacy" (p. 21).

Luckily, there are several ways out of this impasse of credibility. Let us return to those old mass tests undertaken before the stacking effect was elucidated—that is, lack of statistical independence due to many percipients sharing common biases trying to guess the same targets at the same time. Most of these were long ago considered barren of the least smidgen of evidence for psi. As noted already, one vast series conducted under the auspices of the Zenith Radio Corporation in the United States—more than a million guesses—was thought for a time to contain "telepathically yielded results statistically different from chance expectation." Within the year, detailed studies by both skeptical and open-minded psychologists had ruthlessly exposed the misleading influence of pattern bias, and the scene was set for a melancholy admission by parapsychologists that mass tests were useless instruments in their quest for the paranormal.

But suppose subsequent insights into these despised data showed not only that psi was, probably, happening but also clues on how to put it to work. That would be one interesting and compelling way to step around the problem of incompetence or deliberate fraud. After all, nobody is likely to rig an experiment in a way so subtle that nobody notices its intended effect for more than half a century.

Reanalysis of old data has often played an honorable and fruitful role in scientific inquiry. When fresh cosmological theories emerge, the photographic archives are searched for evidence that has gone unnoticed because until now no one had known where to look, and for what. Indeed, the discovery by Rhine of psychic decline affects was confirmed in just this fashion. J.B. Rhine described how his team located lawful degradation in the scoring rates of subjects tested by Harvard University's G. E. Estabrooks, and observed: "the fact that Estabrooks did not recognize it as evidence at the time even increases its value today... with such evidence, scientific acceptance is a matter of time. These significant internal differences due to position effects are there in the records, fixed material awaiting re-examination."

Under those circumstances, no lingering suspicion can remain that the data have been cooked, or selected because they happen by chance to fit the current hypotheses. Better yet if the old material was thought deficient because of its failure to confirm the hopeful expectations of the original gleaners.

§

The earliest data of this kind that I've been able to unearth was published in the *Proceedings* of Britain's Society for Psychical Research in 1928. Suggested by E.J. Dingwall, a mass radio test was conducted by Dr. V.J. Woolley and the renowned physicist Sir Oliver Lodge, on February 16, 1927. In *Extra-sensory Perception After Sixty Years* (1940), J.G. Pratt, J.B. Rhine, et al., noted: "There are at least four others known, of which no report is available." This still appears to be true. Woolley's is the first they cited as published, with 123,295 trials from 24,659 participants. They added: "The second radio broadcast experiment to be published was made in Germany and reported by Herzberg in 1928. It consisted of 12,552 trials with 2092 subjects responding" (p. 82). I haven't tracked down a translation of that one, so let us proceed with Woolley's pioneering effort.

Seven agents, and Dr. Woolley, were sequestered in the Society's offices. Psi research in those days was still closely linked to the study of spiritualistic mediumship. The senders or "agents" were, therefore, chosen from the ranks of "good sitters"—not themselves mediums, but those who usually obtained more than their fair share of reliable information *from* mediums. At five-minute intervals, Dr. Woolley presented these agents with one of five different objects for them to study and then communicate its mental image to the radio audience.

The first of these objects, presented rather late at night at 11:15 p.m., was "a 2 of Clubs playing card, cut at the time from an 'Arpak' pack in which this suit happened to be printed in green on a black background." The second target object was a Japanese print, showing a small bird perched on a skull. The third was a bunch of three sprays of white lilac. In the fourth test, the object was "a 9 of Hearts playing card, cut at the time [that is, "ten minutes after test 1 was over"] from the same pack as No. 1, this suit being printed in red and also on a black background," while Woolley himself, resplendent in "a bowler hat and a grotesque mask," stood in as the final target.

Simultaneously, in the studios of the British Broadcasting Corporation, Sir Oliver "directed the wireless listeners to record any impression they were able to form of the objects so produced." Once they had jotted down their impressions, they were asked to mail them at the end of the program to the Society's office. "The agents remained on the Society's premises throughout the night, without access to a telephone, until after the morning clearances of the letter boxes had taken place."

(Given that more than 20,000 letters were received, one must wistfully conclude—in these days of sluggish postal delivery—that such promptness was itself more miraculous than any degree of psi could possibly be. Of course, were such a mass experiment to be replicated today, guesses could be sent instantly by fax, email attachment or Twitter, along with about a million pieces of unintended spam.)

Since no control series were ever run, the trials that use targets other than playing cards are utterly unquantifiable. In such open-ended conditions, it is quite impossible to estimate how many of the 24,659 respondents might choose the selected targets by chance. All is not lost, though. "The only information given to Sir Oliver Lodge, and by him passed on to listeners, was that numbers 1 and 4 were playing cards of unusual design, and that number 2 was a picture." Because the listeners knew which of the trials represented a familiar playing card, even if the format was slightly different from the customary red or black on white background, each of the two playing card tests might in principle be used as a control for the other.

Pattern bias there was, in profusion. **Table 4.1** displays the accumulated guesses in both tests. The most obvious thing to notice is that the earlier of the two playing card tests registered about 50 percent more guesses than the later test. Perhaps many respondents lost confidence, or became confused, or fell behind and thus failed to record their impressions, or simply went to bed. If alert, intent confidence has any predictive value, we might expect the second playing card trial—that is, Test 4—to be rather more successful, therefore, than the first, Test 1.

Curiously, thousands of people entered guesses for the ineligible Joker card or for cards "not of playing card design." Woolley quite correctly eliminated these improper responses in advance from his matrix of answers. We are left with 23,529 guesses in Test 1, and 15,348 guesses in Test 4. If these are to serve as mutual controls, the numerical disparity must be taken into account; the most obvious way to do that is called *scaling* or *normalizing*: converting the raw guesses for each card into a percentage that can reasonably be compared with the equivalent percentage obtained in the alternate test. (For more on how this process works, see the Appendix that follows Chapter six.)

	CLUBS		SPADES		DIAMONDS		HEARTS		Sum TEST 1	Sum TEST 4
A	1027	577	2255	1636	1600	920	1821	930	6703	4063
2	**190**	145	241	226	257	200	157	156	845	727
3	356	196	348	156	512	237	423	171	1639	760
4	102	155	133	181	157	218	105	157	497	711
5	413	190	510	207	828	329	747	245	2498	971
6	124	84	150	97	224	163	173	86	671	430
7	275	142	349	160	601	234	347	125	1572	661
8	153	100	144	83	175	100	177	91	649	374
9	441	204	478	183	864	288	491	**150**	2274	825
10	235	217	212	185	492	359	210	165	1149	926
J	499	373	460	365	546	454	440	337	1945	1529
Q	254	236	428	404	328	439	784	791	1794	1870
K	353	418	279	290	276	394	385	399	1293	1501
Σ:	4422	3037	5987	4173	6860	4335	6260	3803	23,529	15,348
	T1	T4	T1	T4	T1	T4	T1	T4	Grand Σ: 38,877	

Table 4.1: Raw card votes in the Woolley broadcasting experiment.
Σ (Sigma) is the mathematical expression for Sum.
Targets (**2 of Clubs** and **9 of Hearts**) shown in **Bold.**

For example, the Queen of Clubs received 254 votes in Test 1, but only 236 votes in Test 4. But when we remember that the second test only had two thirds as many votes as the first, we see that the proportion of the vote for Queen of Clubs was *higher* in the second case.

Some other aspects of pattern bias stand out quite blatantly. This is the kind of information that card sharps have known for generations, giving them a useful advantage over innocent gamblers who don't realize how stereotyped their own responses are. In both tests, and in every single suit, Ace was the overwhelming favorite. More than a *quarter* of all guesses went to the Aces.

As you might have guessed, an even more striking population preference was shown for the Ace of Spades, a card rich in traditional symbolic significance, springing easily and quickly to mind. The Queen of Hearts (she of the tarts) also attracted more than her fair share of votes.

Less obviously to the naked eye, although powerfully apparent once noticed, odd numbers proved three times as attractive as even numbers. But these marked pattern biases are themselves not entirely stable. The ratio of odd to even, for example, changed between tests.

§

Woolley's analyst, a once celebrated parapsychologist named S.G. Soal, many years later accused of fraud in certain other psi experiments, quailed in the face of these population pattern biases. Woolley's conclusion was uncompromising: "it is this preference which has made it impossible in this experiment to determine the number of correct guesses to be expected by chance... it is clear from these tables that so far as the card tests go there is no evidence to all of any telepathic transmission."

Today, anticipating just such distorting preferences, a careful anomalies design would incorporate sufficient target redundancy to allow for correction. As we'll see, Soal and Woolley were wise to write off this experiment. Still, there is much we can learn from their mistakes.

Looking at their data today, where would a parapsychologist hope to find any kind of psi influence? To begin with, it's well-established that psi is sporadic and unreliable. The unnuanced question Woolley posed deprived him of valuable data. He asked bluntly how many votes went to **2 of Clubs** in Test 1, and to **9 of Hearts** in Test 4. But if psi exists, and acts fleetingly and without conscious awareness, you might be sitting at home by the wireless and pick up the number but not the suit, or vice versa. So it might make more sense to separate out these elements: you might expect to see the influence of psi on *all* **2**s in Test 1, irrespective of suit, and similarly for *all* Clubs, irrespective of card number. These elements could then be recombined to nominate one card out of 52.

Another issue that never occurred to Soal or Woolley is the dreaded peculiarity of psi-missing. Back in the 1920s, the possibility that a significant psi-mediated deviation might be aimed in the wrong direction had never entered anybody's mind. A statistician these days would use what's called a two-tailed rather than a one-tailed test of significance—that is, apply a much more stringent test of significance to allow for the possibility that the target playing cards were conspicuously *avoided.*

§

Annoyingly, a close look at the raw data—scrutiny that could easily have been conducted *before* the targets were known—shows this logical program breaking down at the crucial point. You might hope that the guesses on one test could serve as a control on the other, that the same biases and preferences would show up in both sets of guesses. That approach would be reasonable if two separate groups of rather similar respondents had guessed only once at the playing cards. But in this experiment, it's unlikely, on the face of it, that listeners would generate an identical pattern of preference in two consecutive trials on the same evening. People don't like to make the same guess twice. And indeed, a study of the data shows that they haven't done so.

This isn't the sort of thing you can appreciate just by running your eye over the table of listeners' responses. I'll save you the trouble. The data fall readily into three intuitively distinct groups. The first is the *odd* numbers (Ace, 3, 5, 7, and 9). The second is the *even* numbers (2, 4, 6, 8, and 10). The third is the *court cards* (Jack, Queen and King). We might compare votes between the two tests in the hope of finding a small psi-mediated increase or decrease in the votes for a single number or suit, but that would work only if the proportions of guesses received by each of these three broad categories remains pretty constant.

Bad luck. They don't.

Odd numbers gained 62.4 percent of the votes in Test 1, but only 47.4 percent in Test 4. Such a massive swing could not conceivably be due to psi. A marked shift in those selecting court cards also occurred, with only 21.4 percent doing so in Test 1, rising to 31.9 percent in Test 4. But court cards were *never* targets in either test, so psi *cannot* be responsible for this swing in preference. Granted, this last fact would not have been known for sure until the announcement of the true targets (**2 of Clubs** and **9 of Hearts,** you'll recall), but the magnitude of the swing is enough to show that preferences have altered from one test for the next. Or does it just mean that there aren't any such biases, that people are doing whatever they damned well like?

No. The BBC's radio listeners were not acting entirely randomly—very far from it. By and large, a constant relationship or proportion is retained by each card number from one suit to the next, *within its category*. Nearly parallel zigzag curves are shown when the data are graphed, which reveals that the *internal proportions*, particularly of the odd numbers, are strikingly consistent. Leaving the court cards aside, the most dramatic departure from this regularity is the comparatively huge boost that *number four* received in Test *4*. As we shall see, this can be accounted for in terms of psychological, not psychic, influence.

The upshot, alas, is that we must now reluctantly agree with the original experimenters. When such grand swings of preference are conspicuously visible in the data, there's little point in trying to use the two tests for mutual control. But the Woolley data are not entirely without value. They show that internal regularities can be expected, *despite* shifts of category preference. In the following chapters, we will examine experiments that employ this fact to great advantage.

§

What's especially valuable for its cautionary character is a curious and disproportionate interest in number 4 in the second cards' trial, a.k.a. Test 4. Although I have no proof of the following conjecture, I strongly suspect that Woolley fell into a classical trap—the introduction of an inadvertent cue to a group of respondents.

This variety of self-inflicted injury is now so notorious that the administrators of psychological tests are warned against it in their first year of college. Here's the account of the error given in 1938 by Louis D. Goodfellow of Northwestern University, in a paper where he made good use of the concept to lambaste the Zenith Radio ESP experiments, which we'll examine in the next chapter.

> As experimentalists, we are always concerned over the suggested nature of our instructions. Most persons recognize the great influence of subtle suggestions on human behavior, but many of us do not appear to recognize fully the effects on psychological experiments. In our laboratory, we have demonstrated that a threshold may be altered by suggestion in the instructions. Since the radio participants had no obvious criterion upon which to base their responses, it does not seem unreasonable to suspect them of using any slight cue or suggestion as a basis for their responses. (p. 615)

Indeed, and it's my guess that this is exactly what happened to Woolley subjects when Sir Oliver Lodge told them to prepare for... Test 4. In the absence of any other cues, a small proportion of listeners bent away from the multitude of conscious and unconscious preferences, and cast their vote for number 4.

By the same token, perhaps, we might expect a certain proportion to favor card No. 1 in Test 1. That's less convincing as an example of instruction artifact, though, since for many people the numerical value of the card will surely be lost in the special name "Ace." As it happens, card No. 1 *is* preferred in the first test, with the notable exception that the numinous Ace of Spades did somewhat better in Test 4. But we're dealing with complex human minds here (Ace of Spades is traditionally seen as the highest card in the deck, and the "death card"). Minds are not as mechanically predictable as Skinnerian psychologists used to claim.

Supposing that card No. 4 was indeed skewed in this fashion simply by the mention of "Test 4," how do we explain the heavy shift to King and Queen in the second test? I can imagine no instruction that would have this effect unless Sir Oliver took the opportunity to send a cheerful message to the crowned heads of Europe. But there is a faint hint in the anomalous ascendancy of the dreaded Ace of Spades in Test 4, together with the heavy voting for Joker and "others not of playing card design." A quite remarkable number of people were attracted in the second test to cards of symbolic significance, generally non-numeric ones. Might this have been the tendency of people under increasing stress (or, perhaps, boredom and frustration) to relapse into habit, superstitious patterns, and archetypes? It's worth noting again that the effect is concentrated almost entirely in such non-numeric cards, but does not discriminate particularly between them.

What we find in the Woolley data, then, is evidence both of strong internal consistency from test to test—which might encourage our hopes for measures using internal control—and of powerful, nonpredictable and nonquantifiable aberrations, which spoil those hopes as soon as they have been encouraged.

Additional techniques such as parity ratios are only appropriate (and therefore passed over silently here) when the underlying preferences of those attempting a psychic task are fairly stable—what statisticians call "stationary." Despite the broad "category" stability in the Woolley data, too much unaccountable noise or preference movement manifests itself to depend upon these methods, in this case at any rate.

Happily, though, another radio broadcast trying to elicit mass psi was undertaken a decade after the abortive Woolley experiment. We'll turn now to these far more extensive tests, and see if our technique of internal control estimates can breathe new life into the old, discarded data.

Five: Zenith

Any Sunday evening between September 26, 1937, and January 2, 1938, listeners tuned to one of the radio stations of the US-wide Zenith network were invited to join a massive write-in telepathy experiment. The time was ripe. Europe was coming rapidly to a pre-global war boil, and dread has always encouraged a fervent interest in the paranormal. But that fascination, to some degree at least, had been focused away from the diffuse vapors of the occult toward the new craze—"extrasensory perception" or ESP.

The Zenith programs carefully involved both orthodox academic psychologists and their parapsychological colleagues. Designed as popular entertainment, they were nonetheless intended by the Zenith Foundation to provide substantial and watertight scientific data. At the end of 76 individual trials, about three-quarters of the audience's attempts showed apparent ESP success.

Zenith were delighted to announce that ESP was proved—with odds against chance explanation of 10,000,000,000,000,000,000 (10 quintillion) to one.

Within months, that astronomical estimate had turned to ashes in their mouths. A team of psychologists from Northwestern University, sponsored by the Zenith Foundation to interpret the data with full scientific rigor, declared: "Neither coincidence nor telepathy, but the natural response of an audience to secondary cues caused the 'highly successful' results of the Zenith radio experiments in telepathy" (Goodfellow, p. 610).

How could such a disaster happen? And what can we learn from it?

§

Each broadcast began with a dramatized vignette of historical anti-scientific intolerance, of the Galileo versus the Religious Establishment variety, meant to hype up the listeners' suspension of disbelief. Instructions of the following type were interspersed:

Narrator: Tonight the experiment will make use of two of the characters on the Duke University ESP cards. A square and a circle! I'll repeat the characters to be used tonight. A circle—and a square.

Announcer: Behind a locked door in a room near the studio are ten telepathic senders. Five are men—five are women. By means of a specially-prepared selecting machine one of the two ESP characters will be chosen at random. The ten senders will concentrate upon the character selected—they will try to send the impression of either circle or square to you. During the intervals denoted by the taps of a bell—see if the single thought in the minds of these ten senders comes through space to you. The machine will operate five times.

Narrator: It is best to write down your impression as soon as you receive it. Do not think about it or try to reason that out. Write down your impressions in consecutive order—as rapidly as you get them. The machine is now ready to select number one.

SPIN... or STOP... BELL... INTERVAL... BELL

Narrator: That was number one. The machine will now select number two. (p. 602)

And so on. The "telepathic senders" were students from Northwestern, believers all, gifted with vivid mental imagery. The selecting device was a special roulette wheel; "the actual selections were unknown to anyone except the senders until after the closing of the polls" (p. 602). Most of the options offered binary choices (Black or White, Circle or Cross, etc), with the targets generated by spins of the wheel. For purposes of standardization in the following reanalysis, I have discarded the few exceptions: two tests with only three trials ("Ship-Sounds"; Hot or Cold), the excess trials in four tests comprising more than five trials each (one with six trials, three with seven); and a single test with three options per trial rather than two (Carrots or Corn or Beans). The results, indicating targets and the audience's collective percentage vote—with a theoretical chance mean of 50 percent—are shown in **Table 5.1**. Note that the number of respondents is listed at the left, ranging from 46,433 on September 26, through to a seriously diminished 4,521 on Jan 2.

	1	*2*	*3*	*4*	*5*
Sep. 26 B/W 46,433	52.60 w	53.04 w	51.81 (b)	52.74 w	51.37 w
Oct. 10 B/W 12,388	52.88 b	53.28 w	52.52 w	49.55 b	52.29 w
Oct. 17 B/W 17,239	55.06 w	47.72 b	51.83 b	52.09 w	47.64 b
Oct. 24 o/+ 15,447	55.11 o	50.16 +	53.50 +	50.97 o	53.06 +
Nov. 21 o/+ 19,178	43.65 o	48.77 o	51.52 o	47.76 o	48.63 o
Nov. 14 */+ 14,697	43.48 +	47.69 +	48.76 *	48.27 +	51.03 *
Nov. 28 +/* 20,367	56.31 *	52.28 *	50.49 *	47.48 +	47.13 +
Dec. 5 D/L 17,548	36.03 D	50.64 L	55.81 D	51.06 L	47.02 D
Jan. 2 L/D 4,521	68.37 L	48.14 D	54.24 D	48.74 D	53.35 L
Oct. 31 ≈/* 14,663	55.45 ≈	52.19 *	52.81 *	47.44 ≈	49.34 *
Nov 7. □ /o 13,886	52.42 □	51.02 □	50.42 o	54.75 □	49.89 □
Dec. 12 H/T 6,644	20.80 T	43.44 T	44.17 H	52.76 H	50.67 H

Table 5.1 Zenith weekly broadcast ESP tests, arranged by target type and percentage vote derived from *z* values (number of standard deviations from mean) given in Goodfellow (1938), Table 1, p. 603, shown above.

Key:

b/w : Black/White
o/+ : Circle/Cross
*/+ : Star/Cross
D/L : Dark/Light
≈/* : Waves/Star
□ /o : Square/Circle
H/T : Heads/Tails

Nearly 40 years ago, when I first learned of the Zenith experiments and how they had been apparently debunked, I contacted the then-editor of the *Journal of Parapsychology*, Ms. Dorothy H. Pope, hoping that Dr. Rhine and his colleagues might still have access to the raw data. She replied: "What records we may have from the Zenith broadcast tests were given, along with all our early data and correspondence, to the Duke University library. They were sealed in the archives..." The Duke archives made a valiant effort to unearth the data, but found only the unpublished paper by Dr. Pratt, cited above in chapter 3.

Lacking the original data, then, I have reconstructed these percentages from a published table (Goodfellow, p. 603) that showed the data in z format: that is, the number of standard deviations.[6] The relevant parts of these are displayed in **Table 5.1**.

It's worth noting that the combined raw data provided in Dr. Pratt's somewhat unreliable typescript shows that among the votes reported by Goodfellow was a small number where participants had written down guesses at *options that were not available*.

For example, on November 7, 1937, there were 35,719 votes cast in favor of Square, 33,585 for Circle—and 126 for "Other."

In the very first experiment, September 26, Black was chosen 152,266 times, White 165,017—and "Other" a surprising 2812 times! Different colors or ethnic groups, perhaps?

In the experiment where Heads versus Tails were the options, a bizarre 932 votes (from a total of 33,220 votes) were cast for "Other" choices.

Who could have sent these unsuitable and perhaps ludicrous responses? Pranksters? Smart alecks writing in "Coin lands on Edge"? We can't know, and in any case these inappropriate responses do not muddle the waters too seriously.

---

6. The back-conversion to percentages will be sufficiently accurate for our exploratory purposes. Reconstructing the number of guesses made for each option is achieved by multiplying the *z* score (provide by Goodfellow and shown in **Table 5.2**) by √N, where N is the *total number of votes*, divided by [chance probability of *success* multiplied by chance probability of *failure*], which in this case is just 1/2 x 1/2, or 1/4.

   Example: on Sept. 26, the first collective vote for White is shown (**Table 5.2**) as 11.2 standard deviations above the notional chance score, which would have been half of 46,433 votes. Now, √(46.433/4) = √11,608.25 = 107.74. Multiplying 11.2 (the *z* score) by 107.74 gives us 1206.71 extra guesses for White, which in turn is 2.6% of the total guesses. And you'll find this excess percentage displayed in the appropriate first place in **Table 5.1**, added to the chance probability of 50%. It sounds ridiculously complicated, but once you get hold of it you'll see that it's really quite simple and direct.

	1	*2*	*3*	*4*	*5*
Sep. 26 B/W 46,433	11.2 w	13.1 w	7.8 (b)	11.8 w	5.9 w
Oct. 10 B/W 12,388	6.4 b	7.3 w	5.6 w	-1.0 b	5.1 w
Oct. 17 B/W 17,239	13.3 w	-6.0 b	4.8 b	5.5 w	-6.2 b
Oct. 24 o/+ 15,447	12.7 o	0.4 +	8.7 +	2.4 o	7.6 +
Nov. 21 o/+ 19,178	-17.6 o	-3.4 o	4.2 o	-6.2 o	-3.8 o
Nov. 14 */+ 14,697	-15.8 +	-5.6 +	-3.0 *	-4.2 +	2.5 *
Nov. 28 +/* 20,367	18.0 *	6.5 *	1.4 *	-7.2 +	-8.2 +
Dec. 5 D/L 17,548	-37.0 D	1.7 L	15.4 D	2.8 L	-7.9 D
Jan. 2 L/D 4,521	24.7 L	-2.5 D	5.7 D	-1.7 D	4.5 L
Oct. 31 ≈/* 14,663	13.2 ≈	5.3 *	6.8 *	-6.2 ≈	-1.6 *
Nov 7. □ /o 13,886	5.7 □	2.4 □	0.98 o	11.2 □	-0.25 □
Dec. 12 H/T 6,644	-47.6 T	-10.7 T	-9.5 H	4.5 H	1.10 H

Table 5.2 Zenith weekly broadcast ESP tests, arranged by target type. Data show *z* values (number of standard deviations from mean) given in Goodfellow (1938), Table 1, p. 603. Number of respondents shown at left below dates.

Key:

b/w : Black/White
o/+ : Circle/Cross
*/+ : Star/Cross
D/L : Dark/Light

≈/* : Waves/Star
□ /o : Square/Circle
H/T : Heads/Tails

I have grouped the data out of chronological order because we are going to use internal controls in the analysis, as we did in the Woolley and Soal tests. Consider again the September 26 run, in which 46,433 people contributed relevant guesses. (There were in total seven trials, two of them duds with no target—3 and 7—but we will ignore all but the first five trials, since that will be our standard yardstick.) We see that the first target was White—and 52.60 percent of listeners voted for it. By contrast, on November 21, when Circle was the first target, only 43.65 percent (a huge negative z of -17.6) voted in its favor; that is, 50 percent (the mean chance expected result) minus the observed extra 6.35 percent vote in favor of Cross.

As noted, there is a peculiar exception in the experimental design that relates to the third and seventh choices in the very first test on September 26, 1937. No third or seventh position targets were selected on this occasion, which was a half-hearted attempt to gauge the influence of color preference. Instead, the senders "counted rapidly to themselves" (p. 604).

A second highly-visible peculiarity, which emerged in the experimental situation, is seen in the hugely distorted votes on the first choice for December 5 and 12, and January 2. A perfectly convincing reason—based on predictable widespread biases—has been found for these anomalies, which will be discussed a little later. In several of our calculations, however, their presence would deform the general pattern of these runs of guesses, and they can safely be set aside for special treatment.

§

What do these guessing data mean? A blunt interpretation, endorsed by Zenith, would simply tally the number of positive deviations attained by targets in excess of 50 percent. I'm not certain if the possibility of psi-missing was taken into account, but this *prima facie* approach would seem to dispel any need to consider it. After all, our Table shows an apparent 36 hits out of 59 targets—11 percent more than would be expected if only chance were operating.

But, inevitably, strong biasing factors *were* present, as they were in the Woolley playing card tests. Might we be able to establish what they were, and their strength, whether general or specific—and take them into account, allowing any tiny influence of psi to show through?

Much of the spadework was done by Dr. Louis Deal Goodfellow and his Northwestern team, in a long paper he published in 1938 in the renowned *Journal of Experimental Psychology.* Its then editor, Samuel W. Fernberger, had already fired a barrage at Zenith in the previous volume. Using the same arguments and methods as Goodfellow, he came to the same critical conclusions by a weirdly contradictory path. Fernberger's foray, however, was admittedly exploratory; we'll return to it briefly at the end of this chapter. Goodfellow's investigation seemed definitive, using all the Zenith data. His negative verdict seemed so conclusive that it is unsurprising to find little mention of Zenith in the parapsychological literature thereafter. In *ESP After Sixty Years,* the notable 1940 summary of the quickening expertise among psi researchers, we find this dismissal: "Whatever importance attaches to Goodfellow's conclusions arises basically from the fact that the methods were inadequate for a good ESP test" (Pratt, Rhine, et al, 1940, p. 195).

However, the Goodfellow analysis was severely flawed. It is a strange farrago of brilliant forensic insight, special pleading, and sheer muddle-headedness. But not without value, as we shall see.

§

Dr. Goodfellow began with two puzzles. Firstly, there were far too many agreements in the audience's votes between targets and positive deviations to be accounted for by chance. Second, the number of respondents who had obtained either perfect accuracy in a given test, or who had failed to identify even one target, was far beyond chance expectation. Could telepathy be the factor responsible for these anomalies?

Goodfellow's previous specialty, the study of psychological patterns, led him at once to an alternative conjecture. In any individual test, the guesses made by a respondent are not independent of each other, particularly when the situation offers a binary choice. If you choose White rather than Black the first time, the likelihood of your choosing it a second time is no longer the same. It might be larger or smaller than one in two; that is a matter for empirical discovery (and in fact people tend unconsciously to be less likely to repeat the same choice). Empirical research with small groups of campus subject revealed the following general pattern:

Having established the first response of a test group, the team then found that usually "the second response [was] the same, but with a smaller deviation from chance. The third response, we discovered, would be the opposite and with about the same deviation from chance as the second. The last two responses were insignificant compared with numbers one and three, but were generally the same as number one. In short, the audience aggregate pattern was **11211**, **1** representing the favorite or suggested symbol and **2** representing the alternative one" (Goodfellow, p. 627).

It's worth expressing some worry about this, since most of the psychological testing literature finds that people unconsciously *avoid* repeating the same guess if an unknown sequence is meant to be random. That is, we generally underestimate the true nature of randomness, in which consecutive numbers have no memory of what came before and hence, in a binary choice, are just as likely to repeat as to differ. Still, in this case the numbers and their overall arrangement were there to be inspected, and **11211** was the collaborative form that emerged.

This **11211** pattern, strikingly, appeared in control tests no matter what the options were. If the same pattern could be found in the Zenith data, half the explanation for the big deviations was provided. The other half was equally clear. If the randomly generated target patterns agreed more often than not with this intrinsic bias, just by sheer chance, no paranormal factors need be invoked.

§

Consider how this might work: If, by chance, the target sequence White/White/Black/White/White had been randomly generated by the selecting machine, a disproportionate number of respondents guessing White for the first target will thereafter get *all* the others right—since this would follow the preference pattern of **11211**—which might account for the excess of "perfect scores."

In the same way, a disproportionate number of respondents who started with Black would get *none* right, accounting for the glut of "zero scores."

On the whole, though, wouldn't these groups cancel each other out? No, not if personal preference for one symbol over another, or some subtle cue that creates the same effect, enhances the vote in the opening trial for one of the two options rather than its rival.

Several consequences are entailed by this line of thought, which tries to explain away what looks like psi as nothing more than population preferences for patterned responses. Firstly, the huge number of Zenith subjects will tend *on average* to follow the pattern **11211** in every test. Second, if the majority correctly picked the first target, they will then hit any targets that conform to the pattern, but miss any that stray from it. Third, in those cases where the first target is *incorrectly* identified by the majority, the reverse will occur.

Now, as it happens, in an astonishing 85 percent of the tests, one of the two alternatives attracted more than half the vote in the first, second, fourth, and fifth positions, while scoring below average in the third position. This conforms superbly to the **11211** pattern. Indeed, the mean result of all 12 tests turned out to be very similar to Goodfellow's expectation, which you will recall was derived from his control experiment. The data are displayed in this format in **Table 5.1**, along with a few gross exceptions to the rule.

As well, 39 of the 59 targets that we are considering *are* compatible with this "most preferred" pattern.

This does not mean, of course, that 85 percent of targets were correctly identified. In some tests, the majority vote in the opening trial went to the *non*-target. In those cases, the rule of **11211** instructs us to look for avoidance or *missing* (not to be confused with *psi-missing*) of the targets compatible with the pattern, and *hitting* on the rest.

Perhaps the surprise discovery of these biasing factors dismayed some early parapsychologists, but it need not have done so. Methods have been designed since then to compensate for such biases retrospectively, and indeed in advance of such an experiment being run. Unfortunately, these methods were unavailable to the Zenith Foundation. Even so, looking at these data, we are not given much to get a grip on. While the pattern is certainly visible, it fluctuates in strength from test to test. Opportunities for precise internal control—for example, comparing the vote for a given option, under identical conditions, when it is target and when it is not are limited. There are not many suitable cases. The remainder, alas, we must discard as lacking the crucial pre-requisites for analysis.

Goodfellow failed to carry his investigation even that far. Instead, he expended much effort in locating subtle cues and preferences that might explain why the audience locked in on one initial choice rather than another. His external control explorations did uncover some interesting facts. The control data were collected from four main sources: (1) university classes, (2) a civic organization of a very small middle western town, (3) customers at the Atlantic and Pacific, and National Tea Stores, and (4) groups of clerks in Chicago business houses. In short, a statistical microcosm of the radio audience.

He found, for example, that on the first trial of five choices—which were content-free, since there was no psi target to aim at—Light received 66.4 percent of the vote, compared with Dark's 33.6 percent. One might suppose that this fact alone would have given him a useful clue. In the Zenith tests, Light's first score on December 5 (when it was *not* target) was 63.96 percent. This may be compared with January 2 (when it *was* target) and it received 68.41 percent.

Think about that for a moment. An estimate from *targetless* control data shows an initial choice of Light by 66.4% of guessers. When Light *was* target, the voters preferred Light by an additional 2.01%. When Dark was target, voters chose Light 2.44% *less often* than its control value.

That dramatically balanced difference was staring Goodfellow's analysts in the face, and they missed it.

§

But wait—can this difference be, after all, one of those cases of subtle, inadvertent instruction? "As a result of our studies in sensitivity," Goodfellow had noted, "we have long suspected that when the judgment becomes difficult, an observer will grasp upon the slightest cue available" (p. 617). Since 1938, this conjecture has been amply confirmed, and formalized in the body of results known as signal detection theory. But despite valiant efforts with respect to some of the other target options, Goodfellow was not able to find any indication of intrusive marginal instruction in the weeks when Light and Dark were targets.

A warning, however: the numbers presented above must not be taken as strong evidence that psi affected these particular votes, since the data from which the control estimate was drawn were very small; the standard error was 2.9 percent. (That is, there are two chances in three that random factors will cause votes for Light to fluctuate within this extra range. Two thirds of the time, Light is likely to attract somewhere between 63.5 percent of the vote and 69.3 percent.) Fortunately, though, we can use internal control in this case to obtain confirmation with much more reliability.

Let's look at a comparable case of extreme bias. In a "mental experiment" with coin-tossing, Goodfellow's controls showed a marked preference, not at all surprisingly, for Heads in the opening trial: 78.2

percent of his respondents picked Heads on their first call. This compares with 79.23 percent in the December 12 Zenith test, where tails was the true target. Here, unhappily, we have no internal control drawn from the Zenith population. Since the standard error for the control was 3.3 percent, we cannot safely draw any conclusions about the presence or absence of psi. Note this, however: the general agreement in magnitude of the vote for Heads shows that neither instruction nor massive psi-missing is needed to account for the December 12 result.

A further set of control preferences isolated by Goodfellow is less directly applicable, but suggestive. The percentage of first trial responses made by 239 subjects to ESP characters presented verbally was as follows:

Circle	32.4
Cross	20.8
Square	19.6
Star	13.9
Waves	13.3

The standard error in this experiment was 2.6 percent.

A caution: We cannot simply extrapolate from these figures to a binary choice, expecting for example that in a Circle/Cross choice, Circle will get 60.9 percent (32.4/53.2) to Cross's 39.1 percent (20.8/53.2). The framework of a binary choice tends to flatten such preferences out, since people are more aware that objectively speaking the chances for either option are equal. (Although, as we've seen, even in an imaginary coin toss, a large majority of people tended to call Heads first.) Still, in the absence of countervailing factors, we can certainly expect Circle to defeat any alternative by a small but distinct margin. Similarly, we might expect Star and Waves to be fairly matched in their vote. Finally, the initial vote for Star is very likely to be well below that for Cross.

In some cases, this pattern is exactly what is seen in the Zenith tests. In others—notably the test where Star and Cross were the options—quite the reverse was found, rather startlingly. These were the cases that impelled the northwestern team to search for unintentional cues in the radio script, artifacts that might explain why so many people would act counter to their collective preference. Some of their ingenious suggestions are convincing, some are implausible (and receive no discussion to substantiate them), and some are so preposterous and inconsistent with the evidence that one is justified in accusing the researchers of undeclared bias of their own.

§

To determine if such objective and intrusive factors skewed the votes, recordings were played of the broadcasts to a panel of "fifteen to twenty professional persons" whose evaluations were collated. This is not necessarily the best way to locate *unconscious* influences, but Goodfellow was unable to run large empirical control tests, and the "judges' choice" method had to suffice.

Let's look at some examples of how such contaminating influences might have affected the guesses. On November 14 and 28, 1938, Star was selected strongly by the audience despite their usual communal preference for the alternative, Cross. In only one of these cases was the target actually Star, so psi hitting cannot be the explanation. Here are some excerpts from the script, with the panel's italics and comments:

> "So jot down on your paper. Cross and *Star*. (Emphasized by announcer.) I'll repeat. A cross and a *star... Alone* in a room *high above the streets of Chicago* are ten *especially selected* ('S' sound) telepathic *senders—five* men and *five* women (Five—characteristic points of star not cross)... either a *star* or a cross... The machine will operate *five* times... either a cross or a *star*..." (pp. 615-16)

As Goodfellow admits, it is not clear that "high above the streets of Chicago" favors Star, "since the cross (on a church) is also frequently seen high above the streets" (p. 616). One might add that stars usually come in bunches—even if they're musical stars, who might frequently be found high, I suppose, above the streets of Chicago. On the whole, though, the panel's specifications seem reasonable.

But if these considerations give Star the heavy weighting in this choice, how are we to account for the victory of Waves over Star in the first trial of October 31, when Waves was the target? The judges simply offered their opinion that Waves was the option cued in by subtle instructions, without justifying this assertion. In the absence of a second Waves/Star test to provide internal control, we have no sound grounds for disputing their evaluation—but it looks like special pleading to me.

§

The important point to retain from all this is that whenever the combined force of preference and cues enhanced a given option, the comparatively tiny influence of psi would inevitably have been masked. Goodfellow does not seem to have understood how small the effect size of ESP was likely to be, perhaps because at that early stage in the development of parapsychology a mixture of sloppy technique, superb subjects, and experimenter enthusiasm was producing very large deviations at Duke University—not uncommonly, of the order of 10 percent different from chance expectation or better. "Apparently," Goodfellow commented, perhaps mockingly, "this suggested material was stronger than telepathy" (p. 619). No doubt it was, since typically it produced variations (from the baseline of 50 percent) of a surprisingly large three to six percent.

One case where we can be grateful for his detective work is the puzzling first trial result of November 21. Whether or not we suspect the intrusion of psi, the public majority choice of Cross is disconcerting. The target was Circle, the option endorsed by collective preference and by the strong vote for Circle in the similar test on October 24. If collective preferences are liable to be altered unpredictably to this extent from one test for the next, we shall be unable to rely on internal control as a method for smoothing out background bias.

As it happens, though, on this particular test the script had been vetted ahead of broadcast by the Northwestern team, in their role as consultants. "We had made a special effort to delete from the instructions any suggested lines." Therefore, in the first place, we cannot expect the influence of cues to be the same as it had been in the "loaded" October 24 broadcast.

In the second place, crucially, a fresh and different bias was introduced despite Goodfellow's valiant efforts:

> The reason for this peculiar phenomenon, we believe, lies in the immediately preceding announcement (inserted at the last moment) of the correct answers for the 'star-cross' test of the previous week. The symbol 'cross' was given a prominent place in the stimulus background of the audience because it had been the correct symbol on three of the five trials. (This was the only test in the series in which this type of suggested script was possible.) (p. 620)

So it seems likely that internal control, for the bulk of the remaining cases, remains a viable proposition. But if Goodfellow earns praise for this disclosure, he deserves censure for a different and amazingly far-fetched effort, to which we'll now turn.

§

Among the encouraging features in the Zenith results is the "first-trial" scores in the Black/White tests of September 26 and October 10 and 17. On two occasions, White was the opening target, attracting scores of 52.6 percent and 55.06 percent. On the single occasion when Black was target, White got only 47.12 percent (so Black scored 52.88 percent). Here, it seems, is a perfect example of internal matching revealing the marginal influence of psi.

Understandably, Goodfellow was alarmed by this discrepancy in his model of random chance modified by bias. His judges felt that the script, if it had any effect at all, would cue in White on all three of the tests. His control group showed a personal preference for White of 52.1 percent, with a standard error of 1.6%—supportive of the psi premise, subversive of the null alternative.

Here is Goodfellow's desperate bid at an explanation: "On October 10th, it happened that, immediately preceding the test, Mr. Gutzom Borglum reported his experience conducting Helen Keller through European art galleries. It may have been possible that this emotional suggestion of blindness, darkness and black carried over to predispose part of the audience to start off with a symbol 'black' " (p. 619).

A moment's examination of the Zenith data shows clearly that if this poignant discussion had any effect it was in the *opposite* direction. Consider: when the dichotomy Dark/Light was *explicitly* presented to listeners, on December 5 and January 2, there was an overwhelming rejection of Dark—even when Dark was the target, although then to a lesser extent. It seems plausible that the color discussion, if it had any influence on the guesses, would have augmented the other bias already in favor of White. Given the results as they stand, I am more inclined to think that it had no noticeable effect at all.

In sum, then, Goodfellow's work can be seen as a mixture of useful insights (recognized as such, at the time, by parapsychologists such as Pratt), and misleading assertions. His most helpful contribution was to show the strength and consistency of the **11211** pattern. Even here, alas, he got himself confused. Using frequency counts "based on samples for six tests aggregating approximately 20,000 cases" (p. 605)—a harrowing undertaking in the days before computers—he believed that Zenith's *most popular* formula was the unsymmetrical **11212**.

This might or might not have been true of the entire million odd guesses, and it's no doubt much too late to process the original data electronically to find out. But Goodfellow appears to have made the elementary error of confounding *most popular pattern* with *mean pattern*, which is what counts in such cases as the Zenith experiment. This lack of coherence between his sample and the overall results, which can be derived from his figures by elementary arithmetic, evidently escaped his attention. (The error arose, incidentally, because he took as three of his six sample tests the most grossly unrepresentative of them all: the Heads/Tails and the Dark/Light choices).

But, as we've seen, there *is* a very common pattern in the choices. Locating it is in some ways an academic exercise, because advanced majority vote methods automatically compensate for such pervasive features. Still, it assures us of an important truth: preferences of the sequential kind are highly durable and persistent. Cueing may alter the personal preference for one option over another, but this fundamental structure will emerge in group studies time and again.

Naturally, that background preference pattern of **11211** will be modulated by the particular circumstances. When Head/Tails is the choice, the sequence is amplified because very strong biases exist; the effect is intensified. In other cases, the impact of pattern bias can be flattened to such an extent that it's barely visible. An instance is the November 7 Square/Circle test, in which the targets actually did fall into the **11211** pattern, with the first option correctly identified by the majority. Here, if anywhere, one would expect conspicuous "hitting." But what actually happened deviated from the generic **11211** pattern. Only the fourth target received conspicuous attention, and the fifth failed to obtain a majority. The most we can say is that almost always the pattern will provide the skeleton, while the amount of fat and muscle will be firmed out according to constitutional factors—personal preferences, subtle instructions... and psi.

§

After all that, is there any good evidence in the Zenith results for the presence of psi? We have seen some scattered examples where controls hint at the small psychic component in addition to the sway of pattern preference factors. Goodfellow's reproof to the Zenith Foundation, rebuking them for their inflated estimates of the significance of the deviations found—on the justified grounds that bias, cues and so on, do account for most of them—is largely well taken. Nonetheless, we can ask whether it is possible for more sophisticated parapsychological techniques to tease out at least some of the right answers, from portions of the data where Goodfellow's policies would hardly expect to find them? That would be a triumph for those who take the paranormal seriously.

Dr. J.B. Rhine did not think so. In 1962, more than two decades after the experiments were debunked, he wrote:

> Persistent difficulty... has been encountered in the past in designing an effective test of ESP for mass application. Generally speaking, there has been no adequate public type of test with sufficient sensitivity and efficiency to be usable... the most common trouble may be illustrated by the most extensive mass test program on record, a test conducted by the Zenith radio program which ran through a 9-month period of 1937-8. The difficulty of having to use a common set of targets for all the participants made it impossible to avoid the obscuring of ESP effects, if any genuinely existed, in the course of necessary corrective statistical procedures. The Greville correction was developed and applied, but the Zenith mass test with the Greville correction did not produce significant results. Either ESP was not present or the test as modified was not sensitive enough. (*J. Parapsychology*, 1962, p. 245)

The Greville correction was published in 1944. It was the first of the statistical methods designed to compensate for the stacking effect. But indeed it was not appropriate to the Zenith tests. Too many elements of bias exist in that data to hope that a general estimate of significance will trace a psi signal through the deafening noise. The same objection applies to Pratt's contingency tables in his unpublished typescript, which ignored the **11211** preference pattern and lumped together all the data for each target option. Careful selection of comparable cases is required, though the criteria of selection must be immune to the charge that they are self-serving. The Greville correction, as Rhine surmised, is an instrument deficient in the fine tuning we will need.

Notice, for instance, a feature of the opening choices that looks lawful but is irrelevant, whether we endorse the psi hypothesis or not. In chronological order, the majorities tend to increase in size. Is this due simply to the fact that the later tests use more emotionally charged options? It is not a function of bigger numbers of subjects causing the deviations to bunch more tightly around theoretical mean: November 28's 20,000 respondents, with a first option vote of 56.31 percent, compared with October 10's 12,000, where the vote for Black was only 52.88 percent.

Since the initial guess in a series is probably the one with the greatest grip on both attention and imagination, it's perhaps most vulnerable to psychological reinforcements and lures. In the first six tests on our table, the majority vote of the first choice was correct. Given the existence of cues, could it be that the tendency to heed them was being cumulatively and unconsciously encouraged by this string of successes? If so, we would have another factor operating to obscure the presence of a small psi effect. The Greville correction, or any rectifying device obliged to take account of *all* the guesses, would simply be flummoxed by these tides of noise.

One can readily appreciate, then, why parapsychologists have for so many years vowed that there is a dearth of evidence for psi in the Zenith data. I believe that reports of this dearth have been much exaggerated.

§

Let us go right back to the empirical discovery of the **11211** preferred sequence. If there is any psi in the data, it will bob up on top of that pattern like a cork on an ocean wave. But since the wave itself will rise and fall—while keeping its overall form—how can we tell what is psi and what are merely the varying fortunes of bias?

We can start, of course, by looking for exceptions to the rule.

Consider again the data displayed in **Table 5.1**.

If Goodfellow were correct, and "any implication substantiating telepathy is an obvious artifact of the experimental set up," we would find that these exceptions to the collective preference pattern are wrong some 56 percent of the time. (This is because, following his dictum, 33 of our 59 targets—that is, 56%—would obtain positive deviations from the mean just by being *consistent* with first choice-plus-**11211**-pattern.) A tally of the nine exceptions to the bias pattern shows quite another proportion.

Three of the exceptions to the **11211** rule are found in percentage of votes in the second position for October 10 (53.28), October 24 (50.16) and October 31 (52.19). All of these correspond to the target, and are *contrary to the general preference pattern.*

One majority-vote preference-pattern deviant is in the third position for November 28 (50.49)—again, a hit.

There are two preference-pattern deviants in the fourth position for October 10 (49.55) and 31 (47.44); these both indicate misses.

In the fifth position, correct answers are given by pattern-deviant calls on October 10 (52.29) and October 24 (53.06), and incorrectly on November 7 (49.89).

So, in total, six majority vote tallies are correct, while only three are wrong. Combined, these nine "crucial exceptions" have a mean deviation from 50 percent of 0.93 percent—extremely satisfying, in view of the most common figure (an excess of about one percent) for visible psi efficiency in many early card-calling tests.

I think this is evidence enough to dispel the myth that the Zenith data are barren of evidence for psi. Although we have examined only selected cases from the 59 available to us, they constitute the entire body of data that is accessible—so far as I can see—to scrutiny of this kind. Our findings so far suggest that using even such crude exploratory tools as these, in a veritable battlefield mined with bias and dangerous artifacts, we found psi more often than not.

It is certainly not unreasonable, in these circumstances, to extrapolate its presence throughout the test—even if it seems difficult to prove this.

But happily, there is another route we can trace. In places, it will join the path just trodden. Elsewhere, it will show us evidence for psi where we have not yet noticed it. I am obliged, though, to repeat what I stressed in the Woolley analysis, and was noted by Rhine and Pratt at the time: these early ESP experiments were not well-constructed. The results we obtain will be provided by features of the Zenith tests that seem to be present more by good luck than by astute planning.

The method we will employ, in fact, is our old standby: internal control. Only three of the Zenith tests—the Black/White discrimination—even begin to approach adequacy in this respect. Another six give us 10 trials where we can use the method with some hope of success. This is a far cry, though, from Rhine's total abandonment of the broadcast data.

§

As a satisfactory minimum, a properly deployed internally controlled psi application must present each available symbol at least three times, with the restriction—ordained in advance—that "target" must not coincide with that symbol on every occasion. Imagine three runs of five trials at the choice Black/White. If Black obtained a majority of around 54 percent in the initial trial of all runs, and the target in each case also happen to be "Black," we would remain uncertain whether this apparent accuracy of the guesses was due to psi, general population preference, or cueing.

External control runs with no targets might help, by showing, say, that Black is usually chosen in the opening position by 52 percent of respondents. For its internal control, however, we must ensure that both Black and White have fairly even chances of being randomly selected as target. This raises a further problem for psi applications. If sensitive subjects know that this restriction is in force, it will tend to make them change their votes from run to run—which could result in excess of apparent "hitting" or "missing," depending on how well they did with their very first guess. So in practice, subjects must be kept in the dark about the experiment format—and will make their guesses at numerous permutations of the target sequence, so that each option becomes target an equal number of times.

Only one Zenith set (Black/White) meets this requirement, but three do have the *absolute* minimum of two appearances. These are Circle/Cross, Star/Cross, and Dark/Light.

With these criteria in mind, we can turn to the results set out in **Table 5.3**, where the deviations from "same symbol" means are shown for all suitable pairs and triplets. What we are comparing is the score for a given symbol (in each given trial position from first through fifth) *when it was target*, versus *when it was* not *target.*

Mean "White" scores:					
	51.60	52.87	49.63	51.76	52.01
Deviations of White votes from their overall means:					
Sept 26 Pred./Targ.	+1.01 W/W	+0.18 W/W	(-1.44) control	+0.98 W/W	-0.64 B/W
Oct 10 Pred./Targ.	-4.48 B/B	+0.41 W/W	+2.89 W/W	-1.31 B/B	+0.28 W/W
Oct 17 Pred./Targ.	+3.46 W/W	-0.59 B/B	-1.46 B/B	+0.33 W/W	+0.35 W/B
Mean relevant "Circle" scores:					
		49.31	49.01	47.79	
Oct 24 Pred./Targ.		+0.53 0/+	-2.51 +/+	-0.85 +/+	
Mean relevant "Star" scores:					
	56.41				51.95
Nov 14 Pred./Targ.	+0.10 */+				-0.92 +/*
Mean relevant "Light" scores:					
	66.19	51.25		51.17	53.17
Dec 5 Pred./Targ.	-2.23 D/D	-0.61 D/L		-0.11 D/L	-0.19 D/D

Table 5.3: Zenith "internal control" analysis: means and deviations (%'s)

For the three sets in which Zenith provided only a single repetition of a given pair of options, the deviation is shown for only one of the pairs. In such cases, as a moment's reflection will prove, success in one test automatically entailed success in the other, and failure in one forced failure upon the other. Each pair of this kind therefore constitutes a single test. In the three Black/White trials, this is no longer true to the same extent, and each predictive deviation can be allowed to stand on its own.

The results are surprisingly impressive for the psi hypothesis. Of the Circle/Cross pairs, two of the three predictions suggest psi-hitting. With Star/Cross, one out of three is correct, and in the Dark/Light choice two out of four are correct. Although this totals five right and five wrong, apparently a chance result, *the mean correct deviation is +1.2 percent*, while the wrong predictions averaged only -0.46 percent. In most of these cases, the standard deviation hovers around 0.4 percent, so we must expect *by chance alone* to see a large number of cases (both right and wrong) in this range. If we consider deviations of about 2.5 times that magnitude—which can be expected by chance only once in 100 times—we're left with only two strong predictions, and both of those are correct.

The White/Black triplet is still more impressive. Here, at last, we meet our minimum adequate standards: three repetitions of the choices, in none of which is the target identical for a given position (that is, first through fifth) in all three cases. The result? *Twelve out of 14 targets deviating in the correct direction from the empirical means.*

If we restrict our attention to deviations of one percent or better, allowing for the skeptics' jibe that some of these successes fall within a range to be expected quite often by chance alone, we find six cases... *all* of which are correct!

Tallying the 14 results in the White/Black trials, we find that the correct deviations from empirical means average +1.42 percent, while deviations in the wrong direction average -0.5 percent. This is remarkably close to the proportions obtained in our analysis of the three "pair" sets, and give us *a psi-hitting estimate of +1.15 percent.*

What's more, using the cut-off point of one percent in each individual case, we have, in all, eight correct positive deviations out of eight—100 percent success!

Dr. Rhine abandoned hope too easily.

§

One further refinement of our method suggests itself. I present it reluctantly, hedged about with cautions and provisos. Despite the conviction of most people that we choose and act from free will, our actions are not infinitely various. They are seldom even arbitrary. In a contained, circumscribed context, people's behavior will tend to fall into limited classes of actions. That is why it is generally possible to enter a store during trading hours and be served, eventually. It is highly predictable that people will not drive their cars backwards down the freeway. One can safely expect to be mugged in certain city streets after dark. But the application of statistics to human affairs remains more an art than a science. We can never be certain that we have isolated the principal determinants governing those classes of action that interest us.

The polarization of votes for "first option" opening choices seems to increase lawfully as the Zenith tests progress, until December 5 when heavy preference factors skew the progression out of all accounting. If this is an authentic, virtually universal factor, we ought to bring it into our analysis and attempt to compensate for it by some sort of scaling or normalization procedure. I have not established to my satisfaction that such a factor does exist. It would require a complex factor analysis on the raw data, which is, as they say, above my pay grade. As a tentative hypothesis, however, let us apply the simplest possible version of this model to the White/Black tests, and see what it looks like.

For there is one rather distressing anomaly in these White/Black figures. As noted earlier, the third trial in the September 26 test was assigned no target and, in accordance with the predominant **11211** pattern, the radio audience favored Black in this run, to the tune of 51.81 percent. This then, would seem to provide a good basis for estimating pure bias for Black when it is in the third position. But in the next such test, where White was the target in the third position, that estimate of Black's bias would give psi credit for a whopping 4.33 percent correct White deviation. In the third such test, Black's inferred psi component would only be 0.02 percent. That is as implausibly low as the previous inferred psi value was implausibly large.

If some factor other than chance augmented White's vote in the last of these three tests, this result becomes more explicable. And there is reason to suppose this factor is a reality. Consider again the opening option votes of September 26 (52.60 percent) and October 17 (55.06 percent). In both these cases, White was target, yet that symbol's deviation was much greater in the latter test—hardly a feature one might attribute to psi alone. Suppose this intensification of preference applied to all the calls in the second test?

Our somewhat questionable adjustment, then, is to rescale the second and third tests in such a way that the "most preferred vote" in the initial position of each run is set at 52.61 percent—so is to bring the two later tests into line with the first. This will yield a conservative estimate, since it must act to *reduce* slightly any psi that is operating in the scaled tests. Still, this is a price worth paying. These rescaled values are displayed in **Table 5.4**.

Sept 26	52.60 T	53.05 T	(48.19)	52.74 T	51.37 T
Oct 10	47.40	53.51 T	52.76 T	50.70	52.53 T
Oct 17	52.60 T	49.98	46.05	49.80 T	50.06

Table 5.4: Black/White tests: Scaled to equalize first–trial majority votes. "White" votes shown, white targets indicated.

And lo and behold! The "third position" anomaly disappears. White's vote, for that third position in the October 17 tests, now safely falls below the control figure—appropriately, since on that occasion Black was the target. Even more satisfactorily, we now have 13 of the 14 targets correctly identified.

Prudence, of course, warns us not to put too much stock in this result. It's worth acknowledging, though, that this adjustment could have been made *in advance of any knowledge of the true targets*, and probably would have been, in any thorough computerized search of the raw data. Alas, such computers were unknown in 1938. Luckily for us, today almost every desk has one or more as does every smart phone.

Dr. Pratt's analysis of the Zenith data made an excellent point while missing the value of what is hidden inside this small treasure trove:

> It cannot be said, from the data, that there does not remain some small amount of agreement between subjects and station explicable by telepathy. But it is clear that this residue, if it exists, must be very small compared to the influences analyzed.
>
> Since it is essentially the public preference for a certain sequence of guesses which thus operates so strongly in producing the present

> data, it would be wise in the future to design experiments to avoid the effect of this phenomenon as far as is possible. Since the effect is clearest in the first four guesses in any experiment, the distortion could be avoided by conducting experiments of sufficient length so that these first four (at least) could be discarded. It is presumable that the tendency of subjects to avoid sequences of more than two similar guesses is strongest in short series. Where the series was long enough, this compunction would not be so strongly felt after the first few choices. It would seem to me that future experiments of this sort should not be attempted with series of less than twelve or fifteen guesses in each experiment. Only then could one begin to analyze the results beyond the effect of preferential sequences." (Pratt typescript, pp. 11-12).

Even if we admit that this survey of the Zenith data does suggest, to everyone's surprise, that psi actually was operating during the experiment, what of the many trials that were not accessible to any analysis based on internal controls? Strictly speaking, we can say nothing at all about them. But perhaps Occam's Razor permits us to infer the active, but masked, presence of psi throughout the entire Zenith series.

Six: Fisk and West and Michie

NOTHING IN SCIENCE is more vicious and sterile than an unfalsifiable hypothesis. If a conceptual model is capable of "explaining" any number of mutually-exclusive phenomena, it's worthless, and justly suffers the derision and detestation of all right thinking scientists. Yet by invoking the apparently facile notion of two psi contrasting modes—hitting and missing—don't we fling ourselves headlong into this odious quagmire? At the very least, don't we run the grave risk of incorporating any deviation from mean chance expectation, in either direction and of whatever magnitude, as "evidence" for psi?

After all, I have paid attention to deviations of around one percent of the guesses even when the total number of trials in the experiment has been too small for any such excess or deficit to be statistically significant. But even when statistical significance has been achieved, it must seem preposterous to claim both negative deviations and the Zenith positive deviations as indicators of a single anomalous agency.

The most notable early attempts to use multiple guesses and majority-vote were conducted in Britain during the mid-1950s by D.J. West (b. 1924 and still alive at 91 as I write this), G.W. Fisk (1882-1972, then a retired businessman and inventor), and D. Michie (pronounced "Mickey," perhaps unfortunately given that his first name was Donald; he was born in 1923 and died in 2007). Despite some early hints of success, Dr. West rapidly became disillusioned with this method. By 1964, as noted above, he was stating publicly: "attempts to extract significance from the guesses of large numbers of subjects... have not proved fruitful." Perhaps this authoritative statement from a man who had clearly invested great hopes in the method is one of the key factors in turning parapsychologists away from the many guesses/majority vote approach. It's true that repeated failure on the part of a credible team of researchers must greatly damage any prospects for a *reliable* process of psychic application.

The first of these experiments was conducted over 56 weeks, from January 1954 to February 1955. It was not originally intended to test the majority vote approach, but to discover "any relationship that might exist between a subject's ESP score and his mood at the time when he took part in the test" (Fisk & West, 1956, p. 320).

Designed jointly by Fisk and West, it made use of a novel set of target cards devised by Fisk to allow for the statistical study of possible displacement effects. Each card showed a clock face with the hour hand pointed at one or other of the twelve hour positions. This was the theory: a blurred sidelong impression might confuse the two o'clock with say one o'clock or three o'clock, but it was hardly likely to do so with an hour further removed.

(Actually, given what we have subsequently learned from remote viewing, it quite often happens that a psychic image is flipped right to left, like a mirror image. If that happens, you might find a target at one o'clock being misunderstood as one at eleven o'clock. But this is something that the experimenters knew nothing of, so they failed to keep the appropriate records that would allow us to check for such effects.)

For simplicity, Fisk displayed three target cards each day (drawn from a randomized deck of 12) on the wall of his study, while distant volunteers mailed in their guesses each day, together with indications of their "feeling-tone" at the time. (106 came from various parts of Great Britain, 27 from the USA and Canada, 21 from Spain, and 8 from France.) In total, they notched up 35,716 calls. "Nearly 200 volunteers started the 'Daily Three' routine and of these 162 completed at least half of the course of 192 calls... a minimum of 96 calls were required for a score to be included"(p. 321). For simplicity, let's call the accumulated guesses made each day a *run*.

The overall result was bitterly disappointing. Fisk and West found that their respondents had accumulated a negative deviation from chance expectation with a probability of less than 0.05 percent.

Then West had a bright idea.

"It occurred to D.J.W. that it would be worthwhile in this case, in which there is a fairly long target series, to work out for each trial the most popular guess or 'majority vote'" (pp. 322-23). Since this was merely an adjunct to the search for mood correlations, subjects who had failed to note their mood had already been excluded, leaving 34,869 calls for 143 subjects.

The exact details of how the "Daily Three" predictions were judged are somewhat obscured in their paper, but it seems to have worked this way:

As a participant, you received a bundle of documents that included instructions, and a "mood" questionnaire plus score sheets to be filled out each day and mailed back. These score sheets would have shown three empty places, and your task was to write in your guesses for the hour cards sitting far away in Long Ditton, Surrey, on Fisk's mantelpiece in the left, central and right positions.

So you might meditate for a moment and then write down (say) 7, 9, 2, then post this form back to the experimenters along with your mood estimate. (Since these cards were all drawn from the same mini-pack of 12, you should not write 7, 7, 7, because once you'd chosen a certain hour for one card the next had to be drawn from the remaining cards.)

When he had received all that day's guesses, Fisk would tally the votes for each position, drawn from the twelve options. Quite often, a plurality of voters—that is, enough voters selecting a number more often than any other but without gaining an absolute majority—would prefer one particular hour for position one, perhaps by only a small collective margin, then another for position two, then a third for position three. If so, those preferred options would be accepted as the three "majority" votes on that day. But note that the published details are not absolutely clear about this. Presumably if the three cards were, from left to right, 6, 9, and 4, you would not be credited with *any* hits if you wrote on your score-sheet "4, 6, 9."

Let's suppose that's how it worked. Then sometimes an equal number of participants would select two or more of the hours as their choice for a given position. If 100 votes were mailed in on a certain day, the left-hand square might get 15 votes for Hour Three, but also 15 votes for Hour Two. All the rest would gain fewer votes—but West's method forced him not only to ignore those losers, but also to throw out the votes for Three and Two... just because neither of them constituted a "majority vote" that day. He wrote: "sometimes two or more guesses were equally popular and no majority vote could then be recorded... the majority vote method caused a lot of null data to be eliminated. All these occasions of which there was a tie, that is to say no absolute majority for any particular target, were excluded from the count (p. 323-24)."

This move by West left me aghast. Instead of totaling the votes obtained for each hour, day after day throughout this long experiment, and thereby constructing a filter used to counter the preference biases for and against choosing each hour, West had insisted on a simple majority in each card position... and thrown out all votes in all the runs that had no such clear majority! After this appalling defoliation, he was left with 657 "majority" predictions, and not nearly as much background information about general preferences as he could have retained and used to calibrate his results.

From his table (**Table 6.1**, below) it is clear that Hour Three (three o'clock) was particularly favored, due to the widespread preference or bias in favor of that "magic" number. It was chosen more than 10 percent of the time *whether or not it corresponded on that day with the displayed target.*

Since there were 12 candidate Hours, mean chance expectation is 8.3 percent of the vote for each. Response biases—the preferences for or against each number swaying those who provided the guesses—shifted the scores for each Hour away from this mean. Hour Ten was chosen most frequently in only 6 percent of runs, Hour Eleven 6.6 percent, and Hour Twelve (or midnight, with its negative "witching hour" emotional charge) got only 5.8 percent of the calls.

Hour	Number of Votes
1	2972
2	3261
3	3524
4	3366
5	3118
6	2665
7	3454
8	2901
9	3171
10	2113
11	2314
12	2010
Total	34869

Table 6.1
"ESP and Mood" experiment. Votes shown for each Hour.

The targets randomly generated for these trials also varied somewhat in frequency, though not nearly to the same extent. If we match target frequencies against response bias frequencies, it turns out that by chance this skewed population ought to have correctly identified slightly *less* than one twelfth of all targets. This is an important point—had the target frequencies, purely by chance, coincided with bias frequencies (as happened by chance in the Zenith experiment), the results might have looked like psihitting. That confusion, at least, did not arise.

§

The real problem in combining groups of guesses that are distorted by bias can easily be demonstrated. Consider what happens with a pattern of responses distorted by the cultural preferences shared by many of the respondents. Since Hour Three was usually favored by a small margin, this *could* have led to a plurality vote for the popular Hour Three *in every single one* of the 657 runs! And since Hour Seven was nearly as popular, it also could have been chosen in every run. It was not impossible that every day a majority of voters in the "Daily Three" task would have chosen Hour Three, Hour Seven, and either Hour Two or Four.

In reality, not quite. Without bias, each hour would have the same chance of being chosen by the majority: roughly 55 times (657 divided by 12). Actually, Hour Three was guessed as a target by the majority just twice that often. At the other extreme, Hour Twelve failed to get anything like its fair share—instead, it was voted as one of the three targets by the majority just 12 times, less than a quarter of its fair share. (See **Table 6.2**, below).

Despite this intrusive skew due to bias, West found to his delight that the majority choices of his respondents correctly tipped 77 of the 657 targets examined. The mean number expected purely by chance coincidence, as we have seen, would have been about 55. The probability of a deviation of +/22 is about one in 100—modest evidence, in the absence of orthodox explanation, of paranormal success.

Sadly, the experimenters did not grasp the merits of their approach. In their paper, as noted above and repeated here for emphasis, Fisk and West stated: "It may be that the majority vote method is a good one to use when dealing with mass ESP tests, but the reason for its effectiveness is not at all clear."

§

Reading these published but more or less forgotten results more than 30 years ago, I could hardly believe that West had given up so easily. It seemed to me that if he had understood the impact of response bias, he might have looked for correlations it seems reasonable, in hindsight, to expect. In 1978, more than two decades after their paper was published, I asked Dr. West if he would send me the original unpublished data. While he could not find the old trialbytrial score sheets, he kindly provided a summary of the data. This data is startling and illuminating when examined with the tools that have been devised since the tests were conducted. Indeed, of all the classic ESP tests I've subjected to close scrutiny, this one comes closest to providing a convincing proof of the reality of psi, and a means whereby we might come to know the apparently unknowable. Why? Because its most compelling features were *not even reported* in the original paper, having been deemed entirely unimportant by the experimenters.

Dyed-in-the-wool skeptics will assume this is a typical instance of parapsychological fraud. If so, it must surely be one of the most extraordinary demonstrations of patience in the annals of imposture. True, West might have invented his data summaries upon my request in 1978. What is also at issue, therefore, if his probity is put in question, is the credibility of the Emeritus Professor of Clinical Criminology at the University of Cambridge. I leave further investigation of that line to others, and proceed on the basis of assumed good faith.

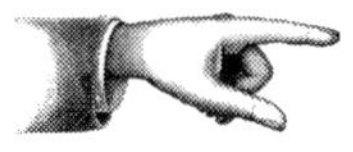

Table 6.2
FiskWest "ESP and Mood" test

Data after majority vote taken in aggregated daily calls. The gray-shaded **bold** numbers on the diagonal from 1-1 to 12-12 show how many times the target Hour was correctly identified by majority calls. Note that when all-time favorite Hour *3* was the target card, it was correctly called by majority vote 12 times. But Hour *6* was incorrectly called 13 times as *3*. When Hour *11* was target, it was mistakenly called 14 times as *3*. (People love calling *3*.) When the popular Hour *7* was target, it received 14 majority votes, but when Hour *12* was target it received only 2 majority calls but got 12 *wrong* majority calls as Hour *7*. There is a lot of noise and bias disrupting the signal.

Target Hours

MAJORITY CALLS	*1*	*2*	*3*	*4*	*5*	*6*	*7*	*8*	*9*	*10*	*11*	*12*	CALL FREQ.
1	**3**	4	1	4	9	8	3	6	4	6	5	7	60
2	10	**10**	2	3	9	4	6	9	7	3	8	3	79
3	12	7	**12**	8	5	13	11	6	7	7	14	3	110
4	9	4	8	**7**	9	8	4	8	2	6	7	5	77
5	2	6	6	8	**9**	2	2	7	2	5	5	4	58
6	4	5	1	4	2	**7**	4	4	4	3	1	1	40
7	7	5	8	2	6	8	**14**	8	5	7	4	12	86
8	4	4	5	4	4	2	3	**3**	6	7	2	4	48
9	3	2	2	4	6	5	9	5	**8**	6	5	1	56
10	1	0	1	0	1	1	1	2	1	**1**	1	0	10
11	1	1	4	2	1	1	2	3	3	2	**1**	0	21
12	0	3	0	0	1	0	2	1	1	1	1	**2**	12
COLUMN SUMS	56	51	50	46	62	59	61	62	50	54	54	52	657

Table 6.2
FiskWest "ESP and Mood" test

The most interesting feature of these results is not that West failed to see any evidence of psi in his participants' calls. On the contrary, he was encouraged by finding an overall excess in hits, scattered among the actual targets, of 77 correct majority votes. But these accurate calls did not seem to provide any evidence of practical benefit from the majority vote protocol. I suspect this was because his evaluation of success or failure was pitched at too high a degree of mathematical abstraction. Charting the numbers reveals a more dramatic effect.

Table 6.2 (above) matches targets against aggregated majority votes. Each call marks the hour chosen by the greatest number of participants in the "Daily Three" tests, judged on a clear majority-vote basis. At first glance, the 12 by 12 tabulation looks like a random shotgun pattern, with values scattered in no obviously intelligible manner. Look more closely, and consistencies emerge.

Majority calls for Hour Ten, Eleven and Twelve, as we might guess from the summary data, are never numerous. For this group, the high point is 4 calls for Hour Eleven—though the actual target corresponding to that mini-peak was the usually popular Hour Three.

Small sample size is to blame for the "shotgun" effect. The sample is too small to smooth out the graininess of random fluctuations in the respondents' massed guesses. Had there been thousands of majority calls instead of a few hundred, much of this bumpy granulation would have subsided.

(If nothing but chance were operating, in a very large sample, each cell would show close to 1/144th of the massed vote. In this experiment, the mean chance expectation is 4.56 calls per cell. However, as noted, people prefer some numbers over others. If only *those* biases were operating, Hour Three cells would have shown 110/12, or about 9, calls and Hour Twelve 12/12, or 1, call per cell. As it is, the "random walk" scatter allowed by the small sample size piles on extra confusion.)

Rows show how many times calls were assigned to each of the 12 possible choices for a given Hour. Consider Hour One. It was chosen 3 times by majority vote when One was indeed the target; 4 times when Hour Two was the target; 1 time when Hour Three was target; and so on. Strikingly (and, of course, incorrectly) there were 9 majorityvote calls for Hour One when the target was really Hour Five, and 8 when Hour Six was target.

In short, there is great variation in the number of calls allocated to the different options. In the case of Hour One, there's no hint at all in this "mediumgrained" data that majority opinion favored either the correct Hour or even any Hour in its immediate vicinity.

Columns list how often each Hour was called when each of the twelve hours was target.

There were 51 occasions when Hour Two chanced to be target. During those occasions, it accrued 4 erroneous Hour One calls, 10 correct Hour Two calls, 7 erroneous Hour Three calls, and so on. In this case, no other Hour was granted a greater tally of calls in its target column than Hour Two itself, which is consistent with the operation of psihitting in this test (although naturally this does not *prove* its action).

The diagonal running from upper left to lower right shows the cells where call rows and target columns intersect. The psi hypothesis is that these cells will show a significant numerical difference from the background nontarget cells. Summed, as we've seen, they do: they add up to 77 correct. But it is clearly *not* the case that these cells show the highest possible scores (though some of them do).

The point to notice is this:

If psi does not exist, there should be no intrinsic difference between the 12 "calls when target" diagonal and any other sample of 12 cells from the matrix.

A graphic way of checking to see if this is true is to arrange the 12 "target" cells in order, from fewest to most calls per cell, and compare this with a similar ordering of the 132 "nontarget" cells.

For example, out of 132 "nontarget" cells there are 8 with zero calls, and 6 with doublefigure calls (that is, 10 or greater). As against this, out of 12 "target" cells there are none with zero calls, and 3 with doublefigure calls. The "target" diagonal has the same underlying "random walk" appearance as the "nontarget" array, but it does not look like a mere sample from that array. (Warning: this is a simplification, since samples tend to wander a bit under the umbrella of the population curve; still, the point remains broadly valid.)

To make this more concrete, imagine you have 100 Grenadier guardsmen, the kind that stand motionless outside the gates of Buckingham Palace. Before they don their famous ceremonial "bearskins" or high furry headgear, line them up in order of height, from shortest on the left to tallest on the right. Then have 10 of them, picked at random, put their caps on, and reorganize the squad by visible altitude. Several of the shorter guards shuffle to the right, and the taller guards in bearskins cluster at that end.

Cell Contents (= number of majority votes)	Total Number of Cells Containing Cell Contents	
	Non-Target (incorrect) Vote	Target (correct) Vote
0	8	0
1	21	2
2	17	1
3	9	2
4	20	0
5	12	0
6	11	0
7	10	2
8	12	1
9	6	1
10	1	1
11	1	0
12	2	1
13	1	0
14	1	1
Sum	132	12

Table 6.3
Data displayed by number of calls per cell

Now, adapting that graphic image, take the "non target" rank ordering in groups of 11, from the lowest to the highest, and find their mean values. The lowest, as you can see at once, contains (8 x 0) + (3 x 1). The mean value is 3/11, or 0.27. By comparison, the lowest "target" cell contains 1 vote. The next highest cells in each case contain 1 vote, showing no difference between the two populations. Thereafter, the values diverge in exactly the way one would predict on the basis of the majority vote model of psi perception. The highest nontarget group contains (5 x 9) + (10) + (11) + (2 x 12) + (13) + (14). The mean is therefore 117/11, or 10.64. The highest target cell is, however, 14.

0.27	1
1	1
1.36	2
2	3
2.82	3
4	7
4.18	7
5.09	8
6.09	9
7.18	10
8.09	12
10.64	14
Means:	
4.39	6.42

Table 6.4

Means of consecutive groups of 11

"When not Target" on left, compared to raw scores "When Target" on right.

The upshot is simple: in this experiment, after account is taken of response biases and random walk variation, 11 out of the 12 "when target" cells show a small but definite excess of correct calls over and above the values we would expect to see by chance. The average majority vote for all 657 calls was 4.56 (657/144). The nontarget cells average a vote of 4.39 calls (580/132), while the target cells average 6.42 (77/12). And this disparity fits in with the model derived from information theory—that is, psienhanced calls should look like any other randomly selected batch of calls in a given test population, plus [in the "psi-hitting" mode] *a significant increment of correct calls added in on top.*

In other words, looking at the graph below (**Figure 6.1**), it is exactly as if each targetmatched cell is a perfectly ordinary representative or "shotgun scattered" cell plucked from the background of nontarget cells and then given a boost of several percent.

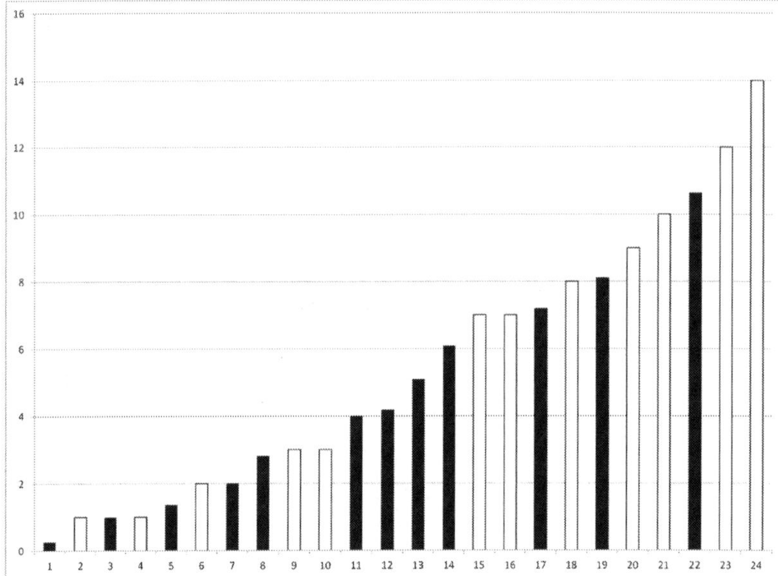

Figure 6.1. Mean Value sorted by Magnitude

Black bars show the range of mean values of non-Target majority votes taken in consecutive groups of 11, from lowest to highest, while **White bars** show the Target votes. It is vividly apparent that the Target votes are drawn from the same largely random array, but given a small additional boost by psi.

§

A more sophisticated treatment must normalize the data to remove the influence of response bias. Recall how this works: instead of staying with the raw votes, each Hour's tally is rescaled to its proportion of the 100 percent gained overall by that Hour. The numerals Three and Seven are known to be significantly preferred when people are instructed to make a quick guess at a random number between, say, 1 and 10.

Suppose, then, that Hour Three almost *always* gains a plurality of votes, whether it's actually a target or not. In this case, it turns out that Three was guessed 3524 times, while the disliked Twelve only captured 2010 votes. So Hour Three, whether or not it's a target, gained 75 percent more votes than Hour Twelve. To cancel out this influence of preference or bias, we simply turn all the raw votes to percentages.

How does that look in practice? Well, the 110 votes attained by Hour Three in this experiment (Row 3 in **Table 6.3** above) look like this:

1	*2*	*3*	*4*	*5*	*6*	*7*	*8*	*9*	*10*	*11*	*12*
12	7	12	8	5	13	11	6	7	7	14	8

While the scant votes for Hour Twelve are:

0	3	0	0	1	0	2	1	1	1	1	2

When normalized to 100 percent of the total votes in their rows, these become

10.9	6.4	10.9	7.3	4.5	11.8	10.0	5.5	6.4	6.4	12.7	7.3

and

0	25.0	0	0	8.3	0	16.7	8.3	8.3	8.3	8.3	16.7

We see at once that the scaled votes for Hour Twelve—because of the absence of *any* competing votes in positions One, Three, Four, and Six—have become absurdly bloated, and no longer remotely comparable to those for Hour Three. And alas, in this experiment, Hours Ten and Eleven, as well as Hour Twelve, all contain cells with zero votes, which artificially inflates the normalized scores of these Hours. So those three Hours must reluctantly be discarded in advance of further analysis. Nor is this a dubious *post hoc* decision—it is a consequence of the method itself that all usable data must share the same characteristics, allowing rows to be fairly scaled on an equal basis.

§

We can see the impact of this problem in **Table 6.5**, where the raw votes for all twelve Hours (shown in horizontal ranks) are displayed as percentages of the total votes gained by each target. Such scaling to percentages is intended to make the individual votes more comparable—see the Appendix at the end of this chapter for more details on this procedure. Ignoring for a moment the problem of the empty cells, compare the values in each column, which show the scaled percentages gained by each target from Hour One to Hour Twelve. Targets are shown in **bold** for easier identification. And look! In this blizzard of numbers, the targets get the largest (scaled) accumulated vote in four of the columns (Hours Five, Six, Nine and Twelve), rather than the single majority vote expected by chance.

But wait. We've already noted that the eight zero votes for Ten, Eleven and Twelve badly distort the results of this comparison. When attention is restricted to Hours One through Nine—the only Hours where *all* cells contain one or more votes—the apparent "psiconcentrating" effect I just described is even more marked and striking.

Now, comparing the normalized and aggregated majority votes for each candidate target (the column entries), no less than *six* of these nine Hours were correctly selected by the majority submitting their "Daily Three" votes. (Note that deleting rows containing zero calls has the side effect of trimming away the inflated majority vote for Hour Twelve while boosting Hour Two's—so the result is no net change. We're not trying to fool ourselves here.)

That is intensely more interesting than knowing merely that there were 77 correct majority votes overall, rather than the expected 55 or so. Why? Because, using this data on a psihitting model, one would have been able to match majority votes accurately against targets on Hours Two, Three, Five, Six, Seven and Nine. By chance, one would expect to get only *one* right; the chance probability of getting even as many as three correct is rather small.

The majority vote method, therefore, was used by West to concentrate scant overall trialbytrial success into an extra 22 correct calls where 55 would be expected—a gain of 40 percent in accuracy. But I have now shown how the data could have been concentrated still further, to obtain six correct matches when one would be expected by chance: a 500 percent gain, rather than just 40 percent!

The chance probability of this result is moderately small, 0.00011, or about 1 in 9,000.

Unabashed, a skeptic will doubtless ask: "Why not 9 out of 9, or better still 12 out of 12, if paranormal cognition is at work here?"

Take another look at the "shotgun scatter" in **Table 6.5**. Now that

Major. Calls	Target option 1	2	3	4	5	6	7	8	9	10	11	12
1	**5.0**	6.7	1.7	6.7	15.0	13.3	5.0	10.0	6.7	10.0	8.3	11.7
2	12.7	**12.7**	2.5	3.8	11.4	5.1	7.6	11.4	8.9	3.8	10.1	10.1
3	10.9	6.4	**10.9**	7.3	4.5	11.8	10.0	5.5	6.4	6.4	12.7	7.3
4	11.7	5.2	10.4	**9.1**	11.7	10.4	5.2	10.4	2.6	7.8	9.1	6.5
5	3.4	10.3	10.3	13.8	**15.5**	3.4	3.4	12.1	3.4	8.6	8.6	6.9
6	10.0	12.5	2.5	10.0	5.0	**17.5**	10.0	10.0	10.0	7.5	2.5	2.5
7	8.1	5.8	9.3	2.3	7.0	9.3	**16.3**	9.3	5.8	8.1	4.7	14.0
8	8.3	8.3	10.4	8.3	8.3	4.2	6.3	**6.3**	12.5	14.6	4.2	8.3
9	5.4	3.6	3.6	7.1	10.7	8.9	16.1	8.9	**14.3**	10.7	8.9	1.8
10	10.0	0	10.0	0	10.0	10.0	10.0	20.0	10.0	**10.0**	10.0	0
11	4.8	4.8	19.0	9.5	4.8	4.8	9.5	14.3	14.3	9.5	**4.8**	0
12	0	25.0	0	0	8.3	0	16.7	8.3	8.3	8.3	8.3	**16.7**

Table 6.5: Normalized votes display majorities gained by each Hour when it was target (**bold on gray**) and when it was not. Data normalized across rows (to percentages) to remove Hour preference.

normalization compensates for response preferences (although at the minor cost of introducing some new distortions due to the zero-vote cells), the underlying *randomness* of guessing at unseen targets is the most visible effect. Any impact from occasional, fleeting psi inputs is obliged to stand out *above* that turbulence.

It's as if we took a crowd of 81 people with the usual assortment of heights, gave one person in nine a small box to stand on, shuffled them all up, and made everyone stand behind a fence in order of visible height. Could you tell which nine people looked taller than they really were? For that matter, could you be sure any of them were standing on boxes?

What is the significance of this discovery? Strictly speaking, it's impossible to say, since this analysis is conducted with 20-20 hindsight. Still, despite the lack of a formal probability estimate, it seems to me that the qualitative insights suggested by this reanalysis are provocative. Investigating claims of dramatic "miracles," whether as evidence for psi or as a paradigm for shooting down psychic pretentions (as James Randi and other skeptics do), is almost wholly pointless.

The bulk of reliable laboratory evidence indicates that psi influences are marginal, barely identifiable above the flux of other random or "noisy" processes of cognition and perception. This statement is not a copout but an obvious experimental constraint. Broadly similar noise effects hamper the monitoring of high-energy physics predictions, such as the discovery of the Higgs particle which had to be carefully picked out of a torrential gale of noise.

The FiskWest test shows, I think, that psi *was* present in their tally of raw votes—and not just in the spectacular correct majorities for Hours Three and Seven (12 and 14 majority votes respectively) which were mostly due to the general preference or bias favoring those numbers... but also as a small increment in the other stochastically scattered cell tallies as well.

§

Fired by what they did manage to observe in this modest victory, Fisk and West (*JSPR*, 1957) set out to refine the majority vote method. Fourteen volunteers, who "had all shown evidence of the ESP ability on previous occasions" (p. 157), were invited to guess at a fresh series of clock face cards. This time, twelve cards were used in each run, one for each hour. Sealed in opaque envelopes, and coded by letters so that cumulative scores could be credited, they were shuffled every day and laid out in a row on a mantelpiece in West's London consulting room.

From a geographical distance, each of the respondents tried six days a week "to divine the order of the row of 12 cards from left to right." In a useful *aide-mémoire*,

> Sets of twelve clock cards were also sent to the subjects with the suggestion that they try to arrange the specimen cards in the same order as the [distant, cloaked] targets, and then record the order on their forms. This advice was meant to prevent the distraction inherent in the mental effort of avoiding guessing the same number twice. (p. 158)

This went on from September 2 to November 17, 1956. During the last seven of those eleven weeks, West added a new twist. On alternate days, instead of using the cards hidden inside envelopes, "he shuffled a separate set of 12 clock cards, arranging them in a row as usual, but open and visible. The intention was to provide a control series under 'telepathy' conditions which would also give the experimenters some guide as to which subjects, if any, were scoring successfully" (p. 158).

Providing this interleaved index series is a considerable methodological advance, as we now have a clear-cut opportunity to assay in advance the size and direction of any deviation.

But wait, not so fast. *Is* it clear-cut?

Of the 14 respondents, only eight contributed to the index series. Worse, as West indicates, the two subsets are now differentiated in a possibly crucial manner. Testing in alternation for telepathy and clairvoyance with one of his star subjects, Soal had previously found strong psi in one condition and not the other. In hindsight, it might have been preferable simply to have drawn out a quarter of the sealed envelopes and evaluated them, as an index of any psi shown in the experiment, in advance of the principal analysis.

By the end of the experiment, West had received 3696 guesses at the sealed targets, and 1332 at the open targets. Regrettably, he scored them in the same self-defeating way as before. "By considering only those envelopes associated with a substantial preference for a particular guess, we hoped to be able to make an unusually accurate forecast of the contents of some of the envelopes" (p. 158-9).

The first inadequacy to note here is that West neglected position preference. If you ask a roomful of people to secretly and freely write down a number between one and 10, a ridiculously large proportion of them, as noted previously, will write down the number three. Similarly, it seems highly likely that definite, if more subtle, preferences will warp the allocation of numbers from left to right. The experimenters failed to present the relevant data in their paper. That leaves us only one way to compensate for such possible influences: by combining the scores gained by target clock faces in a number of runs. That way, the influence of position will tend to wash out. Not perfectly, by any means, but every little helps.

Actually, it's necessary to do this anyway. If psi is present at its usual low level of efficiency, we'd only expect to find a statistically significant deviation if all 5028 guesses were lumped together. By dividing his guesses into 24 predictions (12 on the sealed targets and 12 on the open control set) West made it impossible for the kind of small deviations we can expect to attain statistical meaning. The power of the experiment is too low.

To a degree, looking for the majority vote skirts this issue, trading confidence in prediction against the necessity for arduous repeated guessing. That is, we can be fairly certain that predictions developed on the basis of, say, 300 votes will still contain a lot of random noise—but we can be more confident that in the long run such methods will increase the number of correct predictions above the level of chance. West failed to appreciate this distinction. He demanded significant deviations, when the best he was likely to find was just an excess of accurate majority votes.

In any event, West isolated four large positive majorities from sealed envelopes and duly made his forecasts of the clock faces within those envelopes.

He was wrong each time.

And the control series? West analyzed these next (instead of in advance, as one might expect), and found "some suggestion of negative scoring... This would mean that the subjects were consistently making guesses away from the actual target" (p. 160). With belated insight, he observes: "But if any consistent trend that may have been present in the guessing was in a negative direction, the failure of the 'majority votes' to correspond with the targets no longer appears surprising" (p. 161).

Reading this report years later, I waited breathlessly for him to turn back to the sealed envelopes and looked there for majority *misses*. No such luck. West hared off instead after "systematic miscalling of certain targets... calling six for 4, 5 for two and four for 12" (p. 161). This apparent pattern is almost certainly an artifact, the result of not matching target series against position bias. But had West followed through on his original observation of psi-missing in the sample series, he would have found that *two* targets were avoided by the majority: four o'clock and 12 o'clock. By chance, only one target should have been correctly identified.

This hardly seems a stupendous victory, and indeed it is not. But it is incredible that West didn't even notice this logical implication of his original method. Instead, the best he could manage was the discovery that when all votes from both series were pooled, statistical evaluation "gives a more comfortable significant result, confirming the existence over the experiment as a whole of a nonrandom association between targets and calls, and providing evidence that the subjects were manifesting (misguided) ESP" (p. 161)

Can anything be salvaged from this mess? Taking a majority vote on less than about a thousand votes per target is not likely to be reliable. For good confidence, indeed, one would wish to have 10,000 guesses at each choice. Since this is hardly practicable, or at any rate was in the days before online tests using the World Wide Web, a thousand guesses is the best compromise. Now, as it happens, this test breaks quite nicely into four segments of about that size. The "open envelope" series provides a good index sample, while the sealed targets can be divided into three groups, each of four targets.

Our method is by now familiar. Votes for Hours when they happen to be target are aggregated, and compared with the average vote gained by the same Hours when they are not targets. This can only be done after the experiment is concluded, of course, and could not be used to yield predictions prior to target disclosure. Still, it serves nicely as a test of this method.

In the open-card series, the 12 targets had a total of 100 votes. Non-targets notched up 1232 votes, a mean of 112 votes per target. In a rough and ready way, we might infer that this lower score for targets was due to overall psi-missing, plus the usual admixture of noise.

With some reservations—since the index series was not precisely similar to the sealed-target series—we therefore look for psi-missing on the main group of clock faces. To get our thousand-odd guesses per trial, we will add together without prejudice the votes for targets 1 through 4, 5 through 8, and 9 through 12.

In group one, targets gained 93 votes; non-targets a mean of 103.6.
In group two, targets gained 102 votes; non-targets a mean of 102.8.
In group three, targets gained 94 votes; non-targets a mean of 103.3.

In each case, then, the aggregated targets scored in accordance with the index forecast, although in the second group the deviation is too small to take seriously. In a real-life application, results of this kind would probably lead to two correct predictions out of two, with the targets in the second group being presented again to the guessing team for further guesses.

§

In itself, the extent of this correspondence of observation and theoretical prediction is not startling. Sealed targets scored a negative deviation of about 0.6 percent, not much greater than a single standard deviation, and hence not statistically significant. And our target/not target comparisons, being binary, show a success that could have happened by chance once in eight times. Cumulatively, though, this modest but perfect score contributes effectively to the tenor of these rare analyses.

Having failed to witness the merit in their own tests, were Fisk and West discouraged? Well, they were not best pleased. "The results of this preliminary experiment," they concluded, "were not without promise." The best they could find to say, with a touch of pained bafflement, was this: "Something was happening."

As far as I know, the team thereafter deserted majority-vote research. Yet, in retrospect, it seems that they were very close to an advance in methodology. In between the two series described above, they had seized the opportunity to run a truly pivotal mass media experiment during a popular science feature produced by Science Television Services Ltd. The design of the experiment was far from ideal, as we can judge with hindsight, but it was a dream by comparison with the earlier material.

For expert statistical evaluation, and specification of the target array, West and Fisk were joined again by Donald Michie. In subsequent years, Michie would become known as one of the most important British pioneer theorists of machine intelligence, having worked with the celebrated Alan Turing during and after the Second World War.

The on-air test was conducted on April 19, 1956, and attracted responses from 1367 viewers, who each sent in 20 guesses on a prepared form.

And the results, after Michie's complicated analysis, seemed so destructive that the team was driven back in disappointment to the hopeless clock-face protocols, and from there, finally, to bafflement and anathemas.

§

In the week preceding the TV test, the *Television Times* in Britain published a coupon with spaces for 20 guesses, as well as name, address, sex, and most importantly the subject's self-evaluation of how well or poorly s/he had done. The announcement stated: "Viewers on Thursday will have three pictures before them on the TV screen—a wheelbarrow, trumpet and canoe. The agent, hidden by screen, will concentrate on each of them in turn in a random order, while a viewer will be asked to mark on the coupon on this page the pictures they think he is passing on to them by 'thought transference'."

In the absence of excellent external controlled data, against which one might calibrate the calls made by the viewers, this method has many drawbacks. As we found in those binary Zenith tests in which targets were selected randomly from the same pair of options, a strong most-common mean pattern tends to emerge. In that case it was **11211**. But we have no way of estimating how a mass audience will pattern their guesses in a ternary (three-choice) run of 20 trials.

Conscious of this problem, West and Michie devised a target array governed by certain restrictions. Anxious for some measure of internal control, to offset just such pattern bias, they used a "serially balanced sequence": that is, one in which each of the options appeared an equal number of times, and in which "the different parts of the series are homogenous with respect to the frequency of occurrence" of the three target-options. This rather opaque technical description will become clearer as we see the actual target pattern emerge.

A preferable method might have been to use a diverse set of ternary target-options for, say, five or six trials, and then to repeat this group of 15 or 18 symbols a number of times. You might hope, in the light of the Zenith experience, that the audience's biased pattern preferences would tend to be recycled from set to set, and hence more readily isolated.

Using the serially balanced sequence obliged the experimenters to throw away the guesses made on two of the 20 trials, for if each of the three options was to be target an equal number of times, the maximum number of targets, obviously, would be 18. This was considered no great loss, since the first or opening trial was "expected to be peculiarly subject to 'position preference' and it was decided to ignore it." This suspicion was very well justified when the data came in: Canoe, Trumpet and Wheelbarrow "were guessed with frequencies 156, 806 and 402" in that first trial, "in contrast with the approximate equality of frequencies prevailing throughout the remainder of the series" (p. 123). That is, in their initial confrontation with the three options, the middle image was overwhelmingly selected, with substantial vote to the image on the right-hand side of the screen, leaving the image on the left-hand or "sinister" side to be chosen by hardly more than a 10th of the audience respondents.

While the design of the test was meticulous, its conduct was less so—hardly surprising news to anyone who's had the nerve-jangling experience of presenting a scientific experiment through the mass media (as I've done a couple of times). Interestingly, Michie and West single out one feature for peculiar emphasis. "The experiment itself was a trifle hurried, so that the agent, Mr. G.W. Fisk, was somewhat distracted by the effort to keep in step with the signals."

The program began with a personal anecdote by a woman psychic, and West spoke briefly on the need for scientific experiments in paranormal phenomena. Fisk, serving as agent, explained that he would retire behind a screen and "look at the series of picture cards, canoe, wheelbarrow and trumpet. An announcer would call out 'one,' 'two,' 'three'... and he would look at the pictures one by one keeping time with the voice." Viewers were asked to record their guesses simultaneously with each announcement, and then mail them in for analysis. They were not informed of the special properties of the target series.

The test started, and Fisk began to do nothing of the kind.

Instead of looking "at a series of picture cards," he instead conjured them up before his mind's eye. "It was intended to call the numbers at five-second intervals, so as to leave ample time for each guess, but in the event it seemed as if the series was run through faster than planned, although the producer said that the five-second interval was strictly kept." Presumably British television in the mid-1950s did not keep tape recordings of their on-air programs, and of course the home video recorder or Tivo was decades in the future. At any rate, there is no way now to time the proceedings, so the issue of strict intervals is left open.

The agent was not told in advance what the target series would be. "Behind the screen, G.W. Fisk first opened the paper bearing the target series in the form of a typewritten column of initial letters of the names of the three pictures. Keeping in time with the voice, he ran down the column with his eye, using a stencil to blot out from view the preceding and succeeding letters. As he looked at a letter, so he tried to visualize the corresponding picture card" (p. 116).

Subsequently, he "reported that on the first card the voice called out 'one' before he opened out the paper and was ready to begin" (p. 116). The experimenters comment: "since the first target was in any case the dummy and not utilized in the assessment, this was not an important point."

These departures from the planned protocol are stressed at length by Michie and West in their paper. One anticipates, reading it, that this emphasis portends some peculiarity in their analysis of the results. That does not eventuate, although it is interesting to note that they seek partial correspondences not only with the real-time target in each trial, but also with those immediately preceding and following it. The search for displacement scoring seems to have passed out of fashion these days, but it was popular in 1956. Soal's claims of precognitive displacement effects in card calling by Basil Shackleton had been announced publicly only two years earlier, and Fisk's clock cards had been designed precisely to allow the statistical treatment of displaced psi.

In due course, the guesses arrive by mail—an unsatisfactorily low tally of 1367 coupons, but science programs rarely attract large audiences—and were collated, titled, and analyzed.

Once the data was rearranged by target, as in **Table 6.6**, it was noticed at once that Trumpet, in the middle column, was the most favored symbol, with 8830 votes. Canoe, in the left column, was the least liked, with 7365. Since the target-generating procedure had ensured six targets and 12 non-targets for each symbol, this imbalance was clearly not the result of psi. So even if Canoe, on those occasions when it happened to be target, were enhanced by psi-hitting at one percent efficiency, a comparison of raw votes in that draw probably would still not give it the majority. Why? Because the general bias in favor of Trumpet tended to give it a six percent edge over Canoe.

	C	T	W	Total
2 C_1	393	515	459	1367
6 C_2	354	529	484	1367
7 C_3	417	490	460	1367
12 C_4	388	503	476	1367
13 C_5	428	473	466	1367
17 C_6	401	505	461	1367
Subtotal for C	2381	3015	2806	8202
3 T_1	453	463	451	1367
4 T_2	414	503	450	1367
8 T_3	437	468	462	1367
11 T_4	403	513	451	1367
15 T_5	436	487	444	1367
16 T_6	411	500	456	1367
Subtotal for T	2554	2934	2714	8202
1 W_1	442	386	539	1367
5 W_2	395	500	472	1367
9 W_3	404	497	466	1367
10 W_4	390	486	491	1367
14 W_5	386	517	464	1367
18 W_6	413	495	459	1367
Subtotal for W	2430	2881	2891	8202
Grand total	7365	8830	8411	24,606

Table 6.6: Raw data grouped by target type, displaying votes for Canoe, **C**, Trumpet, **T**, and Wheelbarrow, **W**. Numbers at extreme left show the actual order of presentation of the cards. (From Michie and West 1957. p. 120)

As we've seen before, the easiest way to offset bias caused by simple preferences is to revalue the votes accumulated by each symbol in each trial by reference to that symbol's average score. It's a sort of handicapping, making the contestants more evenly matched. Such scaled or normalized values can then be compared with less hazard, for a suitable handicap has been applied to the favorite symbols, and an appropriate boost to those that are usually shunned, target or not.

§

Alas, Michie and West did not employ this direct conversion and comparison. Instead their analysis relied on a measure of variance, an over-sophisticated technique of such byzantine ornateness that they require several pages to describe it. One of their principal conclusions is that "this analysis reveals that position preferences *did* in fact play an important role"—the truth so wonderfully apparent to the naked eye that it's obvious in **Table 6.7** (below) where the calls are shown in the actual raw order. On that basis, we've taken it as a starting point in the decision to normalize the votes (as displayed in **Table 6.8**).

	Canoe		Trumpet		W'barrow	
1	442		386		539	T
2	393		515		459	
3	453	T	463		451	
4	414		503	T	450	
5	395		500	T	472	
6	354		529		484	T
7	417	T	490		460	
8	437	T	468		462	
9	404		497	T	466	
10	390		486		491	T
11	403		513		451	T
12	388	T	503		476	
13	428	T	473		466	
14	386		517		464	T
15	436		487	T	444	
16	411		500	T	456	
17	401	T	505		461	
18	413		495		459	T
Totals: **Means:**	7365 409.17		8830 490.56		8411 467.28	

Table 6.7: Raw votes for each option per call, with correct target shown as **T**.

The result appears to be a devastating failure of our method of comparing votes for each option *when it is target* versus *when it is not.* Whether we consider the real-time psi-hitting or the psi-missing possibility (for there was no preliminary screening in this test, so either is plausible, and requires a two-tailed test of significance), we find no meaningful variation from pure chance expectation!

On the basis of sheer chance, one can predict that the most likely result will be six correct out of 18, give or take a couple. In this experiment, it turns out that seven of the targets correspond to the scaled percentage that's highest of the three per trial, while seven correspond to the lowest. When the percentages of all targets are added together, they scarcely vary from chance to the smallest degree.

The elaborate Michie-West method confirms this, finding "no significant support for the hypothesis of ESP," let alone majority vote. Nor were they satisfied to leave it at that. "We may make similar tests for the occurrence of 'pre-cognitive' or 'post-cognitive' ESP (forward and backward 'displacement')... here again there is no significant evidence of an association between targets and guesses."

Well, we've heard this sort of thing before.

The Zenith data, apparently, could be explained by bias alone. Is it conceivable that Michie and West also overlooked something?

§

As we did with West's previously described test, let's begin afresh by making no assumptions at all, beyond those that are common to the corpus of parapsychological findings plus information provided in their published paper.

No calls were used by the experimenters as an index of psi mode, so let's use Canoe for that purpose. Suppose we take all the guesses at Canoe and examine them, without prejudice, for correspondences between targets and aggregated scores. There's a slight risk here, for it turns out that after scaling there are more "lowest" votes for Canoe than the mean chance expectation of six. There are, in fact, eight "lowest" votes and six "highest." This somewhat increases our chances of uncovering what *looks* like psi-missing, but is merely due to the excess "lowest" votes.

With this caution in mind, we may search for the same possibilities allowed by Michie and West: direct hitting or missing (which as we've just seen were not in play), and one-step displacement forward or back.

If we find such an effect, we shall extrapolate to the other two target options, Trumpet and Wheelbarrow, but now using a stringent, falsifiable one-tailed prediction.

Since there are six targets in every column, each with an associated probability of one in three, we will expect by chance about two correspondences on each of these tests.

Michie and West considered time displacement, so let's look there.

§

Like Frankenstein's monster, psi reveals aspects of ourselves that we might never otherwise have noticed. And, as with all good Frankenstein tales, I have a hunch—I hardly dare call it a hypothesis—that the key to what follows lies in the brain. In this case, specifically, the rattled brain of G.W. Fisk.

Perhaps the galling phenomenon of "postcognitive displacement" that we'll find in this experiment has nothing at all to do with the psi quirk studied by Soal, and everything to do with the simple, unfortunate fact that Fisk "was somewhat distracted by the effort to keep in step with the signals."

It is extraordinary, reading the original report, to observe the extent to which Michie and West reiterate this circumstantial fact—*without* drawing any conclusions from it. Had they noticed the apparent postcognitive significance of their data, one would be inclined to dismiss their emphasis at once, as selective and self-serving. In fact, of course, they state clearly their belief that "The results of this experiment were thus negative as far as concerns the first hypothesis, namely that there is a small amount of ESP widely distributed through the population" (p. 123).

I'm not suggesting that Fisk *literally* remained one target behind throughout the test after he fell out of synch at the start, running his pencil down the list of initial letters that cued in his "visualization." But when we combine the elements spelled out in the paper, it's not absurd to conjecture that his attention was sufficiently diverted to bring about just such an orienting effect in his TV viewing percipients.

Consider: caught off guard, he started on the wrong foot. The five-second intervals seemed shorter. Arguably, the effort of translating a letter into a corresponding word/image created an appreciable lag. And since the declared ambition of the test was for respondents to secure impressions "he is passing on to them by 'thought transference,'" this breach in synchronization with the announcer's numbering might perhaps account for any subsequent psi displacement.

Indeed, since psi is mediated by unconscious processes perhaps to a greater extent than any other human information source, it's not out of the question that authentic displacement was triggered by the initial time-lag, and simply remained in step from there on.

This speculation is presented with due diffidence, as a pilot study. I'm making no strong claims here. My approach will be criticized, perhaps justly, as *data-trawling*, or even *torturing the data until it confesses*. The result, if regarded as valid, needs to be replicated in a double-blind experiment under controlled conditions. Otherwise, it's quite untestable—save for the fact that, like the physicists' virtual particles, the postulated effect makes sense of the observations, which otherwise remain opaque. If the notion has any merit, it might be elaborated by those in neurologists and cognitive psychologists who specialize in the phenomena of attention and imagery.

In any event, Fisk's target was delayed, so to speak, by perhaps one trial. Remember that in this preliminary search we are entertaining six possible patterns, so the likelihood of random coincidence giving us a match with one of them is not inconsiderable. (To do so, we have to reinstate the opening "dummy" target—not its numeric value, which we know to be grossly deformed by the impact of preference factors, but just the fact that the target happened to be Wheelbarrow.)

Considering the matter theoretically, any correlation in a mass test between delayed targets and *later* majorities—that is, what looks like a postcognitive effect, but could be just "sender" and "receivers" getting out of synch) seems ludicrous. It's possible to imagine, however dimly, how a psi genius like Basil Shackleton might develop the baroque habit of consistently and prophetically displacing his guesses one *ahead*. But how could a large group of more than a thousand ordinary people, connected only by their common leisure-time activity viewing television, abruptly decide to divert their guesses, in effect, *backward* by one trial?

This is a difficult idea to get your head around. The key aspect of postcognitive perception is that when you are making your guess in line Y, you mark down the earlier target for line X instead. Only when trial Z arrives do you capture the target in line Y. You are reaching back in time to picture the previous target sent by would-be telepath Fisk.

Look at line 2, in **Table 6.8**. The real-time target is Canoe, but that only gets a column-normalized 32 percent vote. However in the following trial, line 3, Canoe gains an especially large vote (36.9 percent) even though the actual target for that line is Trumpet, which gets a miserable 31.5 percent . It seems that a significantly large number of people are *reaching back in time* to detect the target for the previous line, and belatedly voting for that.

Note that in this experiment this might not have been *literally* due to postcognition, but was actually real-time telepathy with Fisk, if we suppose he had stumbled and fallen one step behind with his pre-arranged targets. Actually I find it implausible that he literally fell behind for *all* the 20 "telepathic sendings" he was trying for—but perhaps participants who unconsciously did what they could to latch onto his "sending" then continued one step behind. It sounds absurd, but Michie and West did consider it as a possibility, so I'm not just making this up myself in an ad hoc fashion.

And as we shall see, this postcognitive version does correlate "next calls" interestingly with "immediately previous targets."

Treating the Canoe column votes as a postcognitive index test, we find no fewer than five cases where Canoe was correctly chosen by the *next* collective response. So we can go ahead and analyze the other two options in the same way, postcognitively. (See **Table 6.8**, where arrows indicate the possibility that targets in each call influence voting for their category in the *subsequent* call.)

In all, in the postcognitive mode interpretation suggested by Fisk's blunder in timing, we find 13 of the 18 targets identified.

How can it be that Michie and West, even when they explicitly considered the displacement possibility, were blind to its occurrence?

The answer seems to lie in their elaborate formulae. Although they were making the relevant corrections for gross bias (in a backhanded fashion), they confounded their scaling with other, unnecessary, misleading analyses of variance. It's notable that in the Table in their paper that sets out the scores for each call (**Table 6.6**), they displayed bunched together the votes for target options of the same kind, which is mildly interesting but throws away the actual order in which viewers experienced the event and recorded their guesses (**Table 6.7**). It is a sure-fire way to miss noticing the postcognitive correspondences.

	CANOE		**TRUMPET**		**WHEELBARROW**	
0		L		H	**T ↘**	
1	36.0		26.2	L	38.5 **T**	H
2	32.0 **T ↘**	L	35.0	H	32.7	
3	36.9	H	31.5 **T ↘**	L	32.2	
4	33.7		34.2 **T ↘**	H	32.1	L
5	32.2	L	34.0	H	33.7 **T**	
6	28.8 **T ↘**	L	35.9	H	34.5	
7	34.0 **T ↘**	H	33.3		32.8	L
8	35.6	H	31.8 **T ↘**	L	33.0	
9	32.9	L	33.8	H	33.2 **T ↘**	
10	31.8	L	33.0		35.0 **T**	H
11	32.8		34.9 **T ↘**	H	32.2	L
12	31.6 **T ↘**	L	34.2	H	34.0	
13	34.9 **T**	H	32.1	L	33.2	
14	31.5	L	35.1	H	33.1 **T**	
15	35.5	H	33.1 **T ↘**		31.7	L
16	33.5		34.0 **T ↘**	H	32.5	L
17	32.7 **T ↘**	L	34.3	H	32.9	
18	33.7	H	33.6		32.7 **T**	L
Raw Total Votes	7365		8830		8411	

Table 6.8: Michie/West mass telepathy experiment (scaled percentage scores)

Chance expectation per target: 33.3 %. Targets tend to gain highest vote in *next* response.

In seeking to expel all chance fluctuations, they washed out the psi as well, as a clumsy launderer might bleached the delicate pattern from a batik while cleansing ink stains.

Granted, this apparently exciting result might itself be an artifact, caused by the disparity of highest, middle and lowest scores in our scaled columns. If so, we would undoubtedly expect the most dramatic proficiency in the six Trumpet targets, and the less impressive score in the six Wheelbarrow results. This is not quite the case. The mean (time-displaced and normalized) target scores were thus:

Canoe: 34.4 percent.
Trumpet: 34.1 percent.
Wheelbarrow 33.1 percent.

This contour yields a mean overall deviation, perhaps attributable to psi, of +0.57 percent.

We are left with a surprising inference that the Michie-West TV test, far from casting gloom on the prospects of mass psychic perception, somewhat enhances our hopes for analyzing majority votes. Perhaps it points the way to a convenient vehicle for its practical use by a mass-media deluged community. These days, of course, computerized selection of targets and evaluation of responses allows for both group and individual treatment via the Internet.

§

Wait, there's more; the payoff is yet to come. However, please bear firmly in mind that what follows is *not meant* as a proof of psi, nor even quite as a pilot experiment in need of strong replication. Think of it more as an exploration of the unknown at the margins of the known, a sort of protocol thought experiment using real if slightly inadequate data.

As always, here is the argument: In accordance with the repeated guessing model, the more votes we supply the more accuracy we *expect* to gain, since the noise of chance fluctuations is thereby diminished.

One way to increase the concentration of votes in this experimental set of data is through using what I'll call the *triplet*.

A triplet, obviously, is simply a grouping of three things of some sort. Here, we will use it to group both Targets and Votes, which come in discrete groups of three: A target for a particular trial comes from a group of three possibilities: Wheelbarrow, Canoe and Trumpet. Votes in each trial are cast as so many for Wheelbarrow, so many for Canoe, so many for Trumpet. We will introduce each variation of triplets for the two classifications as we get to them.

Because the Mickie-West design uses a triplet format, it has the virtue that it can yield accurate identification of the targets prior to their disclosure. A protocol that compresses or compacts each triplet into a single prediction might be used to transmit information. Let's consider the properties of their "serially balanced sequence." In the case of the 18 calls in the TV test (leaving aside the first and last "dummy" trials, renamed 0 and 19), these constraints generated arrays in which each group of three consecutive trials included one target from each of the three options.

Thus, the chance of Canoe, say, being chosen as target in the triplet's first trial is one in three. Once Canoe is selected, either Trumpet or Wheelbarrow has one chance in two of filling the second spot. The remaining holdout must inevitably become the third target.

The serially balanced series in the TV test (which I used to reconstruct the raw data sequence in **Table 6.8**) was:

W/ W C T/ T W C/ C T W/ W T C/ C W T/ T C W / W

In the first triplet group (which happened to be W C T in this case), random selection could have made the initial target of the triplet any of the three symbols (Canoe, say). Thereafter, the symbol to the right would be second target (in this case, Trumpet), and finally we'd have the symbol to the right of the second target (in this case Wheelbarrow).

We have to imagine that the choice-continuum *in any given row* extends forever in a single line, for example C T W C T W C T W..., akin to the traditional endless number line 0, 1, 2, 3, 4... from basic arithmetic. So if the original randomly selected target happens instead to be Wheelbarrow, the option to its "right" is Canoe. It's like a computer game in which an image proceeds to one side of the screen, vanishes, and immediately reappears from the other side.

Using such a rule, we can interpret the Michie-West data without knowing the actual target sequence. Ideally, we do this by simply compacting our sets of calls in groups of three and evaluating the target means against the abstract chance expectation of 33.3 percent. For true information-transmission in coded ternary (or three-fold) form, the compacted target needs to stand out not just in the predicted direction from the mean, but by the largest amount.

In the opening triplet, the first target was Wheelbarrow (W). In the second line, the target was Canoe (C). That meant in the third line, Trumpet (T) had its turn as target. Of course, as noted above, Michie and West could not know that these candidates, in this order, *were* the winning choice in the first triplet—just that W's tally must be added to those of C, and T.

These three normalized percentages, added together, are in competition with two other aggregates: C in the first line, added to T in the second line, and W in the third—and also with T in the first line, added to W in the second, and C in the third line. And that exhausts the possibilities for the first triplet.

Just to ensure we're all still tracking this argument, let's recall my comment from a few pages back:

The key aspect of postcognitive perception is that when you are making your guess in line Y, you call the earlier target for line X instead. Only when trial Z arrives do you capture the target in line Y. You are reaching back in time to picture the previous target.

The clearest way to show how this works is with another Table, **6.9**, which actually displays the targets alongside their postcognitive majority votes. The notation created by Michie and West (WCT, etc) is replaced for ease of recognition by rotating sets of three alphabet codes: first, the letters *a, b* and *c*, then *d, e* and *f*, then *g, h* and *i*. This maneuver will allow us to compress the votes for each letter and compare their mean overall votes.

Wait! Something unexpected happens at this point.

Due to the way Michie and West set up their TV experiment, there's an extra complication: the rest of the tallies are combined in the reverse direction. Instead of *j, k* and *l*, which you might expect to see in that order, the formula of serial balancing starts to run backwards, yielding *l, k, j*, then *o, n, m*, and finally *r, q* and *p*. You can see how this works by looking closely at **Table 6.9** and then at the compacted result in **Table 6.10**.

Your head is probably buzzing. Don't worry—it'll become clearer with a bit of reflection.

Run	C votes		Norm		T votes		Norm		W votes		Norm	
1	393	a	32.17		515	b	34.56		459	c	33.04	T
2	453	c	37.08	T	463	a	31.07		451	b	32.47	
3	414	b	33.89		503	c	33.76	T	450	a	32.39	
4	395	d	32.33		500	e	33.55	T	472	f	33.98	
5	354	f	28.98		529	d	35.50		484	e	34.84	T
6	417	e	34.13	T	490	f	32.88		460	d	33.11	
7	437	g	35.77	T	468	h	31.41		462	l	33.26	
8	404	i	33.07		497	g	33.35	T	466	h	33.55	
9	390	h	31.92		486	i	32.61		491	g	35.34	T
10	403	l	32.99		513	k	34.43		451	j	32.47	T
11	388	k	31.76		503	j	33.76	T	476	l	34.26	
12	428	j	35.03	T	473	l	31.74		466	k	33.55	
13	386	o	31.60	T	517	n	34.70		464	m	33.40	
14	436	n	35.69		487	m	32.68		444	o	31.96	T
15	411	m	33.64		500	o	33.55	T	456	n	32.83	
16	401	r	32.82		505	q	33.89	T	461	p	33.19	
17	413	q	33.81	T	495	p	33.22		459	r	33.04	
Totals	6923				8444				7872			

Table 6.9: T = Target. Norm = votes normalized by column. Targets displaced by one step following Fisk error. Only 7 of 17 Targets correctly identified.

Note that the target order is mirrored from line 10 through line 17, so that the targets appear in reverse order. Therefore it makes sense to mirror/reverse the order in which non-Targets are alphabetically coded. Thus, a, b and c, through g, h and i, proceed to the right, while l, k and j, through r, q and p, proceed to the left.

Lo! We find that five of the six "compacted-targets" are not merely greater than 33 3 percent, but are also the highest scorers in their line:

1 - 3	a	31.88	b	33.64	c	34.63 **T**
4 - 6	d	33.65	e	34.17 **T**	f	31.95
7 - 9	g	34.82 **T**	h	32.29	i	32.98
10 - 12	l	33.00	k	33.25	j	33.75 **T**
13 - 15	o	32.37 **T**	n	34.40	m	33.24
16 - 17	r	32.93	q	33.85 **T**	p	33.21

Table 6.10: Compacted-triplet interpretation of Michie-West TV data. T= target; post-cognitive displaced scores are shown.

§

One of the pleasant aspects of the Michie-West serially balanced formulation is that it encourages this further step. Apart from the dummy runs at top and bottom, each triplet of ternary trials covers all bases: each of the options becomes target (by anti-bias design). If we group our votes in this fashion, starting at postcognitive trial one and advance by threes, we might be able to do even better than the present 7 right out of 18—although, sadly, owing to the lack of a postcognitive score for trial 18, we must either disregard the incomplete postcognitive set (16-17) or use the numbers from those two trials as the uncertain basis for a majority call. Let's be brave and do the latter.

Indeed, we discover that four of the five eligible groups thus constituted, plus the truncated pair at the bottom, not only exceed the mean of 33.3 percent—they are also the largest of the three candidates in their row. The target scores (derived from **Table 6.10**) are:

(1-3)	34.63 percent
(4-6)	34.17 percent
(7-9)	34.82 percent
(10-12)	33.75 percent
(13-15)	32.37 percent
(16-17)	33.85 percent[7]

7. But note that in postcognitive mode, this last result draws on only two rather than three sets of majority votes.

In effect, we've boosted our total accuracy rate from 41.2 percent (7 right out of 17 trials) to 83.3 percent. This is as it should be, because now we have three times as many guesses comprising each triplet's aggregated target: we have reached the realm of numbers large enough for the repeated guessing by a group to function with some confidence.

Had this been a real-time success, rather than a postcognitive event possibly forced by Fisk's tardiness in keeping up, a message encoding 729 exclusive possible outcomes could have been transmitted in this form. Actually, alas, it would have been received in garbled form, due to the incorrect prediction in the fifth compacted line

Even so, considering that the test design was not perfect for psi application use—let alone the horrid fact that its sponsors wrote the results off as meaningless—this was a superb achievement. Had each of these compacted targets been the basis of an individual wager at 3 to 1 (and an independent sampling run indicated postcognitive displacement), Fisk, West and Michie could have been rewarded comfortably for their efforts.

§

Let's summarize our findings in these reanalyses.

We have looked at tests that comprise many hundreds of thousands of guesses. In all of them, the data were published long ago, at least half a century ago and in some cases much further back. Unfortunately, what was published is seldom all the data one would like to have seen. Most of it can be found in the archived journals of any major public library or university stacks. Most of the tests were thought by the experimenters to yield no evidence at all for psi, and the prospects for mass testing seemed bleak. In some cases, majority vote methods of an inadequate kind were explicitly employed but, with the exception of the first Fisk-West mood study, were assumed to be duds.

Under the spotlight of reanalysis, all but the badly devised Woolley experiment has shown better than chance results, even if only marginally.

I have not presented this old wine in new bottles as an example of the best way to explore the paranormal. On the contrary, we have learned in the past three quarters of a century that combining the efforts of thousands or even hundreds of thousands of people in a single psi task is a recipe for frustration, confusion and the risk of obliterating the very phenomenon we're looking for. Still, finding the footprints of psi in dusty old documents where they were thought to be absent encourages us to try once more. The method of multiple guessing adjudicated by majority vote remains a significant component of psi application, even if it can be exhausting to put into practice, as we shall see.

Appendix: Normalizing data

Often, in these experiments in repeated guessing with majority vote evaluation, we get a batch of raw data that is distorted by certain recurrent biases. This is basically "noise" in our data that can overwhelm valuable results. Can we do anything about that?

For example, if people are shown three distinct images and asked to choose one, there is a strong tendency to pick the middle option. If the same or similar set of images is shown repeatedly, the tendency to choose the central item remains dominant, by and large, with a smaller proportion of voters choosing the right hand column, and fewer still choosing the options of the left.

How can we deal with these irrelevant skews? The simplest method is rescaling or normalizing. Here's how it works.

Suppose (as in **Table 6.9**) there were 17 consecutive calls (or guesses), each one choosing one of three alternative words or pictures. Arranged on the page, we might see them as a table with 17 rows and 3 columns. Suppose the first cell in the left column contains 393 votes, out of 17 cells with a total of 6923 votes.

Average chance expectation (a mathematical abstraction, but a useful one) is then

$$\frac{6923}{17} = 407.24$$

or an idealized 407.24 votes per left column cell.

We see at once that 393 votes are fewer than 407.24, although not by much. If we wish to compare this aggregated vote with the aggregated votes for the two other options that were available (515 in the popular central column, and 459 in the right column), we can start by turning each cell's actual collective vote into a percentage of its own chance expected vote.

To do that, we take 393 and divide it by 4.0724 (or, if you prefer, divide 39300 by 407.24) to get **96.504**, which is that cell's percentage of the mean chance expectation *for that column only.*

To get the full benefit of this rescaling, we have to compare that percentage with those created by rescaling the other cells in that row. The center cell, with 515 votes, comes from a much-liked column that has an overall column sum of 8444 votes. Average chance expectation is

$$\frac{8444}{17} = 496.71$$

or 496.71 votes per central column cell. For the percentage, divide 515 by 4.967 to get **103.68**.

We do the same thing with votes in the right column, starting with 459 votes from a total column sum of 7872. Average chance expectation for that column is

$$\frac{7872}{17} = 463.06$$

so the actual vote of 459 is just **99.12** percent of what we'd expect by chance.

This is enough to show that the highest aggregate vote went to the center option, even after the columns had been rescaled to get rid of a lot of the position preference. Here's what happens when we apply this basic procedure to all the relevant data from 17 columns (see **Table 6.11** opposite).

We could leave the rescaling at that point, but I feel that this stark set of numbers hovering around 100 percent is not intuitively easy to understand.

When we see three choices available in each row, we anticipate that each option will earn about one third, or 33.33 percent, of the total vote. Call those *internal comparisons*, with a joint probability of around 100 percent—not *exactly* 100 percent, though, because each cell in the row is normalized to a different column mean, in order to minimize bias.

Let's make one further transformation, then, which displays the results on that basis.

We do this by dividing each of the percentages calculated above (96.5, 103.7 and 99.1, etc) by 3 to get a presentation making more gut sense: left, 32.17; center, 34.56; right, 33.04, and so on down the columns, as displayed in **Table 6.9**.

And such is the way we mostly proceed in this book, as can be seen also in **Table 10.5** (but not in **Tables 12.1-12.4**, since they have no *internal* comparisons to draw).

Set	CANOE		TRUMPET		W-BARROW	
	% of chance	Target	% of chance	Target	% of chance	Target
1	96.5		103.7		99.1	T
2	111.2	T	93.2		97.4	
3	101.7		101.3	T	97.2	
4	97.0		100.7	T	101.9	
5	86.9		106.5		104.5	T
6	102.4	T	98.6		99.3	
7	107.3	T	94.2		99.8	
8	99.2		100.1	T	100.6	
9	95.8		97.8		106.0	T
10	99.0		103.3		97.4	T
11	95.3		101.3	T	102.8	
12	105.1	T	95.2		100.6	
13	94.8	T	104.1		100.2	
14	107.1		98.0		95.9	T
15	100.9		100.7	T	98.5	
16	98.5		101.7	T	99.6	
17	101.4	T	99.7		99.1	

Table 6.11:
Actual votes shown as a percentage of chance expectation per column

Seven: Rýzl and Stepanek

ONE OF THE few scientists who deliberately pursued the method of majority vote on repeated trials was the late Dr. Milan Rýzl (1928-2011), who changed his address from Czechoslovakia to the United States in 1967. "The Czech secret police visited me," he told journalists Sheila Ostrander and Lynn Schroeder. "This was before Dubček. They wanted me to look for information... They were so insistent, I decided I'd try to get out and take my chances in America" (Ostrander and Schroeder, 1970, p. 342).

In 1964, a report on his successful experiments with the psi adept Pavel Stepanek had been published by Rýzl in the Czech technical journal *Sdelovaci Technika* (*Communication Technique*, Vol. 12, No. 8, pp. 299-302).Two years later, shortly before his defection to the West, an adaptation of that paper appeared in the *Journal of Parapsychology* (1966, 30, pp. 18-30). In the first paragraph of this seminal work, Rýzl posed the question "whether, for strategic reasons, some of the more recent scientific findings have been suppressed." It's a question one might still ponder. Certainly the answer became "Yes" a few years later, with the creation of deeply classified psi research and military intelligence operational programs in the then-Soviet Union and the USA (the latter program known today by one of its code names, Star Gate).

Rýzl's earliest repeated guessing pilot experiments were with a young woman he had trained using hypnotic procedures. Her name, Josefka K., has a suitably Kafkaesque ring to it. Although the technique "proved to yield an increase in the reliability of ESP calls," Miss J. K. had to abandon the tests for domestic reasons. In 1962, Rýzl began a fresh series with Stepanek alone.

Since the psychic had previously shown a stable and marked psi response when aiming at the binary distinction between white and green cards, he was given five coded messages in that form, binary translations from three-digit decimal numbers. (As an example of this kind of coding, which has been widespread now for two generations in computer programming languages, the decimal number 137 is written in binary code as 10001001. In Rýzl's day this was still rather new and shiny.) The experimental protocols were clever, stringent, and highly involved.

Stepanek got all five three-digit numbers right.

§

It seemed a major breakthrough in psi methodology, but his work was effectively unknown in the West. This was two years before Dr. D.J. West, whose efforts we've explored in some detail already, announced his gloomy (and erroneous) repudiation of the repeated guessing approach to psi application.

Here's how it operated:

It takes 10 binary choices (Yes/No, or 1/0, or +/0, or Green/White) to encode the range of familiar decimal numbers 000 to 999. Rýzl's assistant chose a number from this range at random, encoded it into a sequence of green and white cards (that is, as a series of binary targets), and sealed them into opaque covers. These covers were marked A, B, C... K (J was omitted) on the back, allowing the accumulating guesses at each card to be correctly attributed.

A second series of 10 cards, in the inverse or complementary order—White replacing Green, Green replacing White, to compensate for preference bias, and to ensure equal representation of each color—were sealed and labeled a, b, c... k (j was omitted). Star Gate scientists later called this "Complement Targeting Statistical Enhancement."

Finally, Rýzl himself selected a different pattern of 10 cards, sealed them, and marked them 1 to 10. These last would serve as an advance index for sampling purposes. The protocol required in advance that if the numbered index cards did not show sufficient evidence of psi, that series would be declared a dud.

As it happened, these index cards demonstrated psi-hitting in each case, suggesting that the test trials might also be in that mode. (This, as we'll see, might be an uncertain assumption—but it worked for Rýzl.)

These tests were of close-range clairvoyance. Fifty times, all 30 cards were shuffled and presented to Stepanek for psychic identification. Naturally, he was not shown the letters and numbers on the backs of the envelopes. But even if a subtle sensory discrimination allowed him to segregate one envelope from another, as seems likely, he still had no way of knowing—by other than paranormal means—which color, green or white, was present in each cover. This was disputed, but without proof, by the late skeptic Martin Gardner, in *How Not to Test a Psychic*, a slyly insinuating monograph from 1989. Gardner, according to Rýzl. suggested that the Czech psychic "write an article or give an interview in which [Stepanek] would reveal how he cheated. Gardner went on to offer his good offices and his connection with an organization to help publicize his report and arrange to produce a documentary film that would make him at once internationally famous and at the same time enable him to receive substantial honoraria" (Rýzl, Letter to the Editor, *Journal of Parapsychology*, 54, September 1990, p. 284). Stepanek declined this offer.

For most ordinary subjects, 50 calls per card would be grossly inadequate. Stepanek, though, was apparently a psychic superstar (if rather monomaniacal—binary card guessing was his only psi feat, and even this faded with time). In this series, his overall visible psi efficiency was reportedly +23.8 percent beyond the chance mean of 50 percent! Even so, Rýzl knew that it was unlikely that significant deviations would be obtained on each card in such a small number of calls. So he devised a safeguard. Unless an outstanding score for either Green or White was achieved for each given card, it was returned to the pool (bulked out with new index cards to replace those cards that met the test), and these went back to Stepanek for another 50 runs.

The chief drawback was the time consumed, a difficulty for solo implementation that has never been resolved. Majority vote psi using repeated trials takes a *lot* of effort; there's not really any way around that (other than calling on the effort of many volunteers, and that can have its own drawbacks, as we'll see). Stepanek's stable and powerful psi response mitigated the usual bane of boring psi tasks, those wretched decline effects that weaken accuracy over time. But even with that stunning 23 percent efficiency, to get the five three-digit numbers "it was necessary," wrote Rýzl in "A Model of Parapsychological Communication," "to make 19,350 single color-calls (of which 11,978 were hits and 7,372 were misses.)"

He added ruefully: "The average speed on the whole was about 40 calls per hour so that the mere accumulation of the data took some 50 hours (with two persons participating). To this we must also add the time necessary for evaluation of results."

§

Let us consider the first run of 50 calls per card that Stepanek made on the target-number "242," encoded as the sequence: G W W W W G W G G W. (At first this looks like a translation into standard binary code of the number 242, which would be 11110010. But this string differs from that—GWWWWGWGGW would be 0111101001—because in creating the alphabetical string Rýzl's assistant used some kind of private code.) In that first attempt, involving 1500 guesses, Rýzl was only satisfied that one of the ten binary options (the card *H* and its opposite *h*) had accrued sufficient votes to make a firm prediction.

The remainder, therefore, went back for further paranormal scrutiny. Three of these cards, and their inverse or complement forms, required as many as four runs to gain a clear majority: a total of 400 guesses apiece.

Index run - White	Calls	Prediction	Target
1	33	W	W
2	15	G	G
3	23	G	W
4	25	?	G
5	16	G	G
6	25	?	W
7	27	W	G
8	27	W	W
9	32	W	W
10	22	G	G
Message run - White	Calls	Prediction	Target
A	18	G	G
B	34	W	W
C	35	W	W
D	29	W	W
E	33	W	W
F	27	***W***	G
G	29	W	W
H	15	G	G
I	21	G	G
K	39	W	W

Inverse run - Green	Calls	Prediction	Target
a	23	W	W
b	33	G	G
c	18	***W***	G
d	23	***W***	G
e	20	***W***	G
f	16	W	W
g	24	***W***	G
h	5	W	W
i	22	W	W
k	27	G	G
Combined message		Index of Preference	
A	41	G	0.84
B	67	W	1.34
C	53	W	1.04
D	52	W	1.04
E	53	W	1.05
F	43	G	0.85
G	53	W	1.06
H	20	G	0.39
I	43	G	0.87
K	66	W	1.32

Table 7.1: Rýzl-Stepanek Protocol
The first 50 trials, plus preliminary index calls

Total White calls—
Index (245/500), Message (280/500), Inverse (289/500)
Combined White mean: 27.13 calls per card (of 50)
Incorrect simple majority votes *Italicized Bold*
(Adapted from *Journal of Parapsychology,* 1966, 30, p. 25)

Two of the ten *index* cards, which used a different and random sequence of green and white cards, scored exactly at chance level (25 out of 50), and so were ignored, treated as "pass" calls. Of the predictions arising from the remainder, six proved correct. If we construe this index score as six of eight correct, we can go on with some small confidence to the *test* sequence plus its color-inverse. That inverse sequence can be added to the straightforward version to produce a score with a theoretical mean of 50 percent—a move incorporated into the Reswick/Vodovnik telepathy experiment to be discussed in the next chapter,.

In the first run, the test sequence lost only one bit of information. Six out of 10 were correctly obtained in the inverse form. Combined, all 10 bits of the message received majorities—although, admittedly, in four of them that majority was too small to impart much confidence.

The number of guesses is quite staggering, as is the improbability that the successful identifications were made by sheer chance. In all, Stepanek made 19,350 calls, and 11,978 were hits. His overall score was nearly 62 percent, rather than close to 50 percent as chance would have it. The mathematical likelihood of this outcome is given by skeptic Martin Gardner as 1 in one quadrillion, 125 trillion, 899 billion, 906 million, 842 thousand 624. That is the full and extraordinary decimal expansion of $1/2^{50}$. The whole experiment, as noted above, took 50 hours, plus additional time and toil to process the results.

One additional feature of these figures deserves attention. It was just as well that Rýzl incorporated an inverse form of the message, since overall Stepanek called "white" eight percent more frequently than "green". This helps to explain his comparative failure with the inverse message, which had six green targets to four white ones. By adding each straight white vote and its equivalent (but inverse) green vote, this imbalance tends to even out.

Another method of handling the eruption of this unpredictable problem, which we shall discuss shortly in some detail, is the "Index of Preference," which adjusts the scores according to the overall ratios obtained. When this Index is applied to the figures in the table, the aggregated result is unchanged but two of the incorrect predictions in the sub-groups are repaired. (This fact has the unanticipated merit of casting doubt on Martin Gardner's implication that Stepanek cheated by peeking at the colors of the cards.)

§

Rýzl was not the only Soviet to apply this methodology. A Bulgarian, Dr. Georgi Lozanov, ran an extended telepathy test based on majority vote, which was described at the 1966 Parapsychology Conference in Moscow. Using two telegraph keys to record binary decisions, his percipient attempted to ascertain by ESP whether the sender was asking him to press the right or left key.

Unlike most programs of this kind, each command was presented ten times. If, in any of these brackets, the percipient struck one key six times or more, that key became his vote. Dr. Lozanov reportedly claimed that his participant was enabled, by this screening procedure, to get 70 percent of the commands correct.

As we've seen, though, majority vote taken on only ten guesses is not a terribly good guide. If Lozanov's life had hung on the accurate reception of any particular command, his prospects would not have been encouraging.

§

Fortunately, our general rule can be read another way, one less taxing to the individual participant, and producing many more guesses. My own experience of majority vote methods has led me, on the whole, to follow this alternative path. I believe it's the route most likely to be taken whenever paranormally-derived data is required by a community. Circumventing decline effects of the most noxious variety, it has its own drawbacks but does give fast results. It is also, I fear, the method even more attractive than remote viewing to the military and what we might dub ESPionage organization (if there are any in operation these days), media and lottery plutocrats, computerized pollsters and totalitarian regimes of every hue. It's this, an approach to finding and training psi superstars such as Stepanek, potentially handier in every way but more difficult logistically to put into practice:

> *A large number of respondents shall each guess a number of times at a single sequence of coded, indexed targets. As always, these respondents and the experimenters must be blind to both the targets and the precise decoding protocols until the guesses are completed.*

In other words, two heads are better than one—so long as you can find out, without intruding upon them, where those heads are at.

One problem is that a thousand luminous psi talents functioning at peak efficiency will get you nowhere if half of them are brilliantly psi-hitting and half are superbly psi-missing. Their guesses will tend to obliterate each other, leaving you a low variance, net chance result—and no useful information.

On the face of it, preliminary evaluation of a sample index message will not *guarantee* segregating hitters from missers, or what in the next chapter we shall call *phi* mode from *mu* mode. After all, if each respondent makes only 10 calls, the chances of a single psi event (in the general case) will be only one in 10 if psi functions in about one percent of calls. Sometimes it's more effective than that, but often far more fleeting. The likelihood of an individual obtaining two psi hits, one in the sample and one in the message itself, is therefore rather small. Other techniques are needed to filter hitters from missers, such as tests of personality characteristics or typical cognitive mode—topics that have been researched extensively by parapsychologists, but with no absolutely sure results. (We'll return in a later chapter to attempts by Dr. James Carpenter to achieve this goal.)

Before he left Czechoslovakia (as his homeland was then called), Rýzl reportedly put his stable of talented psychics to work in a group repeated guessing exercise aimed at winning a lottery. The results were gratifying, if not entirely satisfactory.

Unlike most traditional Western lotteries, where you are simply allocated a ticket bearing a given number, the Czech lottery was similar to the British Pools system or US varieties such as Powerball and Mega Millions. Bettors *specify* the numbers that will be drawn. Of 49 candidate numbers, six were selected at random in each Czech lottery draw. If Rýzl's team guessed those six correctly, they would win a handsome prize. For five right, their share would diminish; four correct, or less, and the winnings were still more reduced.

To my knowledge, Rýzl did not publish the details of these experiments, at least in English. We are told that he drew up a sequence of binary options able to encode the lottery numbers. Pavel Stepanek, Miss J. K. and others made their (hopefully) precognitive guesses, which were then pooled. These generated predictions for the coming draw.

In the first week the team reportedly got one number right, the following week three, and on the third attempt they got four correct and made a pleasant profit. It would be interesting to know how many subjects made how many guesses. Presumably both numbers were low, since their success rate was far inferior to the 100 percent accuracy achieved once by Stepanek in his lone trials.

Did Dr. Rýzl subsequently make his fortune as a result of this approach? Alas, apparently not. Sheila Ostrander and Lynn Schroeder commented coyly, in their 1970 book on Soviet psi research, *Psychic Discoveries Behind the Iron Curtain*: "Rýzl doesn't mention taking any high-scoring coeds off to the races to help him make his way in the new world," and he did not die a wildly wealthy man. The difficulty is, of course, that high-powered use of majority vote psi requires a large number of psi-effective participants. As Rýzl pointed out in "A Model of Parapsychological Communication":

> parapsychologists have given considerable attention to the problem of finding a way to make ESP practically applicable. It seems that the difficulty has mainly been the fact that no way has been found to make the ESP performance so perfect and constant that lawful control can be obtained. This is the impression one would get from the studies generally accessible in the scientific press. It has been only in the experiments with the subject [Pavel Stepanek]... that a sufficiently stable ESP response was attained to warrant an attempt at the reliable conveyance of information by ESP with a real hope of success.

§

A cautionary note is needed before we get too excited. The amazing 50 right out of 50 calls has been repeatedly mentioned by parapsychologists as proof not just of the reality of psi but also of its capacity to drive real-world applications. What is usually overlooked, or even swept under the carpet, is Dr. Rýzl's failure to replicate this feat with Stepanek—or with anyone else. He did try, three times (with slightly different protocols—but had little success.

The best available source for information about these duds is probably Martin Gardner's book on Stepanek, which draws on both published and unpublished documents. Despite his confident, urbane air of even-handedness, Gardner's mocking tone, as if with one eyebrow raised, makes it clear that he considers Stepanek a fraud. He offers various hypotheses for how this remarkable success could have been achieved, but none of this shows why Stepanek and his somewhat clumsy experimenters *failed* in their attempts to replicate the first fine careless rapture.

It is not, though, as if Stepanek plummeted at once to random levels of performance. The first replication tried to match ten white/green cards in a sequence set by tossing a coin. A bias-countering color-reversed set was also created, and unless all were correctly identified (a very stringent requirement), the test would be regarded as a failure.

Six cards were correctly identified. Three did not reach the needed level of confidence and so were regarded as "passes." One was simply wrong. That single error was sufficient to ruin Rýzl's hope of a clean sweep—and so, annoyingly, the experiment was abandoned. For Rýzl, there was no point in seeing if further repeated guessing could be condensed into correct majority calls for the three undecided cards. In effect, therefore, Stepanek scored six right and one wrong out of seven. Is it fair to dismiss this as nothing more than chance?

Surely not.

The second attempted replication used a single three-digit number, coded to a binary pattern of ten hidden cards (and their inverse ten). Calls continued on and off for nearly a year, and the psychic ended by making 24,000 guesses. Gardner, without giving any numbers, says only that

> The criteria used for evaluating the results were even more complicated than before, and require three pages of typescript to explain.... The experiment was another failure. PS showed no ESP success on the actual colors (p. 52).

What's more, in Gardner's correspondence with Rýzl some two decades later, it was said that the original records had been stored in Czechoslovakia when he and his wife fled, and were now lost. Rýzl in 1987 now found the results of the second and third replication runs "confusing" and "quite worthless" (p. 53).

That third attempt was even more ambitious, and tried to convey in coded form (now using yellow and white cards) the phrase "Peace and Freedom" or perhaps "Freedom and Peace," probably with the two gaps between the words filled with another character for a total of 17 letters. (By a curious coincidence, the word "Peace" was also chosen some years later by Dr. Jim Carpenter in his successful attempt at repeated guessing psi messaging.) Now Stepanek made a total of 30,600 calls, but obtained an overall a negative score. It would be helpful to have more details, but they are unavailable. Might this have been significant psi-missing? We'd need to know the magnitude of the errors to decide that.

Not long after, Stepanek chose to cease working with Rýzl and continued as a paid parapsychological subject with the US researcher Dr. Gaither Pratt, one of Rhine's long-time colleagues, and with the German-Australian Dr. H. H. Jürgen Keil. No further attempts were made to repeat the dramatic 100 percent success.

It's my suspicion that Rýzl was guilty of ever more over-elaborate designs in his tests, trying to cover all possible stumbling-blocks and instead getting caught in the weeds. Dr. Edwin May, the former scientific director of the US government Star Gate program, told me, "Of the many ways he could have encoded things, his was among the least effective." He added: "We jumped on this and went for 2 x 5 BCH code which was 100% single bit error correcting with some 2-bit correcting to send a 2-bit message." Now, this statement is not immediately clear to most of us, so just for the joy of it I'm going to make your eyes bleed for a moment. BCH code is based on the names of Raj Bose, D. K. Ray-Chaudhuri and Alexis Hocquenghem, its inventors at the turn of the 1960s. As Wikipedia (a reliable-enough source for such technical topics) puts it:

> Given a prime power q and positive integers m and d with $d \leq q^m - 1$, a primitive narrow-sense BCH code over the finite field GF(q) with code length $n = q^m - 1$ and distance at least d is constructed by the following method.
>
> Let α be a primitive element of GF(q^m). For any positive integer i, let $m_i(x)$ be the minimal polynomial of α^i. The generator polynomial of the BCH code is defined as the least common multiple $g(x) = \mathrm{lcm}(m_1(x),\ldots,m_{d-1}(x))$. It can be seen that $g(x)$ is a polynomial with coefficients in GF(q) and divides $x^n - 1$. Therefore, the polynomial code defined by $g(x)$ is a cyclic code.

Relax: There will not be an exam on this. It is easy to see why Rýzl might have avoided taking the BCH code path and settled instead for his own elaborate but unsuperscripted and unsubscripted protocols.

As well, Rýzl's own preferred scheme of training participants under hypnosis, which is not known to work for other parapsychologists (mostly using unsophisticated methods), plainly didn't turn out a stable of superhumans. Another psi investigator, Dr. Charles T. Tart, a founder of Transpersonal Psychology with an abiding interest in paranormal and spiritual phenomena, endeavored to train psychic ability. His teaching devices, developed from the mid 1960s, provided instant feedback and excitement to his participants. His Ten Choice Trainer, with its valuable option of allowing participants to pass on any particular call, immediately let them know if their spontaneous button push corresponded with the randomized intention of a "telepathic sender" revealed by the lighting of one of ten bulbs on a circular display 15 inches across. He told me: "My percipients were encouraged to examine their reasons for wanting to push or not push a particular button at a particular time and try to see if they started to find associations between feeling certain ways and being right, and so develop those, or being wrong, and so not respond at those times" (private communication, May 23, 2015). You can find a brief account in Tart's *PSI: Scientific Studies in the Psychic Realm*, 1977, pp. 144-46, where his papers on the topic are summarized and cited, and more extensively in his 1976 University of Chicago press monograph, *Learning To Use Extrasensory Perception*.

At roughly the same time, Russell Targ was developing a four-choice ESP teaching machine allowing feedback, reinforcement, and a pass button to prevent the task from becoming one of wearying *forced choice*—the classic ESP routine that seems to have become passé by that time. Targ had demonstrated this to NASA administrators (and spaceflight pioneer Wernher von Braun), and NASA had funded his continuing work. He found that his device not only improved performance but, even more encouraging, "*none* of the 147 volunteers showed a systematic decrease in their scoring" (Targ 2012, 89-90).

Charley Tart realized before he started that a certain measure of raw ability is always needed before learning could take place, and that instant feedback could help confirm subtle cues from psi-modified guesses. He wrote in 2015: "The concept in the classical era was that you were *testing* how much ESP a particular person had. My insight was to recognize this was an unfamiliar task that had to be *learned*, and that testing without immediate feedback actually constituted a classical psychological extinction paradigm. Voila! The more you tested people, the more they declined to chance, ESP could be extinguished with a known technique!" (private communication).

It was a clever insight, based in orthodox learning theory, but for some reason—to Tart's chagrin—it was not generally followed up by others. Even today, there is a tendency to run psi trials with college students as part of their course work, whether or not they have provided previous evidence of psychic talent. It's arguably one reason why experiments by skeptical academics tend to fail—like pulling in random people off the street to find out if training can teach them to run a four minute mile. For most of them, not so likely.

By the same token, only more so, volunteers for the task of replicating Stepanek's famous feat are still in short supply. This book, though, might help swell their numbers, and perhaps their success rate. So, too, might a 21st-century version of Targ's teaching device, a 7.2 Megabyte, four color app, released in November, 2009:

> You can now have an ESP machine for yourself at no cost... as a free application for the iPhone. It is called ESP Trainer. After a year, we have had more than ten thousand downloads from Apple's iTunes store. (Targ, 2012, p. 93).

And other psi-related computer programs are under experimental development.

Eight: Differential

WHEN AN EXPERIMENTER muddles along in advance of a comprehensive theoretical understanding, the universe is not always obliging enough to fetch forth just the results she or he needs to clarify a quest for insight and evidence. Even a dazzlingly accurate hunch can get lost in the vast complexity of reality. It is not easy to exclude unwanted variables, when you are almost entirely ignorant of the mechanisms involved in your chosen phenomenon.

Chance can play as large a role in the unfolding of a useful discovery as does rigorous planning and ingenious insight. Consider the case of Gregor Mendel's theory of how physical characteristics are inherited genetically. Human prejudice, ignoring his findings, helped to retard scientific progress for a full generation. Even so, Mendel's empirical observations in his monastery garden might never have been made in the first place had it not been for a stroke of luck equal to the misfortune that later plagued his breakthrough.

The plant Mendel selected for study in his monastery garden was a variety of pea that showed several distinct characteristics, notably flower color, inherited in sharply different ways. The purple-red kind, crossed with a white kind, produced in several generations only red or white offspring—never shades of pink. The plants came with round or wrinkled seeds, short stems or tall, yellow seeds and green, and so forth, Mendel examined seven such variables and in every case he found that the characteristic was passed on discretely, without shading off into intermediate forms.

This clear proof that inheritance is governed by specific genes led to Mendel's "law of independent assortment," and later became the capstone for the genetic development of neo-Darwinian evolutionary theory. Yet, as geneticists were later to learn to their chagrin, it turns out that very few interesting characteristics are passed down by this simple process. All the gene loci in which Mendel had been interested just happen to be situated on different chromosomes of the pea, permitting the beautifully elegant mechanism to be manifested cleanly. For genes located on the same chromosome, Mendel's straightforward law no longer applies.

In short: had Mendel not been lucky enough to choose just these seven characteristics of his pea for scrutiny, he might never have discovered the profound truth they exemplify so lucidly. (Actually I wouldn't be surprised if he also studied other features of the plant, found them less easily explained, and quietly shelved those confounded results.)

With the conjecture of psi mode—hitting and missing to a greater extent than chance—we are faced with this sort of difficulty. Nobody yet knows for sure why people tested for psi respond sometimes with statistically significant psi-hitting and sometimes with significant psi-missing, or why "sheep" (believers) tend to hit while "goats" (skeptics) tend to miss. The phenomenon of displacement (to the extent that it's real and not just an artifact of data-trawling) only makes matters worse.

In practical terms, as we've seen, multiple guesses at the same target can mitigate the problem, when allowance is made for stacking effects, where common biases brought to bear on a single shared target can reinforce the wrong answer. When it works properly, though, redundancy methods can concentrate a tiny amount of psi into the correct reception of information. But if every psi-hitting manifestation in a group response is the blurry resultant of diametrically opposed psi-hitting and psi-missing events, any practical applications seems doomed to be inefficient and unreliable.

What's needed is a way to force participants into acting psychically in a predictable manner. Preliminary testing might identify those who predominantly hit or miss (assuming this feature is consistent in individuals, which it probably isn't), and allow their guesses to be segregated. But large-scale undertakings of this magnitude seem out of the question at this time, although military and intelligence applications might do it routinely. For future generations, perhaps, the administration of such tests might become as ordinary as IQ tests and blood-type or genomic tests, or perhaps magnetic resonance imaging and PET scans. In the meanwhile, it would be enormously helpful to find a simple test that can sort the majority of hitting responses into one group and the majority of missing into another. Perhaps we can find ways to force such a psychic *differential effect*.

§

In 1969, Dr. J.B. Rhine described such differential effects as follows: "When in a psi test the subject is confronted with two features in a comparative way, he tends to react differentially to the two in his psi responses; that is, he generally scores above chance on one and below on the other with significant consistency, if he shows psi ability at all."

Amplifying this dictum, Alan D. Price wrote in the *Journal of Parapsychology* (1973): "In brief, the evidence suggests that when a dual-target (or more generally, a dual condition) situation is employed in an ESP experiment, one target type (condition) tends to 'attract' psi-hitting tendencies and the other, psi-missing tendencies. Thus, an 'inherent' bidirectionality in the psi process seems to be differentiated and controlled to some extent by introducing a dual-condition into the experimental situation. Carpenter... found evidence that a differential effect can occur even when subjects are not consciously aware that the target difference exists."

The effect has been known for more than 70 years; in early work by Foster, Rhine noted, "the two-aspect test required a response involving both a symbol and a color choice." This must immediately give us pause. Doesn't this mean that the hitting/missing mode of subjects trying to identify playing-cards should be split by the two-fold nature of the targets: suit and number—although this generally doesn't happen?

This is not so, pointed out Rhine, when the subject's response "integrates the individual elements... The point seems to be that if the subject mentally unifies the two elements, there is no differential effect; and if not, there usually is." In the identification of a playing-card, of course, the two elements are clearly integrated into one target—even if we can distinguish them in later analysis.

§

The best indicator seems to be cognitive style—the way in which an individual prefers to make sense of the world. Some people are strikingly verbal, talking a problem out, making written notes. (As you might guess, I'm one of these.) Others are principally pictorial in their approach, "getting the picture," drawing graphs. Some delight in numerical analysis, manipulating abstract symbols, while others "feel out" the situation, seek gut reactions, fly by the seat of their pants.

Now it happens that, in the Western culture of most of the last century and perhaps even today, despite serious gains for women in education and the workplace, gender was a fairly reliable indicator of a tested population's dominant cognitive style.

When tests of Verbal Reasoning and Spatial Relations were studied in the 1950s and 1960s, it was usually found that women tended to have greater Verbal facility than Spatial, and men tended to show the reverse scores. There was nothing implicitly sexist in this observation. The distinction is not primarily between the cognitive styles of *individual* men and women, but between the average Verbal and Spatial scores of women as a group, and the Verbal and Spatial scores of men as a group. It's like height: on average, women are shorter than men, even though there are short men and towering women.

Similarly, of course, some women are better at Spatial thinking than they are at Verbal, and better than most men, while some men score higher on Verbal than on Spatial. (I am one of those.) Some are proficient at both (like my brilliant wife Barbara, a mathematician and a writer), or equally inept. All that mattered, for the purpose of this exploration, was that group *averages* correlated in this way.

§

The late Dr. John A. Freeman, a researcher with Rhine's Institute, became interested during the 1960s in possible relationships between psi-mode, sex, and dominant cognitive mode. His pioneering studies—though they were based, unfortunately, on the intensive investigation in only a few school classrooms—suggested that this gender correlation might still prove a useful adjunct to psi applications employing hundreds of thousands of unscreened respondents.

If it could be shown that the average psi-mediated deviation of women on Verbal guessing tests tends to be in the opposite direction from that of men, Freeman thought, and if we knew in advance what that direction is likely to be (hitting or missing), and its level of apparent efficiency, then separating the test results by gender might greatly enhance our capacity to isolate the psi component in a mass test.

Of course, such a discrimination would be even more fruitful if it could be based on *individual* scores for Verbal, Spatial and Reasoning skills. But such personalized tests, to be in any way accurate, are laborious and time-consuming. Modest correlations with gender alone might be more convenient than superior measures that require one-on-one administration of aptitude tests.

We must regard Freeman's findings as provisional and somewhat culture-bound, the tentative results of "work in progress" that has never really been developed. Another of Rhine's colleagues, Dr. Jim Carpenter, told me: "No one exactly followed up on his work. Other differential work was done by Rao, Kanthamani, Palmer, me a bit, and I'm sure some others too during that period." He added: "Parapsychology research has always been so fitful and unprogrammatic, guided by the bright ideas of whatever the new crop of people is. Lacking strong theoretical ideas we have lacked programs. Who knows if it could have been replicated, or how specific it might have proved to be to John, his samples, his kind of rapport with kids, etc. etc. I think also that the findings were getting so complicated that Rhine probably lost interest in them, and John was working under Rhine's thumb" (private email communication, December 24, 2009, cited with permission).

Freeman found his most interesting distinctions in groups of early adolescents. This is the age-group in which cognitive differences emerge strongly. It is likely that in adults the dissimilarity between males and females becomes less striking. Still, it is the best we have to go on.

Before I summarize Freeman's empirical findings, it is valuable to clarify this proposed distinction. I have chosen the Greek letters *phi* and *mu* as useful mnemonic devices, reminding us gently that while more females are *phi* than *mu*, and more males are *mu* than *phi*, sex as such is not the point. Freeman's original search for psi-mode correlates focused on scores from boys versus girls; his later work indicated that his correlations pertain rather to *phi*-ness and *mu*-ness.

Therefore, we shall dub as *Phi* subjects individuals who score higher on Verbal than on Spatial tests, whether they are men or women, girls or boys. Those people who score higher on Spatial than on Verbal tests we'll call *Mu* subjects. So, any given man or woman might be either *phi* or *mu*; only the scores on a test like the Thurstone Primary Mental Abilities battery can tell you whether you are one or the other.

Freeman's ESP booklets asked his young participants to pick out which option in each line of a test would be chosen later as the target. He made it clear that each participant would get a different, individualized set of targets, which neatly avoided at least some stacking effects.

The booklets offered four kinds of choices:

Some lines showed the same identical picture five times in a row.

Others showed five different pictures.

Some showed the same geometrical figure repeated five times.

Others showed five different figures.

Some lines showed the same word repeated.

Others had five different words.

In pilot studies, Freeman found that when students were given these varying target options, it forced a differential effect, with some kinds of array yielded higher than chance results and others lower than chance—psi-hitting and psi-missing forced by design, and not just at random.

§

Here are the predicted outcomes:

Phi *hits*, and mu *misses*, targets from a line showing:

> The SAME repeated PICTORIAL IMAGE or WORD, or
> DIFFERENT geometric SHAPES or abstract SYMBOLS.

Mu *hits*, and Phi *misses*, targets from a line showing:

> The SAME geometric SHAPE or SYMBOL, or
> DIFFERENT PICTORIAL IMAGES or WORDS.

This model was confirmed (within the limits set by the necessarily small number of classroom participants) in several replicated tests.

For example, in 1969, Freeman administered a precognition test to eighth-grade classes at Rogers-Herr Junior High School, in Durham, North Carolina, where Rhine's Institute is still located. His test booklet "was designed to see if geometrical figures could be substituted for [the five classic] ESP symbols, and if pictures of familiar objects could be substituted for words." With the latter test options, he had already established the pattern shown in the table above.

In a preliminary analysis, with the responses segregated by sex alone, results were somewhat promising. For this approximation, the girls' consolidated votes were interpreted by *phi* (female-like) criteria, and the boys' by *mu* (male-like). In 1680 trials, the 28 girls missed the *phi*-hit targets by an insignificant 0.1 percent, deviating from mean chance expectation by only one vote (a statistically meaningless result). On *phi*-miss targets, they missed much more convincingly, by 3.0 percent.

And in 1500 trials, the boys obtained a positive deviation of 1.7 percent on *mu*-hit targets, and a predicted (though low) negative deviation of 0.4 percent on *mu*-miss targets.

So far, then, the results failed to disprove Freeman's speculation, and indeed corroborated it to some extent.

§

Freeman then divided his subjects into true *phi* and true *mu* groups on the basis of each individual's scores on the Verbal Reasoning, Spatial Relations, and some Reasoning subtests of the Primary Mental Abilities battery. His *mu* group then comprised 20 males and four females, and his *phi* group 23 females and five males. (One of the girls was away from class when the PMA tests were given.)

Mu subjects, in 1440 guesses, had an excess of predicted *mu*-hit targets of 3.5 percent, and a negative deviation of 1.8 percent on *mu*-missed targets. Overall, this was an apparent mean psi effect, in the predicted direction, of 2.6 percent.

Phi subjects, in 1680 guesses, obtained a positive deviation on *phi*-hit targets of 1.0 percent, and were 4.2 percent below chance on *phi*-miss targets. Again, the mean psi effect is about 2.6 percent.

This is a remarkably strong effect, and has rarely been equaled in more routine tests of ESP such as the decades-long studies by PEAR researchers at Princeton, where psi-attributed deviations tend to be closer to one anomalous information bit per 1000 calls or worse.

§

Freeman's protocols are a paradigm in the deliberate evocation of a differential effect. What he found more than four decades ago is that if we lump together both groups, and consider only the combined result, the differential effect is lost. Majority vote taken on both groups together has a faintly psi-missing look to it, though statistically insignificant. The deviations from chance, to a great degree, have cancelled out. "Different symbols-same picture" targets are missed by a tiny 0.3 percent, and "different pictures-same symbol" missed by 0.6 percent. Without the differential sorting, we're left with a total overall negative deviation of only 15 votes out of 31,201 calls—an utterly misleading result.

Is it any wonder that in ordinary life, where one must suppose the bidirectionality of psi is not usually polarized in this convenient, artificial fashion, there is so little daily evidence of our paranormal capacities?

Freeman's exciting results were, admittedly, no more than hints. The standard error for the groups cited above is on the order of 1.5 percent, which helps account for the variation on the hitting and missing targets of the *phi* clan. It is plausible to conjecture that chance fluctuations boosted the missing effect and hindered the hitting mode. Even so, it seems clear that in truly massive group psi applications, a preliminary screening of participants into *phi* and *mu* categories might greatly enhance the efficiency of paranormal effectiveness, if target options are structured to elicit a differential effect.

As we've seen, even without individual screening the division of subjects according to gender is slightly better than doing nothing. Freeman's figures suggest that about one fifth of males will test out *phi*, and one fifth of females prove to be *mu*. I do not know if this proportion holds true for the world beyond the 1969 eighth-grade of Rogers-Herr. If so, we might hope to employ the male/female distinction as a clumsy but useful approximation to the *mu*/*phi* distinction.

Freeman continued these experiments, clarifying and refining his test instruments and hypotheses, and it seemed clear he was onto something quite important. But, as we shall see, the reigning paradigm in experimental parapsychology moved away from this approach. I have reason to think that there was virtue in Freeman's method. A fully developed psi technology would reduce these generalized trends to a battery of highly reliable correlations, so that each psi subject can be screened in advance. Perhaps estimates could then be made of the direction in which his or her psi responses might be expected to function. But such estimates would in turn have to be modulated according to other factors such as those proposed in Dr. Jim Carpenter's "First Sight" theory of psi, as we shall see later.

§

These are far from exhausting the list of useful distinctions that were found. Asked, for example, to write down half their guesses and announce the rest aloud, 20 subjects in a 1962 experiment showed a significant difference in the scoring according to the method they preferred. Interestingly, once again, the total aggregate score of the group was not significantly different from chance, so a simple analysis would not have revealed any psi at all.

Nor was there much difference between written and called guesses. Yet the combined values for the individually favored methods scored positively, while those for the methods disliked scored negatively.

Another statistical measure, *variance*, expresses the amount of internal variability in a series of guesses. It's a

> statistic for the degree to which a group of scores are scattered or dispersed around their average; formally, it is the average of the squared deviations from the [empirical] mean; in parapsychology, the term is often used somewhat idiosyncratically to refer to the variance around the theoretical mean of a group of scores (e.g., MCE) rather than around the actual, obtained mean.[8]

(This unusual definition permits the measure to indicate the extremity of the response, in terms of either psi-hitting or psi-missing.) Probability theory provides expected values for this variation and, if a run of guesses has significantly more or less internal variation than is expected by chance, it suggests (all other known factors being controlled) that psi is at work in "pushing" the scores in either a psi-hitting or psi-missing direction.

In rare cases, one curious feature, dubbed by its discoverers the *focusing effect*, operates endearingly. Here a particular target in a range of options is favored by the percipient. If you operate this way, your ability to identify that numinous target correctly is greater than your degree of success with other targets. With Pavel Stepanek, this sometimes applied to a single card, then to the card plus the envelope it's wrapped in, then the cover *that's* placed in. Nor can this effect necessarily be attributed to near-subliminal awareness of markings on the back of the card, or its envelope, etc (although Martin Gardner implied that it did with Stepanek). Careful precautions can rule out this easy explanation.

It seems preposterous that someone should be more attuned psychically to one specific card than to any others. Perhaps this effect is a version of the phenomenon often notable in "spontaneous," uncontrolled psychic experiences: a person's special rapport with, say, a particular person or place.

§

We've seen that if psi for one task drops away, it can still saunter back in a fresh role. Thouless elevated this observation to the rank of a principle: the *change effect*. He allied it with the *witness effect*, a failure of psi that has often been found in the laboratory if a stranger (especially a hostile,

8. http://psiphen.colorado.edu/Glossary.htm
"MCE" is the abbreviation for "mean chance expectation."

skeptical stranger) is brought in to observe proceedings. On the face of it, this alleged "witness effect" sounds like a convenient plea. Surely, the skeptic will surmise, failure to maintain impressive scores stems from the increasing abandonment of slack protocols favored among the gullible.

This is not the case, however. If interlopers remain on the scene long enough for the subject to become accustomed to their presence, results will usually reappear. Alas, hostile critics are not often so generous with their time. Scrutiny need not be relaxed (although it could be argued that this will happen unconsciously), but a decent degree of patience must be exercised.

§

Clearly, then, an important requirement for a psi technology aimed at knowing the currently unknown will be screening procedures that allow a group to be split in advance into psi-hitters and psi-missers, assuming that distinction has any stability. Paralleling Freeman's work with children is the classic study, later confirmed by the study of variance, of the *sheep/goats effect.*

First noticed by Dr. Gertrude Schmeidler (who died aged 96, in 2009), this is a distinction between those who are convinced of the reality of ESP (the "believing" sheep) and those who are convinced that it's probably or even certainly nonsense (the "skeptical" goats). Schmeidler found that sheep tended to hit the target, goats to miss. That is, the goats did not simply score at chance level—they *failed* significantly.

It is still not known why this occurs, when it does. One might imagine that folk who have had striking experiences of accurate psi prior to the experiment would become sheep, likely to believe in ESP. Those who have not (or, if psi missing is a deeply ingrained inhibition against accepting psi mediated information, those who *will* not), probably would not believe in it. Schmeidler tested more than 1000 subjects for this effect. In Thouless's words, "calculation shows that the difference between the 'sheep' and the 'goats' is unquestionably significant ($p = 0.00003$)." Curiously, this promising effect has not been replicated consistently in later research.

A number of attempts have also been made at matching psi ability, mode of hitting or missing, and certain personality traits. These parameters are not identical with those investigated by Freeman, though they might interact to some extent. Certainly, success in this search would advance the day when a battery of IQ and personality inventories would offer experimenters a well-defined profile of any given individual group.

Typical early work along these lines was presented by B. K. Kanthamani and K. Ramakrishna Rao, who examined 14 basic personality factors and found that four of them correlated with ESP performance.

Subjects rated as warm and sociable scored higher on psi tests than the critical and aloof. Dominant people psi-hit, while submissives psi-missed. "Happy-go-lucky" individuals scored positively, "serious minded" folk scored negatively. Finally, tough realists were psi-hitters, while sensitive aesthetes were psi-missers (perhaps a surprising discovery).

Kanthamani and Rao put these factors together in a single test—the Combined Personality Measure—and it not only screened hitters and missers, it did so better than any of the individual component factors. To a large extent this confirmed a conjecture by Professor Hans Eysenck (1916-1997) that extraverts are more attuned to psi (in a directly useful sense) than are introverts.

It is possible, as we'll see, to put psi to work without knowing or assessing these factors, but it's rather more arduous. More importantly, from a scientific viewpoint, this kind of correlation might help us formulate a valid paradigm for psi: find out *how* and *why* it works, rather than simply using it.

§

If psi behavior is modified by personality, we'd expect many psychosocial variations to be matched by differences in psi response. More than a century ago, Sir Francis Galton studied the effects of birth order on personality traits, and found that more eminent scientists had been eldest or only children than chance would allow. Havelock Ellis confirmed this in 1904, after surveying 975 famous men and 55 celebrated women. That conclusion has since been reinforced in many other studies worldwide, most notably in the controversial study from Frank Sulloway, *Born to Rebel* (1997).

Members of the Institute of Psychophysical Research, Oxford, thought birth order might be a good place to look for distinctions in psi subjects. Their expectations were cautious. It was not predicted that eldest or only children would score best at ESP tasks, but simply that they'd be different psychically from siblings born later in the family.

In 1964, the Institute organized a write-in guessing experiment through the British magazine *Queen*, and received 756 entries. Using the same target order of 25 ESP cards, prepared by Professor H. H. Price and secured in his house, they appealed for further guesses through the *Daily Mirror* newspaper, and got 5055 replies.

"It was predicted that any birth order effects would be less marked in the population of lower socio-economic status (the *Mirror* readership) than in the population of higher socio-economic status (the *Queen* readership). This prediction was made in the belief that the differential treatment of the first-born may be less likely to occur in lower-middle and working-class families than in middle class ones," a prediction based on previous sociological observation (and perhaps some upper-middle-class prejudice).

In the event, the *Mirror* respondents were not significantly differentiated in scores by birth order, but the *Queen* group broke up satisfactorily into eldest (average score: 5.50), only child (4.70), and younger siblings (5.11), where mean chance expectation was 5.0 correct. Odds against this result occurring by chance are greater than 300 to 1.

A number of other experiments were conducted by the Institute along these lines, though with much smaller test populations. In the three most significant ones, the eldest children again did best. This, the researchers stressed, might not follow for all types of psi situations, but it was clearly a stimulating hint.

§

Ingenious psychological correlations, strange to tell, have a way of losing their validity as the years pass. Yet scrutiny of the original, promising studies does not support the obvious conjecture that the effects were a product of wishful thinking or slack precautions. Dr. D.J. West has made vivid comparison with the diminishing effectiveness of placebo drugs, those useful concoctions that often provide medical relief despite their lack of pharmacological properties. Their efficacy is psychogenic, and their reliability is to some extent a function of a lack of sophistication in patients. As the public has become familiar with the names of behavior-altering pharmaceuticals, often advertised by expensive television commercials, placebo medications have to keep pace with more elaborate mumbo-jumbo in terminology and methods of administration. Placebos, let me stress, are *not* the snake-oil panaceas of quacks; they are a legitimate technique of healing. But their power depends, to an enormous extent, on the patient's trust in the medical practitioner.

"From sheer biological necessity," Dr. West points out, "life is organized around a limited but sharply focused morsel of environment presented by the senses. Anything coming from beyond this familiar focus must constitute a deep psychological shock... The mere possibility of extra-sensory contact outside the individual's focus. threatens the whole basis of personal identity." Psi produces internal conflict, and as this grows "resistance builds up."

As with placebo effects, then, the psychical researcher will find the best results in situations where "reality" does not press too fiercely on subjects. West notes that most high scorers in card-guessing tests have failed conspicuously to make a fortune in the stock-market or the race track, which one must suppose would call on the same paranormal talents. The same applies to entrants in lotteries where the bettor chooses the numbers.

"Where subjects are asked to choose between a small number of fixed choices," Dr. West noted, "the prospect of any particular guess turning out correct presents no threat to reality sense, since it might so easily prove correct by sheer chance... In the case of betting, although the situation is statistical, the practical consequences of supernormal success, even though highly gratifying in themselves, would serve to underline the unreal quality of the phenomenon, and hence invoke resistance."

As a believer in ESP, Dr. West did not mean "unreality" to be taken literally, of course. To the sophisticated mind, delicately encapsulated in its ego defenses, anything that breaches the wall between self and not-self is perceived as unreal, threatening. It is no accident that the rise of the New Age, getting on now for half a century ago, came at a time when many young people in the West were rebelling against "the prison of the ego," and finding joyous possibilities of openness in the teachings of gurus like Alan Watts and, a bit later, Werner Hans Erhard (born John Paul Rosenberg) of *est*.

A testable consequence of Dr. West's tentative hypothesis is that psi will be found most strongly in children, whose ego boundaries are still fluid, and in so-called "primitive" or shamanistic cultures that have never emphasized our brittle aversion to ego loss. Alternatively, the psi subject must be "tricked" into supposing that his guesses have only some commonplace psychological significance, when actually the array of possible choices is coded to offer genuine information.

Another method is to provide subliminal cues interpolated randomly with telepathic or precognitive messages, while permitting participants to believe their efforts are directed purely to the sub-threshold or subliminal targets. Since this latter ambition is "legitimate," psi might intrude without resistance. Some experiments of this sort were run by Dr. Joseph Rush, though with only ambiguous results.

§

Clearly, then, the painstaking work of parapsychologists during the last half-century and more has not been barren, for all its lack of public impact in a time when millions will believe almost anything preposterous—vampires, zombies, magical Secrets that bring you your heart's desire, angels at your beck and call, the rediscovery of Atlantis, abduction by UFO aliens... The major disciplinary finding is that psi *does* exist—at least in some people, possibly in all—and that it follows certain regularities observed elsewhere in orthodox psychological phenomena.

We know that psi, by whatever unknown mechanism it functions, is a "stochastic process." That means its manifestations occur in a way that (like radioactive decay) can only be described by a law of probability, not of causality. In the case of perceptual psi (ESP or precognition), for example, this means that in any successful series of guesses overall results will deviate significantly from mean chance expectation—but there is no sure way to determine exactly *which* individual guesses will be guided by paranormal knowledge rather than by chance factors inside the workings of our complex brains and minds.

It is the stochastic character of psi that for so long has hindered efforts to apply paranormal abilities to problems in the mundane world, allowing us to know the apparently unknowable.

Still, this stochastic process obeys, in a general way, a number of lawful decline effects. Although this deterioration is highly frustrating, it's a feature we can use to estimate which parts of a run of guesses are most likely to be influenced by psi, and in which direction.

Even more significantly, perhaps we can devise useful psi applications that circumvent the decline effects, by employing signal-detection techniques designed by information theorists precisely to cope with stochastic data flows. Let us turn our gaze on these attempts.

§

In 1887, at the Case Institute of Technology, Ohio, the death-blow to 19th century physics was struck by A. A. Michelson and E. W. Morley. Their sensitive equipment established the staggering fact which was to underpin Einstein's Relativity theories—that light radiation in vacuum always propagates at a constant limiting velocity. It cannot travel slower than that, and nothing energetic or material in the universe can travel faster. That discovery is one of the mainstays of the critic of psi, since psi does not respect the light-speed limit.

Ironically, in the mid-1960s, several engineers at Case performed a crucial experiment that sought to boost the confidence with which each "bit" of psychic information could be concentrated into visible and usable form.

The test was conducted jointly by Professor James B. Reswick, Director of the Engineering Design Centre at Case Institute of Technology, and Lojze Vodovnik, Assistant Professor in Biomedical Engineering at the same campus. Vodovnik was also an associate professor of Electrical Engineering at the University of Ljubliana, Yugoslavia. Perhaps it is auspicious that this remarkable pioneering use of majority vote psi should have been carried out by such a team—rather as if Neil Armstrong's companion on the first moonwalk had been a Soviet cosmonaut.

Although their intention was modest—to convey by psi the number "13" in binary code—the experiment's design was complex. Their set-up was well-conceived and elaborate, for they meant to elude the major pitfalls of psi application.

Coding their message in binary notation meant the subject was offered only two choices per call (three if you consider the null option of making no choice, but this was not permitted). In computer binary code, the decimal number "13" is written "1101." To guess "13" in binary, then, you make four consecutive decisions of "one" or "zero."

Lacking access to any proven psychics, Reswick and Vodovnik invited two young romantically-involved students, Warren Oksman and Judy Scher, to serve as their subjects. It seemed possible that their warm emotional bond might help elicit psi between them. Warren was selected as agent or sender, Judy as percipient. (Tragically, in 1979, Oksman took his own life at 35; he was a well liked assistant professor at the Harvard Business School. The *Harvard Crimson* reported: "Oksman came to Harvard as a graduate student after earning a masters degree in engineering from Case Western University. He was a teaching fellow from 1970 to 1974 while working for advanced degrees in applied mathematics.")

§

Many years later, in December 1991, a remarkable PEAR paper by Dunne on "co-operator experiments" with random event generators showed what happens when two people try to combine forces in influencing a machine. The results are baffling by the usual standards of "non-intentional" laboratory practice, but quite familiar to anyone who knows the parapsychological literature or, indeed, the wider psychological literature.

In brief, fifteen pairs completed 42 test series, notching up more than a quarter million trials. The results were "consistent with those of a benchmark database of 2,520,000 trials generated on the same device by 91 individual operators." It's the details that are fascinating. "Pair-specific patterns" or signatures were identified, Dunne claimed, but these bore no resemblance to the individual or combined signatures of the two co-operating subjects. It's as if two people, blending their would-be-psychic intentions, merge to create something different from either alone, as elementary particles do when they coalesce into atoms. Indeed, Dunne took this as evidence in support of PEAR's "quantum mechanical model of consciousness," which proposed a "wave mechanical character of the human/machine interaction."

Most interesting of all, though perhaps culturally determined, was the impact of sex and bonding. Eight operator pairs of the *same* sex produced an overall "psi-missing" *negative* result, though not to a significant degree. Seven *opposite* sex pairs produced a statistically significant "psi-hitting" effect.

The best news is that these male-plus-female psi-hitting teams did nearly four times better than their individual results would have predicted. Moreover, within that general finding, it turned out that "four 'bonded' couples achieved on average effects more than twice those of three unbonded opposite sex pairs, and nearly six times those of the single operators." Love might not make the world go 'round (except in the movie *Interstellar*), but it seems to have a serious impact on micro-electronic circuits.)

§

Warren Oksman, as sender, saw his console lamps switch automatically again and again between red and green in the sequence comprising his coded target string. Although the binary code could have been presented literally as ones and zeroes, it was realized that colors might have more emotional overtones, heightening any psychic zing. Whenever either the red or the green light flashed on, he registered the fact that he was mentally "sending" the right color by pushing the appropriate data punch button.

At the same moment, in an insulated part of the building, a neutral light alerted Judy that she must now make and register a choice. She had two electric keys available, one at each hand. Left was coded "red," right was coded "green." Depending on what she felt Warren was looking at on this trial, she registered her guess and it was recorded automatically by an IBM 026 card-punch machine. (These were the old, old days.)

But what of the risk of psi-mode inversion? In an ingenious solution to this eternal problem, Reswick and Vodovnik simply added a single index zero to the start of the message, making it "01101." Now, knowing the first digit signified zero, they could assume that any significant excess of one color in the first position could be interpreted as representing that zero.

In other words, they no longer needed to match up Warren's red lamp with Judy's guess of "red," Warren's green lamp with Judy's "green." Psi-missing might invert the calls—but the deep code was now invulnerable. As long as any such inversion due to psi-mode remained consistent throughout the long experimental runs (a feature that could not be guaranteed, of course), the binary message could be deciphered from the sequence of preferred colors: merely construe as a zero Judy's majority vote choice for the first item in each repeated set.

There remained the bugbear of bias and preference skews. Suppose Judy had a solid predilection for choosing, say, red rather than green. Since psi is so inefficient, no expectable psychic input would be able to compensate for the bias. The message, whatever it was, would be bound to come out as a string of reds.

Then again, her preference factors might shift slowly or abruptly during the course of the experiment, out of sheer boredom. During the total of 13 stunningly dull hours at her console, it would be surprising if she didn't make unconscious arabesques of her choices, skewing them misleadingly from the lofty ideal of pure independent "mean chance expectation."

To control for bias, Reswick and Vodovnik came up with a two-pronged attack.

§

Firstly, they extended the core message by including its inverse form. That is, to the first part—now reading "01101"—they added "10010." The full message now ran: "0110110010."

Doing this meant that *whatever* sequence they had chosen as core message, however many zeroes or ones it contained, the full sequence was now assured of having exactly as many ones as zeroes, reds as greens. Any consistent bias would cancel out. To interpret the coded string produced by Judy's guesses, they merely had to invert the values gained in the second half of the package and add them to their twins in the first half.

To put flesh on these bones, let's take an idealized example. Say Judy prefers red (coding "0') over green (coding "1') by a factor of 6 to 4. And let's posit a psi-hitting element of one percent. For every 100 repetitions of the core target sequence, "01101," she'll guess like this:

61 red (0)	41 green (1)	41 green (1)	61 red (0)	41 green (1)

Throw in the inverse component, "10010," and the sequence will continue:

41 green (1)	61 red (0)	61 red (0)	41 green (1)	61 red (0)

Inverting the coded values of this second short string, we get:

41 green (0)	61 red (1)	61 red (1)	41 green (0)	61 red (1)

Add this debugged version of the second half of the string to the first, and we get this:

102 (0)	102 (1)	102 (1)	102 (0)	102 (1)

and the consistent color bias has gone, while the modest psi component shows forth bravely (though not by much).

Sadly, in the real world it's likely, as we've noted, that Judy's bias will actually *change* during the course of a long session. In a clever move, the experimenters added one further wrinkle—a yellow light, seen only by Warren at the sender's console. When this yellow light flashed on, he was instructed to "send" nothing at all. Since Judy was obliged to make a choice at this point, and since her only options were the standard red or green, there was no way for her call to be influenced by psi.

(Unless, I suppose, she started picking up *Warren's* daydreaming bias pattern. But even if this occurred, it would probably have only a minimal effect—because psi is a very infrequent influence, unfortunately.)

Any blatant, shifting bias pattern could thus be tracked, at the end of all the trial runs, by noting how Judy called when "yellow" was Warren's target.

Using * to denote a yellow, or null, light—an absence of transmitted information—the whole message string now read:

"*01101*10010*."

Each repetition of the message called for 13 decisions on Judy's part (could this be why the decimal number "13" was chosen as target?). Since each target lamp was displayed to Warren for two seconds, it took Judy 26 seconds to guess her way through each cycle.

And just to make sure she wasn't unconsciously building up distracting and erroneous patterns 13 bits long, Judy was not *told* the length of the cycle. As far as she knew, there was just a vast, endlessly random snake of binary choices coming through the psychic ether from her lover.

Nor did she know there were any "nonsense bits"—those yellow lights. For Judy, there was just a white light flashing on every two seconds, telling her to make another guess. These neutral signals came at her without pause for 10 minutes at a stretch. Then the two subjects, still secluded from each other in their separate locations, were allowed to rest for three to five minutes before returning to their consoles for the next session.

The same test message of 13 bits was presented to Warren Oksman 790 times in various sessions that went on for two weeks.

When Judy's responses were collated, inverted, checked for bias, and finally decoded, *all four digits of the binary code for "13" had been chosen correctly a majority of the times.*

§

The brilliance of this applications protocol is seen when we learn that Judy demonstrated consistent psi-missing during the two weeks. Using the index bits—the first "zero" digit, and the fourth "one"—the experimenters were made aware of this feature. Happily, their protocol compensated automatically for psi-missing mode.

What's more, a graph of Judy's guesses at the yellow "null bit" also revealed a developing trend to select red rather than green. Although the message, as it happens, was clearly interpretable without needing to take this bias trend into account, it was proof that in some future psi applications such a barometer of shifting preference might be crucially important—and easy to arrange.

§

So the attempt at psi communication by Reswick and Vodovnik must be counted a success. But how much confidence should they be permitted to hold toward their prediction, prior to disclosure of the true target sequence? How statistically significant was their result?

Well, the crudest way to look at this is to say that a binary message four bits long can only encode 16 different numbers, 0 through 15. So the *a priori* odds against guessing the right target number purely by chance would appear to be only 15 to 1, hardly startling odds.

But of course the matter is more complex, since each of these bits of information is built up from many more binary choices. If Judy's majority votes had only exceeded her minority votes by one or two guesses, this would be much less remarkable than an imaginary case where she got every single one of her 7900 targeted guesses right (we can leave out the yellow target calls).

In fact, after decoding, Judy's results were as follows:

1st symbol	2nd symbol	3rd symbol	4th symbol	5th symbol
22 Red	46 Green	20 Green	17 Red	13 Green

Each of these figures shows the difference from the mean of 790. We can easily calculate the likelihood of such deviations from the mean. In a binary-choice sequence of 1580 guesses, the standard deviation is about 20. That is, an excess of 20 guesses above or below the mean, 790, will occur just by chance about one-third of the time. Put it another way—any time a coin is tossed 1580 times, there's one chance in three that heads will come up between 770 and 810 times—the mean, plus or minus 20.

Two standard deviations covers a lot more ground. This extends the likely range out to plus or minus 40 from the mean of 790. Only in 5 percent of experiments will you expect so great a deviation from the mean purely by chance. This is the celebrated 0.05 level of confidence usually required as a very minimum by social and psychological scientists looking to demonstrate a causal effect at work skewing probabilistic results.

In the Reswick-Vodovnik test, only the second symbol (with 46 more Greens than the mean) meets this minimally rigorous standard. Two of the other symbols are only a single standard deviation away from the mean, and the fourth and fifth symbols do not vary from the average by even this much.

If we were betting on this information, we would hardly wager heavily at such odds.

§

Now it's true that *taken all together* the combined results are far more significant than this, as we found earlier with the Canoe-Trumpet-Wheelbarrow set of targets. The chances of varying by even this modest degree from the mean *four times in a predicted direction* (we must leave out the index bit from this calculation) are quite small. We can be satisfied, as the experimenters were, that psi was shown overall by Judy and Warren. Even so, we might not wish to rely on any single bit of the message string taken by itself.

How much psi? The usual amount. In all, apparent psi was 1.49 percent (in this case in psi-miss mode, significantly *below* the mean).

These results still seem to me tremendously exciting. If we could ensure that all digits are received with the clarity of symbol 2—either by extending the already arduous run into the high thousands of guesses, or by screening for subjects with a superior psi efficiency—we would now possess in this protocol a thorough-going basis for regular applications of psi to real-world information problems.

Perhaps you can recapture my enthusiasm, reading a report of this experiment more than four decades ago. My God, I thought. If this method of redundancy analysis could be applied to precognition, even at the unsatisfactory confidence level attained in the Reswick-Vodovnik test, our power to know, encompass, and direct the consequences of our actions would be spectacularly enhanced.

It seemed a literally Promethean prospect.

Nine: Casino

WALTER V. TYMINSKI was active in early explorations of majority vote psi precognition. Tyminski was president of *Rouge et Noir*, one of the world's few corporations specializing in advice on the mathematics of casino gambling.

During 1968, Walter Tyminski partnered Robert Brier, a philosopher and now Egyptologist who was then a young Fellow of the Institute of Parapsychology, in a series of real life casino psi blitzes. Their results were published in the March, 1970, issue of the *Journal of Parapsychology*, and suggested that there was a killing to be made for gamblers who used the emerging psi technology... at least, until everyone else started using it too.

Nearly half a century later, I don't see the high rollers using Brier and Tyminski's methods at the roulette table. What went wrong?

§

Tyminski and Brier tested their binary code method on three different games of chance: roulette, craps and baccarat. In each case, they were able to satisfy three crucial requirements. Firstly, a preliminary index sampling of their operator's repeated guesses, completed before the play-by-play predictions were decoded, hinted whether a given series of calls had been enriched by any attested psi-mediated information.

Even star psychic percipients have off-days when scoring falls to chance levels. At other times, the fluctuations due to chance will hide any small excess of correct guesses (or deficit, in the case of psi-missing) due to ESP. By taking preliminary samples, as we've seen with other protocols of this sort, the researchers hoped to infer the presence or absence of psi before they put their money down.

Second, they used the same sampling runs to check for psi-mode. Thus, they could estimate beforehand if their operators were psi-hitting or psi-missing. If the missing mode were in play, why, they could get valid forecasts just by inverting the binary coded predictions.

Third, they achieved consistent above-chance results. Even so, due to a fundamental limitation in their method, those results were not spectacular. But as any professional gambler knows, winning is always better than losing, even if the winnings are moderate.

Indeed, with a careful staking plan (ideally, one devised by a mathematician and structured along the same lines as an efficient "noise reducing" code), *any* edge over house odds must lead, in time, to colossal winnings. Dividends snowball, protected by a rational betting plan, so that marginal winnings can grow by geometric progression. All it takes is time.

For any deeply proper souls who considered a gaming house an improper venue for legitimate scientific research, Brier and Tyminski had a brisk retort:

> A real-life [psi-application] must be of such a nature that a subject can sustain interest through a long series of tests. Further, the events predicted must be such that they allow for clear statistical treatment. For these purposes the gambling casino seemed most suitable.

In these sessions, 5 guesses were made at each separate target. All the targets required binary choices, so a majority was registered in favor of one option or the other if it gained 3, 4, or 5 of the votes.

This is a ridiculously meager poll compared with Reswick and Vodovnik's 1580 guesses at each target digit—and even in that experiment, statistical significance was attained in only one of the four message bits. But Brier and Tyminski were prepared to sacrifice ideal accuracy for high turn-over and quick feedback to the psi operators. They wanted a large sequences of different targets, and results that didn't take weeks or months (or thousands of operators) to generate. A small but reliable excess of wins over chance expectation would satisfy them nicely.

§

Here's their roulette method:

Their casino used a wheel marked around the rim with 18 black, 18 red, and 2 green numbers. Bets were laid on either red or black—a binary choice. If the ball clattered into one of the green slots, the house took all.

So the casino cleaned up, on the whole, twice for every 38 spins. As players had one chance in two of winning on the remaining 36 spins, they'd average, by chance, 11.84 wins in every 25 bets placed.

The psi application tried to predict 25 spins of the casino wheel. With a majority vote taken on 5 guesses per bet, 125 guesses were needed. To check on psi-mode, the number of both targets and guesses was doubled—so now the first sequence of 25 majority calls served as "sample" for the second, or "play," sequence, which was independent of the first.

The researchers' operator, HB, wrote down 10 groups of 25 calls. Although she knew that redundancy was involved, and that guesses would be pooled, she was not informed which particular blocks of 25 would be combined with which. Neat. In one stroke, any unconscious, misleading pattern HB might develop in her calls was defused.

But if she didn't know what the precise targets were in any group of 25 calls, what was she aiming at?

The protocol set up a kind of time loop. HB "was instructed to visualize what would be written down next to her guesses, and this would be entered after the wheel had been spun."

Thus, she was not *directly* attempting to forecast the fall of the ball on the spinning wheel, but rather the symbol (R or B, red or black) that later would be written down in the adjacent column on her record-sheet.

Of the 10 runs of 25 guesses HB made, it was decided for simplicity to pool the odd runs as the database for the first 25 spins of the wheel, while the even runs coded the results of the next 25. The first group could thus serve as an index to the potential success of the remainder.

For each string of 25 majority calls, you will remember, HB's most likely chance score was 12 (well, 11.84). If the sample run turned up close to 12 matches, this would be taken as evidence that there was no useful psi in that whole batch—and hence Brier and Tyminski would expect only a chance number of winners in the second run, and thus decline to place any bets.

But if the sample forecasts were correct rather more often than you'd expect by chance, they'd assume the second run also contained an excess of psi hits. If HB's sample forecasts were conspicuously *wrong*, of course, they'd assume she was psi-missing and simply invert her predictions for the second or "play" run. So when her majority vote said "Black," they'd back "Red," and vice versa.

It worked. It actually worked.

§

In four pilot runs, HB's "index" scores were close to chance (12 hits both times), and the associated "play" sequences were also near chance (10 hits the first time, 12 the second). In two other runs, HB scored 13 on one sample string and 15 on the other. These were accepted as indications of psi-hitting, and indeed this was confirmed: 18 hits on one "play" run, 13 in the other.

In the most striking of these examples, 18 right out of 25 calls, the benefits of majority vote become vividly evident. These 25 predictions pool and concentrate 125 individual guesses, which themselves were right only 54 percent of the time (still a pretty impressive "psi-hit" effect of 4 percent). Majority vote analysis condensed these scattered hits into a single run of 25 that was right on *72 percent of bets*!

But note, too, the limits of this application. If only it had been possible to make many more guesses before the trials were pooled—without losing the overall continued success rate—perhaps all of the eventual 25 predictions would have been right. Anyone insisting on 100 percent accuracy, even using majority vote, will need to make a lot more guesses than 5 per throw.

§

Attempting to confirm these encouraging findings, Tyminski himself made a series of guesses targeted at a casino craps (dice) game.

A striking feature of this series is that Tyminski did not specify in advance exactly which craps game he was trying to predict. More causal time loops. "The predictions were to be for the first 40 hands when WT was present, whenever that was. Thus... he would not have the problem of arriving on time."

This sounds comical, but it addresses a real hassle in the real world. WT's repeated guesses would be matched against just one set of craps hands, but which set would remain indeterminate until the last moment. For a gambler, who may have to wait for a seat at the game, this is a very important proviso. It's just the sort of issue psi application engineers are going to need to resolve. And for philosophers of science, it is the vertiginous gateway into paradox, although eerily reminiscent of quantum measurement problems.

The first 20 hands were taken as a sample for the second 20. Only 9 hits were achieved in the sample sequence, so Tyminski inverted his predictions on the assumption (a remarkably weak one, I would have thought, given the minimal size of the deviation) that he'd been psi-missing. The gambit paid off: his forecasts were right 14 times out of 20.

§

Baccarat provided the final confirmatory series. It's a card game in which either banker or player wins at roughly equal odds. This time the woman operator, ADK, was an attested psi-hitter. Living some distance from the researchers, she made her guesses at home and posted them in. Mail-order psi gambling!

ADK provided majority vote predictions for 5 separate sessions at the card table, each comprising 200 hands of cards. At 5 guesses per hand, this was a laborious total of 5000 guesses. These were recorded on 20 separate sheets, each with space for 250 guesses. Each sheet therefore contained data on 50 hands of cards played on a given evening at the casino.

Again, ADK knew that some guesses would be used as a sampling index and some used to play—but she didn't know which. She, too, aimed at the correct answers that would be entered next to her guesses on the record-sheet after the real outcome was known.

The protocol was familiar. If the index scores were close to chance expectation—between 11 and 14 right—Tyminski would decline to bet. Only if sample predictions were right 15 times or more, or (psi-missing) 10 or less, would subsequent majority calls be trusted. Thus, this series was at least a little more rigorous than previous experiments.

Annoyingly, despite ADK's prodigious efforts, her predictions had to be scrapped in two of the five sessions. In one case the casino was unexpectedly closed. In the other, the experimenter was detained. Of the remaining three sessions, each comprising four groups of 50 hands, the criterion for psi was reached in only four of the index runs.

But despite all these problems, in the four betting runs corresponding to those index samples ADK got 59 hits. This was 9 hits in excess of the mean—better than nothing, but perhaps not compensating for carefully guessing and writing down 5000 R's and B's on 20 sheets of paper...

§

Is there anything else to be learned from this series of real-life experiments? Just this—subsequent study of the results suggested (paradoxically) that a modest majority gave a more accurate prediction than getting all five pooled guesses right.

Overall success rates in the aggregated Brier-Tyminski majority vote experiments were 70.3 percent for 3-out-of-5 majorities, 47.9 percent for 4-out-of-5, and only 35.7 percent for 5-out-of-5. Chance alone in each case, naturally, would have given close to 50 percent.

This finding was not limited to the grand totals. It was a consistent trend. "The 3-out-of-5 majorities," noted the authors, "gave positive results in each of the seven runs; the 5-out-of-5 majorities gave negative results in five of the six runs in which such majorities occurred." Thirteen years later, when I discussed it with him, Dr. Brier remained bemused by this discovery, but still did not know what to make of it.

So—does it work for everyone? Can it work for you?

Nobody knows—yet. Hardly anyone other than a handful of experimenters has ever tried the redundancy psi methodology. (At least, as far as we know. But if it works better than chance, perhaps those who use it are quite sensibly keeping their mouths firmly shut.) Since we still don't know what psi is, it's not obvious which aptitudes it calls for. Parapsychologists have some interesting correlations, but I think the honest answer remains: Who knows?

In our present state of very partial knowledge, the only sensible working course is to assume that any given individual is most probably a feeble but occasionally effective psi talent. Repeated guessing and majority vote methods will not help such people build better psychic muscles, but it might put the ones they've got to best use.

And of course for psychic athletes, it will boost accuracy and power.

Try it and see.

There's a coarse rule to be derived from all this:

To make psi work reliably, guess repeatedly at the same target.

But as we've seen, this formulation in unrealistic. The human mind dotes on patterns. If it's got a dull job to do and it can't detect any nice soothing patterns, why, it'll go ahead and *invent* some. Or it'll remember one and impose it over the top of what's going on. Like those irritating, droning refrains small children sing-song to the clatter of a train's wheels.

Taking into account some of the precautions we discussed, let's rephrase the rule:

> *A single operator shall guess repeatedly at a sequence of options coded to compensate for bias and psi-mode, taking care that the decoding protocols remain unknown to the operator until the series of guesses is completed.*

While this is not an algorithm—a formal set of repeatable procedures—it will serve most purposes. It points the path to psi applications anyone can try.

All that's needed is... the will and patience of Job.

While the method I have outlined is dreary to employ, computer games programmers will have no trouble dressing it up into compulsive and distracting arcade, laptop or smartphone formats, once the word gets out. Today's vast array of vivid simulation games are ideal imaginary landscapes to thread psi applications into.

Ten: Media

In 1962, Dr. Robert Taetzsch offered consolation to impoverished seekers after psychic truth in a seminal article, "Design of a Psi Communications System."

> Parapsychological research work often proves to be very tedious and frustrating, and there is usually very little monetary reward attached to it. What then impels so many men and women to pursue these studies? While there are undoubtedly many reasons, I believe that the strongest is... a possibility that psi phenomena might be controlled or directed for a number of useful purposes... Once we have developed a reliable system for the control of psi phenomena I feel that the efforts to increase the yields of psi processes and to design better control systems will be increased a thousand fold.

If Taetzsch was rather too optimistic in his timetable, it's still true that getting a handle on one good, solid psi application will spur the development of many more. In his elegant solution to some of these problems, published in the *International Journal of Parapsychology*, he wrote: "While we know practically nothing about psi communications channels we do know something about the noise that operates on those channels." The signal detection method he devised was very similar to the program used by Dr. Milan Rýzl in Pavel Stepanek's-style psi applications, described above in chapter 7.

Taetzsch's design also employs binary coding and the random insertion of index calls to test for hitting or missing mode. With each trial, the subject sends a response to a computer through one of two keys. The program records the incoming guesses and incorporates them into a constantly up-dated statistical evaluation. Jahn and Dunne's PEAR protocols adopted this suggestion.

There was a clever additional twist, again akin to Rýzl's but more efficient:

As soon as a given element in the message string accrues a majority *that is significant at a pre-established level of reliability*, the program terminates the count for that element. Since it now has a firm prediction (for that single bit), it doesn't need to bother you for more guesses aimed at that element.

Such *sequential sampling* plans, Taetzsch wrote, "differ from single sampling plans in that the number of samples (trials) is not fixed prior to the actual sampling; but is dependent on the results obtained by each sample. The main advantage... is that, on the average, they require fewer trials per decision for an equivalent degree of reliability."

Taetzsch's paper includes a discussion of cost-effective design, noting: "It is necessary to develop a compromise between the desire to maximize reliability and the desire to minimize redundancy when selecting parameters."

Although Taetzsch had in mind an algorithm for individual applications, in principle there'd be no difficulty entering guesses from many operators at once, using a home computer network or the Cloud. A "Taetzsch machine" would monitor the performance of each respondent independently, as well as the collective scoring of the group, and modify the number of guesses it required to obtain clear majorities for each bit in the message string. This instant feedback from accumulated scores to the monitoring program would also combat biased preferences and individual quirks.

Benefits are always balanced by drawbacks. To gain the very best advantages of any application using this method, specialize software and even hardware might be required. Perhaps we're talking military and intelligence implementation, or very large public or corporate programs akin to meteorological services. On the other hand, a small group of start-up programmers and engineers might be doing it already.

§

The computers that brought multiplayer games into the den are going to make psi application programs easy to play—for fun, as well as profit. Even primitive programmable pocket calculators were used to this end, reportedly with success. In 1985 and 1986, SRI's Dr. Harold Puthoff published brief papers in *Research in Parapsychology* outlining a clever if controversial program.

Reviewing some previous majority vote applications, Puthoff noted two common drawbacks. Firstly, probability estimates are based on independence of guesses, and with almost all repeated guessing protocols the message string has simply cycled through the same set of targets. If the response biases of the operator coincided with the repeated cycle, as we've seen with the Zenith data, there'd be a spurious coincidence of calls with targets: a side consequence of the stacking effect.

And as with Zenith, this would not make the majority votes *correct*, of course, but it would give the experimenter an erroneous sense that something paranormal was going on—until the decoded result failed to match the message. Worse, if the message did by chance agree with the majority calls (as it is bound to from time to time), this chance coincidence would mislead both operator and experimenter into believing that psi had been demonstrated.

A second drawback was that old bugbear, psi-missing. Puthoff had a neat cure that bypassed the need for index calls. This sneaky trick constructed each paranormal call out of *two* concurrent but independent psi-acts, in the hope that in a binary choice two wrongs make a right.

It worked this way. Puthoff's goal was to reduce the number of trials to an absolute minimum, consistent with amplifying a small psi effect. He and his colleagues chose "what we refer to as a 5-bit majority-vote code. Each trial consists of 5 individual subtrials, with a majority vote (3 or more selections out of 5) constituting the overall trial selection."

This meant, you see, that if the calculator program found agreement between the first 3 guesses, or 3 of the first 4, it could register a vote and move on to the next trial—in the long term, a considerable saving in time spent pushing buttons—although the margin is absurdly small and unreliable.

Was this the best that communications theory could devise? Yes, stated Puthoff:

> in the terminology of coding theory, the majority-vote-of-five procedure constitutes a trivial application of block-coding theory in which a (5,1) block code (Block length 5, 1 information bit) is used to correct all single and double errors in the transmission of a 5-unit block. It can be shown that, with regard to error-correcting coding, no better 2-letter, 5-place alphabet than the majority-vote exists (*Bell System Telephone Journal*, 1956, 203-234), and an identical argument holds for all other odd-length (n, 1) block codes.

I hope that sets your mind at rest. I'll spare you the exact binomial distribution.

Combining his two clever wrinkles, Puthoff's scheme is this. The operator may enter one of two choices, 0 or 1, up to five times. For roulette, these are coded red and black (more strictly, red-plus-green versus black-plus-green, allowing for the house numbers). Inside the machine, a randomizing sub-routine "relabels the 0 and 1 buttons, subtrial to subtrial... The percipient's task therefore reduces to one of simply guessing the 'right' button, subtrial to subtrial, to accumulate entries in the 'right' memory location."

Hence, each of the subtrial targets is independent of the others. Even if response bias skews the operator's calls (or button-pushes), relabeling will compensate by giving back on the roundabouts what bias took away on the swings.

§

Could this really short-circuit psi-missing as well as bamboozling preferential bias? I suspect it's too neat, a conjuring trick that might not slip past the wary unconscious for very long. Still, it's rather elegant. "From one viewpoint," Puthoff argued, "each subtrial entry can be seen as an inherently two-stage psi process, viz., what is the ground-truth answer? Which button do I press to answer it? From this viewpoint there exists in this format a double-negative mechanism that would tend to compensate for psi-missing, should it occur at both stages of the process."

Three percipients tried the method, entering 100 trials each into a programmed HP-41C calculator, and gaining feedback on success or failure from the experimenter after every trial (each comprising 3, 4 or 5 subtrials, remember). Results appear promising. Raw or unprocessed votes gained between 2.6 and 10 percent more correct individual calls than mean chance expectation, and this was concentrated by majority-vote into between 10 and 21 percent extra correct answers. Combined, the three operators got 63.7 percent of their majorities right, which would occur by chance only one time in a million.

Puthoff and his associates continued to refine and elaborate this method of sequential sampling techniques with variable length codes, apparently with similar success. I somehow doubt, though, that this is the royal road to psi application success. For starters, the psi efficiency of his selected percipients was already many time greater than one finds in most parapsychology experiments, and as Puthoff notes "the overall probability of error... for the 5-bit majority-vote code decreases dramatically" as the psi-boosted likelihood of correct calls increases. What's more, it is not clear that psi generally functions in this global fashion, allowing us to hoodwink the mind into turning psi-missing against itself. (But perhaps the same objection can be raised against the use of interleaved index calls in more "traditional" repeated guessing protocols.)

§

My own research into high-redundancy perceptual psi techniques was launched in ignorance of previous studies by West, Freeman, and others, let alone Puthoff's work, then more than a decade in the future. In 1971, I began my research in earnest, focusing on the prospect of majority vote conducted on multiple, repeated efforts by an individual to identify each part of a coded message.

But as we've seen in the case of Pavel Stepanek, that is a numbingly boring way to approach any task, especially where the phenomenon is as skittish as psi. So psychologist Len Kane and I developed a simplified analytical method for a large number of people making their guesses at the same time, rather than a single person repeatedly guessing at a small number of targets. It seemed that a newspaper article on ESP would be an obvious way to get a substantial number of participants at the same time. Remember, there was no Internet, no blogs, no Facebook in the early 1970s to carry such an experiment instantly to thousands or millions.

I finally got my experiment into an Australian national newspaper in 1973. Despite strenuous efforts, I was unable to persuade that newspaper or any other to let me try this exhausting feat a second time—a fact that, serendipitously, led me at last to the fruitful reanalysis of old data secured by others and detailed in this book.

The test appeared in a full-page article in the features section of the Australian *Sunday Telegraph* of January 14, 1973. A staff journalist and I had written several hundred words roughing out recent psi discoveries but carefully avoiding any stress on the majority-vote aspects of this experiment.

The test coupon was balanced by a dignified photo of me gazing intently at a typesetting computer, my then-long hair pulled respectably out of the way.

The coupon design is shown below, with the targets marked as shown later (with one horrible error introduced) in the newspaper. I intended it to run from 1 to 18 straight down the page. The layout designer chose to split it in two, somewhat damaging the effect of flow that I'd sought, but that's not the worst mistake.

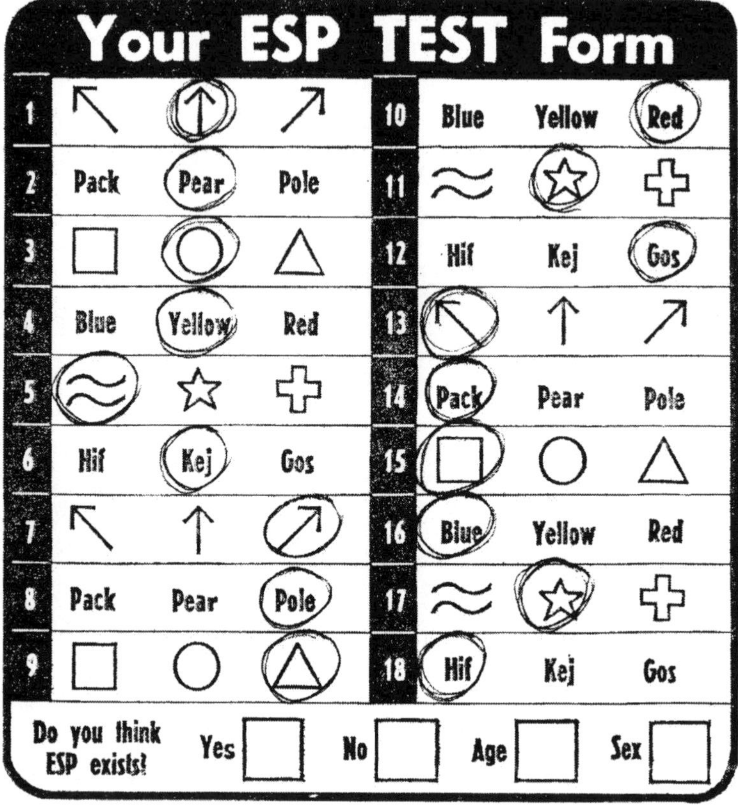

Your ESP TEST Form

1	↖	↑	↗	10	Blue	Yellow	Red
2	Pack	Pear	Pole	11	≈	☆	✣
3	□	○	△	12	Hif	Kej	Gos
4	Blue	Yellow	Red	13	↖	↑	↗
5	≈	☆	✣	14	Pack	Pear	Pole
6	Hif	Kej	Gos	15	□	○	△
7	↖	↑	↗	16	Blue	Yellow	Red
8	Pack	Pear	Pole	17	≈	☆	✣
9	□	○	△	18	Hif	Kej	Gos

Do you think ESP exists? Yes □ No □ Age □ Sex □

Figure 10.1: Newspaper form with targets marked.

On each of 18 lines, three alternative options were offered. In every case, one of these three would later be selected as a target for psychic perception. The first six lines constitute the basic set of options. The next six, and the final six, merely repeat the same pattern of 18 options exactly, in the same order.

What's more, each odd line is made up of three "symbol" or "figure" options (for example, diagrams of a square, a circle and a triangle), while the even lines contain "word" or "lexical" options (such as the instantly familiar and preference-laden words "Blue," "Yellow" and "Red" and the meaningless pseudo-words "Hif," "Kej," and "Gos.").

By 1973, I had learned of John Freeman's *phi/mu* discovery, so I hoped that by alternating "different symbol" targets with "different word" targets I might promote a psi-enhancing differential effect in my participants' guesses. If that happened, I hoped to see contrary hitting and missing by females and males.

Readers were given a straightforward task. Later in the week, they were told, a single item on each line would be selected as "target" by a random process. This target array would be published the following Sunday, when the coupon would be reprinted showing circles surrounding each of the 18 targets.

The task of participants was to predict the random selections, marking their guesses on the coupon by circling their choices, then mail it to the newspaper to arrive by the following Thursday. They were *not* told that the targets would encode a precognitive message, but they were assured that their guesses would not influence the order of the targets.

§

You will have noticed that the triplet, three-part structure of this experiment, with its six rows of three targets, repeated three times, is remarkably similar to the Michie-West protocol—except that in my test there were no intentional "dummy" trials, and much greater variety in the options. This astonishing similarity is entirely coincidental, since I did not learn of West's work for several more years.

Our independent analyses of the optimum deployment for a mass psi application suggests, perhaps, that a triplet test of about this length exemplifies a good working compromise between simplicity and information density.

For the options themselves, I borrowed freely from the patterns devised by Dr. Robert Brier in his 1968 mass school precondition tests, although I elaborated them by introducing those primary color names and meaningless syllables into my "word" lines. Seizing my chance, I was eager to investigate as many independent variables as possible. In retrospect, it's obvious that greater consistency and homogeneity would have been preferable.

So entering one's guesses on the coupon was not a very complicated task, once participants had overcome any disquiet they felt at the apparent absurdity of trying to forecast random events in the future.

This anxiety or "giggle factor," by the way, remains a very real obstacle to psi application, even in these days of resurgent belief in the occult, astrology, alien abductions and heaven knows what all else. Very few "goats" (unbelievers in psi) took part in my test, yet many of the participants added a letter pointing out that the experiment was doomed, for they felt that only meaningful "predestined" events are accessible to psychic foreknowledge. Dr. Rhine's endless card-guessing experiments proving the reality of precognition seemed to have made no larger impact on sheep than on goats.

§

Interpretation of the guesses was rather more complex. I needed to take steps to offset the confusions introduced by position biases and item preferences. West and Michie used their "serially balanced sequence." I wanted something simpler, easily understandable. So I used systematic rotation of targets, in the hope that this might offset any tendency to prefer one column over another.

Here's what I mean. Suppose you could choose from DOG, CAT or HORSE in lines 1, 7 and 13. You might be especially fond of dogs, and hey, look, there's DOG in the left column—but CAT is in the middle column, and you also have a predisposition to choose items from the central position, especially with your first guess. HORSE, in the right hand column, might suffer from your childhood fear of horses, although that in turn could be slightly offset by the way you also have a certain preference for choosing items from the right-most column rather than the left-most. So, by rotating targets among all the options in all the columns, the very format of the coupon itself constituted an attempted precaution against unconscious prejudice and bias—though this fact, naturally, was *not* revealed to the readers.

The randomly generated message, in triplet coded form, would establish the order of targets from the options in the first six lines. In each of these lines it was completely impossible to know in advance, by ordinary means, which option would eventually be marked as target. But thereafter, starting with row 7, target order would *not* be random—although, to stress this again, none of the participants knew *that* either.

In the two sets made up of lines 7-12 and 13-18, the "message pattern" would be repeated, but shifted one step to either the right or left—and the direction of rotation would itself be determined by chance, immediately before interpretation was begun.

If the coded sequence gave "Pear" as the target in line 2, either "Pole" or "Pack" would become target in line 8, and the remaining option would automatically become the target in line 14. The initially random target configuration would rotate from one set to the next, retaining its internal structure intact.

We have seen the same principle applied in a slightly different way in the final stage of reanalyzing the Michie-West data. There, we found a "left-middle-right" position bias, in which options on the left were always somewhat at a disadvantage. Even after normalizing to dilute position preference, a certain amount of variation remained from column to column. Anticipating such an effect, I built into my test a compensatory mechanism akin to that which we imported into our interpretation of the Michie-West study. In compressing the data into majority-vote form, the three sets of guesses in each entry were added together.

In fact, there did prove in my mass media test to be a general tendency to select items from the middle column, similar to that found in the earlier British experiment. As you can see by considering the options in **Figure 10.1** and the votes shown in **Table 10.3**, of Square (in the left column), Circle (central column) and Triangle (in the right column), most votes in my experiment went to Circle each time it appeared—392, 364 and 365. But the average expected purely by chance, given a total of 956 usable entries, was about 319. One must assume that this effect is due to the combined influence of symbol-preference (a strong liking for circles, noted by the Zenith investigators) and position-preference (the fact that the circle was always in the central column). Scaling or standardizing helps obliterate column preferences, while favoritism among options is offset by systematically shifting the target from one alternative to the next in subsequent lines.

Statisticians may be frustrated by this approach, for the targets from lines 7 through 18 are now not independent of the others. But I was not interested in statistical significance as such. My intention was not to establish the reality of psi; that was my premise. Nor was I concerned overmuch with a detailed evaluation of probabilities. I looked for clear majorities in each line (after adjustments to minimize the skews due to bias), and beyond that didn't trouble myself greatly.

I hope that by now the reasoning behind this decision is clear. If psi technology grounded in redundancy and majority vote is to be more than an esoteric field demanding numerically stupendous runs and high-flown analysis, it has to work in a fairly uncomplicated format. (Actually it seemed at the time very likely that it *wouldn't* work, but also seemed worth trying out.)

The gambling predictions of Puthoff or Brier and Tyminski leave much to be desired from the viewpoint of academic certainty—but apparently they did enhance a gambler's odds of winning, and presumably could be replicated by anyone with the inhuman amount of patience needed to fill in sheets and sheets and sheets of guesses week after week...

§

Which brings us to the "message" I hoped would be precognized by my media participants. But bear this crucial proviso in mind: my would-be future-seers did not know (at least by normal means) that there was a message buried in the array of randomly selected targets. They certainly had no clue that gambling would be involved—at the race track, to be exact. What their attempts at precognition tried to identify were just the shapes and symbols in the newspaper form they were about to mark and then mail to me.

Not having a legal casino handy at the time, it seemed a sporting proposition to use horse-racing as the random-target generator, since success would bring its own reward. Recall that readers were instructed to mail their guesses to arrive by Thursday, January 18, 1973, and the newspaper required the targets in good time for the Sunday press. So I chose the principal Australian race meetings available on that Thursday afternoon.

My first notion was a code specifying each horse in the 17 races—218 horses were scheduled to run—and use it to try to predict which one of these horses would win at the highest odds. This seems a convenient route to a substantial return, since in any pair of race meetings there is usually a winner at 40, 50, or even 100 to 1. But I was balked by the philosophical hazards involved, a problem not often thought to bedevil players.

If ordinary betting behavior is governed to a certain extent by precognition, the horse that theoretically ought to be shunned by players might be backed heavily at the last moment, altering its favorable long odds. Precognition of a "surprise high probability future" might thus skew the phenomenon it was forecasting. Analysis indicates that this effect is not likely to have much impact on horseracing, where most of the big money is placed on the basis of fairly rational calculations or inside race fixing. But the possibility could not be written off.

So I decided instead on another difficult goal, one less open to perturbation by psi perception. Australian totalizators offered good prices on the "Daily Double," a bet in which the player specified the winners of two races announced in advance.

In the Double that I chose for my random target generator, 12 horses were scheduled to run in the first race, and 15 in the second. Pre-post scratchings might eliminate some of those candidates, but all 27 had to be incorporated in the experiment. If a predicted fancy never made it to the field, it would be evident that the bugs in high redundancy psi were very far from being ironed out.

It takes a matrix of 180 alternatives to encode all possible pairs of winners in two such races. Five groups of triplet options allow for 243 alternatives (that is, 3 raised to the power 5), more than are needed for the Daily Double. The coupon, of course, had a basic set of six such threesomes, each set capable of encoding 729 alternatives—that is, 3 raised to the power 6. So, one line in the excess was going to waste.

For the same reason that impelled Michie and West to include an initial dummy trial, knowing that bias would cause a huge surge for the first central option whether it was a target or not, I knew that this spare capacity was no bad thing. Psychology tests confirm that the first line in a random guessing task is the one most prone to position biases (as it was for the Michie-West test). So my principal prediction was coded into lines 2-6 (and repeated, in rotated form, in 8-12 and 14-18).

§

For the first row of options, therefore, I used a modified form of my original notion. It would tell us, in general terms, which horse would win at the longest odds. Naturally, the three symbol options in that first line could discriminate between only three alternatives. So I divided the racing form into three sections—the first six races at one track (Seymour); the last three at Seymour and the first three of the other track (Kembla); and the remaining five Kembla races—with the specification that the first target would indicate which of these blocks contained the longest odds winner.

Bear in mind that this first call was, at best, expected to be confused by a powerful preference factor. Thus, if position bias in this line proved overwhelming, it would not foul up the principal predictions. Granted, if majority vote pointed to the correct block, that wouldn't count for much. The chance of being right, after all, was one in three.

§

With these essentials settled, the process of coding began. To simplify analysis, each of the basic 18 options was assigned a letter, from A through R. In the first set of triplet options, "A" would stand in the left-hand column of the second line ("Pack"), "B" in the center "Pear"), and "C" in the right ("Pole"). In the second set, "A" would move to the right (becoming "Pear"). In the final set, "A" would be the right-most item on that line, "Pole."

By adding the three A's, B's and C's, etc, I hoped that any position preference bias favoring left, center or right would wash out, or at least be reduced. Since the major prediction was to start with the second line, it seemed most logical to start our code from that line. The first, seventh and thirteenth lines, representing "highest-odds winner block," completed the rotating alphabetic sequence with "Q," "R" and "P."

At the outset of the experiment, a coin toss determined whether the alphabetic sequence would step once to the right or to the left with each new line. Applied on the day of the experiment, this procedure ordained that the sequence should move right. Instead of having

A B C
D E F
G H I
J K L
M N O,

we had

A B C
F **D** E
H I **G**
J K L
O **M** N

The experiment, then, had three components.

There was the coupon itself, an array alternating "geometrical figure" and "word" options.

There was an intermediate alphabetic code, matching that array, designed for our convenience.

Finally, there was a standard procedure relating the 243 possible combinations of items from five rows of triplet options to the 180 paired-combinations of horses from the two "Daily Double" races; and an ancillary code for the first row, relating to "longest-odds winner" for both race meetings.

Recall that this attempt at knowing the otherwise unknowable was performed long before the existence of the Internet. The experimental task, when the guesses arrived by mail, was to sum the numbers scored for each option, separately for males and females, then, through the appropriate compensatory mechanisms, derive the overall majority and minority votes. Because we were hoping to force a Freeman differential effect, it was hoped that male participants would act in the *mu* fashion, choosing the word targets and avoiding the figure targets, while the female participants would produce a mean *phi* result of the opposite polarity.

Later, and independently of these results, I was pledged to encode the actual race results into an array of symbols, and that configuration would be published. Readers, still blind to the method used to generate the targets, would thus have the opportunity to see the true target array, although only days after all their guesses were mailed in.

In short, the target pattern at which they were aiming would be publicly available "in the future," and in due course they could evaluate their individual accuracy.

The article and the coupon, drawn by a staff artist from my sketch, duly appeared in the newspaper.

And I was confronted at once by the heart-rending horrors of trying to conduct a scientific experiment through the mass media.

§

The coupon had been intended to run directly down the page, from line one to line eighteen. For reasons of newspaper esthetics, however, it had been broken, as noted above, into two segments of nine lines, cheek by jowl, shown above.

Worse was in store. Gremlins had been at work at the printers and, to my disbelief, early (country) editions displayed the coupon *in photographic negative*: white symbols on black background. The mistake had been caught quickly by an alert staff-member, and rectified, but by that time thousands of copies had been printed and distributed.

Have you ever tried to circle words or symbols against an inky black background? Hundreds of interested, puzzled readers did so, to my astonishment, using colored ink, lipstick and substances hitherto unknown to humankind. One schoolteacher, mailing his valiantly inscribed copy, gave me a "fail" mark for my stupidity in choosing that format. Such are the perils of mass media psi experiments.

I had my revenge on the teacher, although it brought me no joy: I discarded his entry, along with all the others submitted on botched coupons. The first rule of scientific experiment is ruthless expulsion of all unwanted variables. The white-on-black coupons had to go.

For one error I did deserve a fail mark, as have others before me. Reading the article over Sunday breakfast, I saw belatedly that my printed instructions committed the crime that long ago blighted the Woolley mass test, as I would learn during my later researches. *Keep a copy of your panel to check your ESP efficiency next week*, I had suggested. *(Use a second copy of the test pattern or note down "Line 1 Item 2, Line 2 Item 3, etc.)*

This was somewhat misleading anyway, since only those few readers who got 10 or more targets right by chance could expect psi to help them over the top to a significant individual deviation. It was, however, I'd thought, a useful red herring, for it helped assure that participants would actually consult the targets when they were printed the following week. But my example had been too specific. I had thrown in one of Goodfellow's subtle (or even flagrant) cues. Almost certainly, I realized, there'd be a gruesome surfeit of guesses for those particular options in the first two lines.

And this did, indeed, occur. Perhaps it would have happened anyway (as it did in the Michie-West TV tests), but line 1, item 2, was favored with more votes (489) than any other item in the entire test. And item 3 in the second line, "Pole," did indeed receive more guesses (366) than all other items in its column (and the same thing happened in the Michie-West test).

§

However, the most distressing and unforgivable blunder of all (but one with a curious philosophical pay-off) did not appear until the following week. As I've shown, the experimental protocol specified stringently that the original coded set of targets would be rotated one step in each of the two subsequent sets of six lines. To my disbelief and horror, I found when the target array was published on January 21, that in the 17th line, *the second item was circled instead of the third, which had been specified by the predetermined rotation rules!*

In line five the target was "Waves," so in line 11 it became "Star"—and in line 17, should have become "Cross," exhausting the possibilities. But as it happens, by some ridiculous miscommunication between experimenters and newspaper staff, in line 17 the wrong option was circled, repeating the target shown in line 11.

In an attempt to rectify this wretched error, we can use one of two *post hoc* changes in our alphabetic code: one is to switch "L" for "J" in line 17. The case for doing this is that "K" has correctly followed the original rotation rule, and must be left where it is. The other possible correction is to begin with "J" in the middle and follow with "K" to its right and "L" to its left. Curiously, whichever alternative is adopted, "J" remains the highest scoring option when items from the fifth, eleventh and seventeenth lines are added together.

Or we can simply throw away lines 5, 11 and 17, discarding one sixth of our data. Strictly speaking, it must be granted, this positional error invalidates those three lines containing "Waves," "Star" and "Cross," if not the entire experiment. (This is the same logic for abandoning rows 10, 11 and 12 in the Michie-West experiment, because they contained very small numbers of majority votes and some cells with no votes at all.) To repeat my cautionary remark at the outset: Regard what follows as nothing better than a test run, a pilot study. Still, what we can learn from it is not necessarily negligible.

Later, I was somewhat comforted by a candid admission of errors that led Dr. Jim Carpenter and several colleagues to get results wrong in an important experiment. He noted of this then-20 year past slip up:

> Unfortunately, errors in using the [purpose-written computer program] in the rush before scheduled class presentations led to false initial results in both cases. In Study One, extreme-quartile cut-off points intended for the two mood scales [...] were switched, resulting in the inappropriate inclusion and exclusion of much data. In Study Two, one of the predictors of hitting was inadvertently omitted. These problems were later realized, but the data lay in a filing cabinet for a long time before a period of leisure permitted them to be analyzed again, carefully and correctly. The results were interesting enough that I am reporting them now. (Carpenter, 2010, p. 674)

I'll adopt the same slightly shame-faced excuse for the blunders in my own experiment.

§

By Thursday, we had received 956 suitable coupons, just enough for acceptable levels of confidence. Of these, 603 were from women, 353 from men. Respondents' ages ranged from 9 to 80. There were 101 boys and 159 girls aged between 9 and 20 (21 then being regarded as the age of majority); from 21-40, 130 men and 202 women; from 41-60, 88 men and 214 women; and from 61-80, 34 men and 28 women.

These are fascinating data in themselves. Popular belief would credit an interest in the paranormal to many more women than to men; in fact, the ratio found was fewer than two to one.

There is clearly a falling-off in interest among men in their middle years, though perhaps this merely reflects the readership of that particular newspaper, or the failure of these men to mail their guesses.

Nearly every reply checked "Yes" to the question "Do you think ESP exists?" and many people wrote (often inanely) describing their previous psychic experiences. This is an important point to bear in mind. It indicates a far greater homogeneity in the test population than would be found in a survey group that was not entirely self-selecting.

The raw or unprocessed numbers of votes for men and women separately are given in **Tables 10.2a** and **10.3a**, together with raw compacted numbers for each derived by combining the three blocks of 18 items, six per sub-column. The coded meaning of each of the 18 items is rotated from block to block (**Tables 10.2b and 10.3b**). You'll see that instead of the arrows, Hifs and Kejs, squares and circles icons, Packs and Poles, etc, on the form itself **(Figure 10.1),** they are replaced by the single letters mentioned above.

These alphabetical labels are for ease of identifying which options are equivalent. For example, as noted above, "Pack" stands in the left-hand column of row 2, and can be coded as "a." In the center, "Pear" is coded "b." And "Pole," on the right, becomes "c." However, and this is the key, in row 8, "a" moves to the right (marking "Pear"). Then in row 14, "a" marks the right-most item on that line, "Pole."

By adding together the numbers associated with each letter, the result helps obviate left-middle-right preference.[9]

9. Note that a, b and c begin the second row, due to our qualms over predictable massive preference for the center position in the first row. In the initial set of six, the last rotated choice is o, m, n, so the "next" set is rotated to q, r, p, at the *top* of the block. I admit, it was a clumsy and unintuitive choice—but it does the job, without ambiguity, easily coded into future machine implementations.

Why is all this fiddly stuff needed? Well, look at the raw votes from both the Male and Female participants. The effects of bias are starkly apparent, both of column position and word or icon preference. We have to compensate for this noisy overlay. Rotating the meaning of the 18 options is one way to attempt that.

1	q	67	r	195	p	91
2	a	100	b	124	c	129
3	f	78	d	134	e	141
4	h	108	i	139	g	106
5	j	134	k	120	l	99
6	o	86	m	111	n	156
Σ		573		823		722
7	p	94	q	166	r	93
8	c	120	a	128	b	105
9	e	99	f	138	d	116
10	g	143	h	129	i	81
11	l	118	j	141	k	94
12	n	104	o	150	m	99
Σ		678		852		588
13	r	114	p	147	q	92
14	b	106	c	144	a	103
15	d	104	e	134	f	115
16	i	110	g	127	h	116
17	k	107	j	156	*l*	90
18	m	102	n	134	o	117
Σ		643		842		633

Table 10.1a:
Total guesses by Males (353 respondents)
Σ (Sigma) indicates column sums

1	325 L	402 H	332
2	331 L	335	393 H
3	331 L	354	374 H
4	353	330 L	376 H
5	431 H	321	307 L
6	353	312 L	394 H

Table 10.1b:
Compacted Male guesses:
H = Highest vote, L = Lowest vote

1	q	116	r	294	p	193
2	a	148	b	218	c	237
3	f	121	d	258	e	224
4	h	204	i	248	g	151
5	j	225	k	214	l	164
6	o	144	m	253	n	206
Σ		958		1485		1175

7	p	182	q	239	r	182
8	c	172	a	252	b	179
9	e	171	f	226	d	206
10	g	235	h	214	i	154
11	l	219	j	258	k	126
12	n	174	o	264	m	165
Σ		1153		1453		1012

13	r	179	p	261	q	163
14	b	178	c	237	a	188
15	d	164	e	231	f	208
16	i	178	g	266	h	159
17	k	192	j	258	l	153
18	m	163	n	271	o	169
Σ		1054		1524		1040

Table 10.2a:
Total guesses by Females (603 respondents)
Σ (Sigma) indicates column sums

1	518 L	655 H	636
2	588	575 L	646 H
3	555 L	628 H	626
4	577 L	580	652 H
5	741 H	532 L	536
6	577 L	581	651 H

Table 10.2b:
Compacted Female guesses:
H = Highest vote, L = Lowest vote

Can we distinguish between gender groups on a *phi*/*mu* basis? On the face of it, we cannot: in the consolidated groups, no symbol is chosen as the clear favorite of one sex while being shunned definitively by the other.

This, though, might be a superficial illusion due to biasing factors much stronger than the modulations that could be attributed to psi. If cultural preferences drive up the vote of a certain option (say, FRIENDLY DOG rather than SLIMY EEL), it could easily remain higher than its competitors every time it appears, even with a "psi-missing" decrement of several percent. The answer, as I've argued above, is rescaling or standardizing the raw data, a simple but tedious step.

In the Michie-West reanalysis, we used an index of position preference derived by standardizing all columns with each other (to offset any gross column preference). That was easy and reasonable, since only one option appeared repeatedly in the same left-middle-right position.

Consider the consolidated votes for all of my 956 respondents (**Table 10.3)**: 5059 votes for options in the leftmost column, 6979 for options in the center column, and 5170 for those in the right-hand column. Can we now apply this column-standardizing procedure directly to the newspaper scores, comparing votes for each symbol or word as transformed by a column index of preference calculated using all 18 lines?

No, we cannot—precisely because that Michie-West index, for all its beautiful simplicity, assumes the column biases remained fairly constant. In this test they clearly did not. There is a significant indication of what might be termed "lateral drift." The overall preference for left, central and right positions is not stable, as it was in the Michie-West test.

A crucial element is the block of six lines that contains, by turns, "word" and "figural symbol" options. Voting patterns in the three blocks vary somewhat. Participants' liking for the central column is pretty persistent. (That is not to say that everyone who placed a vote there once always did so again; merely, that the group tendency as a whole is to favor the center column.) But there are conspicuous tides of fortune affecting scores in the left and right-hand columns. Observe the summed votes in **Table 10.3** of all participants, grouped naturally in the three blocks of alternating symbolic icons and words (here replaced by rotating letters):

183 q	489 r	284 p
248 a	342 b	366 c
199 f	392 d	365 e
312 h	387 i	257 g
359 j	334 k	263 l
230 o	364 m	362 n
1531	**2308**	**1897**
276 p	405 q	275 r
292 c	380 a	284 b
270 e	364 f	322 d
378 g	343 h	235 i
337 l	399 j	220 k
278 n	414 o	264 m
1831	**2305**	**1600**
293 r	408 p	255 q
284 b	381 c	291 a
268 d	365 e	323 f
288 i	393 g	275 h
299 k	414 *j*	243 *l*
265 m	405 n	286 o
1697	**2366**	**1673**
	Column Sums:	
5059	**6979**	**5170**
	Column Means:	
281.06	387.72	287.22

Table 10.3 Newspaper experiment, 956 entrants. Note the switching of *j* and *l* in the 17th row, caused by a wrongly-circled target (Star again, instead of Cross) in the newspaper feedback display.

How are we to take account of the shifting fortunes? (You'll note, I hope, that the following points are all raised *prior* to any disclosure of the actual targets.) We can see that in set two, a left-column option (in lines 7-12, with 1831 votes) tends to be worth more than the same option in set one (1531 votes in total), and set three (1697 votes in total). Recurring votes for the candidates on the left (Left Arrow, Pack, Square, Blue, Waves and Hif) need to be adjusted to make them comparable, just as all the aggregated votes in the middle column need to be adjusted.

But what happens if most of the targets happened to fall in the same column? In this experiment, just by chance, such target clumping did indeed occur. However, since my hypothesis was that psi influence would switch alternately between hitting and missing, that possibility could *also* be self-remedying—unless the *hit* targets chanced to fall into one column and the *miss* targets into another.

The answer is simple and direct: standardize each option's vote in proportion to the average vote gained by each column of six options, thus:

183 Q 23.91	489 R 42.37	284 P 29.94
248 A 32.40	342 B 29.64	366 C 38.59
199 F 26.00	392 D 33.97	365 E 38.48
312 H 40.76	387 I 33.54	257 G 27.10
359 J 46.90	334 K 28.94	263 L 27.73
230 O 30.05	364 M 31.54	362 N 38.17
276 P 30.15	405 Q 35.14	275 R 34.38
292 C 31.90	380 A 32.97	284 B 35.50
270 E 29.49	364 F 31.58	322 D 40.25
378 G 41.29	343 H 29.76	235 I 29.38
337 L 36.81	399 J 34.62	220 K 27.5
278 N 30.37	414 O 35.92	264 M 33.0
293 R 34.53	408 P 34.49	255 Q 30.48
284 B 33.47	381 C 32.21	291 A 34.79
268 D 31.59	365 E 30.85	323 F 38.61
288 I 33.94	393 G 33.22	275 H 32.88
299 K 35.24	414 *J* 35.00	243 *L* 29.05
265 M 31.23	405 N 34.23	286 O 34.19

Table 10.4
Sub-columns scaled to remove column preferences

All that remains is to add together the standardized or rescaled votes using their letter codes. Let me work through an example for you. F, D and E are represented three times, as are all other options. In the case of F, it is coded to Triangle in the third line, to Circle in the ninth line, and to Square in the fifteenth line. But as explained above, each of these appears in a different column, so the marked preferences *for* or *against* left, center and right require some adjustment of the kind used in earlier analyses, variously known as "rescaling" or "standardizing" or "normalizing." The method offering the most intuitive outcome is to rescale each raw vote as a suitable proportion of its subcolumn of six options. When we do this, here's what we find:

	F	D	E
Line 3	Triangle 26.0%	Square 34.0%	Circle 38.5%
Line 9	Circle 31.6%	Triangle 40.3%	Square 29.5%
Line 15	Square 38.6%	Circle 31.6%	Triangle 30.9%
Average score	32.06%	35.27%	32.94%

Now, as you can see, it is much more plausible to compare the rescaled votes for F, D and E, because the changing fortunes of left, center and right columns has been largely erased. If we anticipate *phi*-mode precognition, we look for the highest average vote, which is candidate D. At this point, though, we have not yet decided whether the overall result can be expected to be influenced by a *phi* or *mu* mode, but attentive examination of the data, after standardizing in this manner, provides a promising hint.

Q 29.84	R $37.09^{H\ T}$	P 31.53
A 33.39	B $32.87^{L\ T}$	C 34.23
F 32.06	D $35.27^{H\ T}$	E 32.94
H 34.47	I $32.27^{L\ T}$	G 33.87
J $38.84^{H\ T}$	K 30.56	L 31.20
O 33.39	M $31.92^{L\ T}$	N 34.26

Table 10.5 Compacted results:
Sub-columns scaled, then compacted.
$^{H:}$ Highest score per row, $^{L:}$ Lowest score per row, $^{T:}$ Target
Result: Perfect *phi* accuracy achieved.

Our starting point, you'll recall, was to see if the 353 male participants scored, in aggregate, in the opposite mode to the 603 female participants. It turned out that they did *not*.

If the men and women had been neatly segregated into Freeman-style *mu-phi* categories purely by gender, we'd expect to find that where the males chose an option most strongly the females would avoid it most strongly. If we concentrate only on Highest and Lowest aggregate raw votes, we see that men and women agree completely in 58 percent of their preferences, whereas their choices are mutually incompatible only 11 percent of the time.

It seemed that the self-selecting nature of the test had indeed produced an homogeneity in the groups of respondents. That is, where females psi-hit, so on the whole did the males, and where females psi-missed, males did also. There might still be individuals of either sex whose psi activity operated in the inverse mode, but they were not bunched together by gender.

This outcome need not cast doubt on Freeman's findings, which were valid in the setting that gave rise to them (a co-ed class room), but merely on its applicability to self-selecting mass media participants. Dr. Freeman was studying captive audiences of an age group in which cognitive mode dominance could be expected to follow something like a binomial distribution. In psi tests administered through newspapers—and the *Sunday Telegraph* was, at that time, the most cerebral Australian Sundays, although that is not saying a great deal—we might reflect that the majority of participants will be *phi*: polarized toward verbal amusements like reading. Granted, this is *post hoc* reasoning, and is one more motive for regarding this event as nothing more than an intriguing pilot study in majority vote psi.

§

In any event, since there was no discernible distinction between the guesses of men and women, I aggregated them all into a single analysis. Now, however, we are confronted by a new puzzle. If the males cannot be counted on to guess contrary to the females, should we adopt a *phi* or *mu* interpretation for the lot? On the reasoning sketched above—and because a ratio of two female participants to each male implied that the predominant mode would be *phi*, or "female-like"—I accepted the *phi* pattern: "a choice from three different symbols forces a hit, while a choice from three different words forces a miss." The word *forces*, of course, applies not to each guess but to a subtle and still mysterious tendency that sways the overall outcome by modifying a small number of guesses.

Happily, the compacted configuration (**Table 10.5**) independently confirms this estimate—again, in advance of actual target disclosure. After the standardizing operation, the predicted *phi* mode sequence is

(R) B D I J M,

while the *mu* mode pattern reads

(Q) C F H L N.

But our matrix of five triplet options gave 243 possible combinations of options for the principal prediction, of which only 180 were combinations coded to potential winning pairs. (See the appendix to this chapter for the details of how this works.) The array C F H L N decodes as the number 233, and is an impossible answer, because there were no horses coded to it!

One can interpret this fact either of two ways. Perhaps the experiment is a failure, and so a meaningless pattern had been generated by the 956 participants. Or—more plausibly—the overall response, including the males' contribution, took the *phi* form. In that case, the collective prediction is thus

(R) B D I J M

—which coded for the number 100, safely inside the limit of 180 combinations. In turn, 100 was the coded intersection of race 6, horse 7, and race 9, horse 10.

I frankly admit that this structural side effect of the *phi* interpretation was a fluke. There are many possible combinations in which both the *phi* and the *mu* sequences would have appeared together in the matrix of 180 viable predictions. Psi technology, as a going concern, could not be allowed to depend on such strokes of luck: a sampling series must *always* be built-in to applied designs.

§

So what was the outcome?

The sequence B D I J M translates as the number 100, which in our matrix was the intersection of horse 7 in race 6 of the Daily Double, and horse 10 in race 9. The element (R), the third option in the lines coded "P," "Q" and "R," specifies races 4 to 8 at the Kembla race meeting.

Here are the actual race results:

The first leg started at 3.05 p.m.: the winner was "Hopetoun," horse 7.

The second leg started at 4.45: the winner was "Time to Go," horse 10.

They paid, respectively, 4/1 and 20/1.

The Daily Double dividend was $156 per 25 cent investment.

When both meetings were over, the longest odds winner proved to have been "Revival," paying better than 60/1 on the Totalizator: this horse had run in the sixth race at the second (Kembla) meeting. That is, it fell in the third block of races, coded "R"—although that was probably an artifact of the absurdly large and obviously biased vote for the middle option in the first line of the test, and can safely be dismissed as meaningless.

Even so, the mass prediction, interpreted as *phi* mode, was correct in every detail, with a probability of 0.004.

And yet, extraordinarily, only six of the 18 individual target options were accurately *phi*-identified after subcolumn rescaling, as expected most often just by chance.

§

How significant is this gratifying majority vote result? Leaving aside the sizes of the target-option deviations—which, due to the scaling, now possess conventional rather than literal values—one would estimate on the face of it that the compacted prediction is one of 729 possible sequences. If the valid estimate is taken to be $p<0.003$ (1 in 729, two-tailed), the results are clearly significant by commonly-accepted scientific standards, where one chance in 100 of mere coincidence is seen as significantly unlikely.

If we discard the fifth, eleventh and seventeenth lines we are down to one chance in 243, still a moderately significant result.

If, to be completely certain, we ignore the first, seventh and thirteenth lines as well (the one yielding that "R" prediction), chance probability rises to one in 81. That is not especially remarkable, but better than the traditional parapsychological requirement of $p=.05$, one in 20, or five percent.

§

There are several further ambiguous features of this analysis that need to be examined. For a start, to obtain this pleasing prediction I've had to postulate a preferential factor called "lateral drift," a kind of consistency effect that maintains in each sub-column a certain ratio of proportions between its three words and three symbols.

There might be readers who are still having trouble with this postulate. A simple imaginary case will help to illuminate the notion. Suppose, in such a test, the raw votes in the left-hand column totaled 6000. It could be that the left-hand sum for the first set of six triplet options was 1000 votes, for the second left-hand set 2000, and for the third left-hand 3000. That is, in gross terms there is an increasing tendency to favor the left-hand column.

My postulate is this: such a tendency will not produce a smooth stepwise increase in the number of votes going to consecutive options in the left-hand column, but will represent discontinuous sharp shifts in group preference when a fresh set begins its repetition of the basic ternary symbols. But within that large-scale jump in preference, each option will retain proportionately the same drawing power.

Psi, if present, would raise or lower these numbers by an additional proportion of the total vote per line.

Admittedly, using this assumption has borne fruit but mightn't this be accidental? The postulate—that preferences are conserved *within* the column—is not self-evident.

On a purely intuitive basis, two contradictory possibilities seem equally likely. One is that if "Pack," say, has once proved one and a-half times as attractive as "Arrow," and "Waves" proved three times as attractive—irrespective of the actual number of votes involved—this rank order will continue to persist.

On the other hand, isn't it plausible that the high scorer "Waves" will subsequently be *less* favored, having had its season in the sun, while "Arrow," precisely because it was passed over the first time, will increase its vote dramatically?

Fortunately, we do not have to adjudicate these alternatives. I could go on for a while with charts and additional tables of numbers, but this really is not a book of formal science but rather an entertaining glance (I hope) at some of the hairier patches of fringe science, and frankly I'd rather go off for a brisk walk, don't you agree?

(Unless, of course, you're still wondering about the details of how a bunch of five letters—B D I J M—disclosed the winning horses, in which case you might care to proceed to the Appendix that follows immediately. Or you could skip that and go directly to Chapter 11.)

Appendix: Turning letters into horses

In the fairly complicated discussion above of my 1973 newspaper psi experiment, we went from an array of images and words to coding them for convenience as letters ("a" through "r"), and then using those letter codes as a guide in compacting the votes for those images and words into normalized percentages. As if that weren't enough, we finally have to transform the resulting group of letters a-through-r into numbers, which we'll use to pinpoint the predictions in two horse races.

I know, this is all starting to look like the plot of a Dan Brown concoction starring his "symbologist" Robert Langdon, from *The Da Vinci Code* and its bestselling sequels. Luckily, it's not *that* complicated. But it does take a bit of concentration to follow what I'm doing here.

We start with the basic triplets:

A	B	C
D	E	F
G	H	I
J	K	L
M	N	O

You'll see at once that, unlike in the experiment, the letters are not rotated one step to the right with each new line. That rotation is entirely optional and specific to this particular racing forecast trial. The triplets could have been rotated left instead of right, or moved two steps at a time, or whatever pleased the experimenter. But the basic template for decoding the Targets chosen by the combined votes of 956 participants is the simplest array of triplets shown above.

I've included a chart below that shows how I permutated the available letters five at a time, starting with the left-hand column: A D G J M. I coded that letter sequence to the number 1.

ADGJM	1	ADHJM	10	ADIJM	19
ADGJN	2	ADHJN	11	ADIJN	20
ADGJO	3	ADHJO	12	ADIJO	21
ADGKM	4	ADHKM	13	ADIKM	22
ADGKN	5	ADHKN	14	ADIKN	23
ADGKO	6	ADHKO	15	ADIKO	24
ADGLM	7	ADHLM	16	ADILM	25
ADGLN	8	ADHLN	17	ADILN	26
ADGLO	9	ADHLO	18	ADILO	27

AEGJM	through	AEILO	code 28-54
AFGJM	through	AFILO	code 55-81
BDGJM	through	BDILO	code 82-108
BEGJM	through	BEILO	code 109-135
BFGJM	through	BFILO	code 136-162
CDGJM	through	CDILO	code 163-189
CEGJM	through	CEILO	code 190-216
CFGJM	through	CFILO	code 217-243

How do we get number 2? Easy—replace M, the final letter from the first set, with the letter to its right, N. So number 2 is coded A D G J N.

For number 3, we replace N by O, one step to N's right.

But where can we go from there? Why, take a step upward. Replace J with its immediate neighbor K, and follow the same procedure. Now we have A D G K… completed by first M, then N, then O. Thus, these code for number 4, 5 and 6. For 7, 8 and 9, we replace K by L.

That exhausts the permutations beginning with A D G. How to proceed?

Simple: begin now with A D H, completed with the same sequences as before, for numbers 10 through 18. Then start again at 19 with A D I. That gets us to number 27, and we've run through all the A D varieties.

So we start again with A E, and the first batch runs AEGJM through AEILO, which codes 28 through 54.

This might sound perilously like some madcap numerology, but in fact it's a simple and reliable replacement code. And it allows us to turn any set of these letters A through R into numbers between 1 and 243.

As we saw in the chapter, the *mu* prediction was B D I J M (with an R in front of it, which we can ignore for the moment). How do we find B D I J M in the chart? Without writing down the entire list of 243 combinations, the easy way to do that is to look for the block containing these letters. That will be the fourth group,

BDGJM through BDILO, code 82-108

Since BDILO represents the number 108, just move backward through the permutations:

BDILN = 107
BDILM = 106
BDIKO = 105
BDIKN = 104
BDIKM = 103
BDIJO = 102
BDIJN = 101
BDIJM = 100

And there it is: 100!

But we still are not finished. The number 100, we hope, contains locked within it the information specifying two winning horses in two races. However can we do that?

We knew that Race 6 had 12 horses running. And Race 9 had 15 horses lined up at the starting gate. So I simply drew up a chart listing every possible combination of a winner from Race 6 with one from Race 9. Here it is:

		Race 9														
		1	***2***	***3***	***4***	***5***	***6***	***7***	***8***	***9***	***10***	***11***	***12***	***13***	***14***	***15***
Race 6	***1***	1	2	3	4	5	6	7	8	9	10	11	12	13	14	15
	2	16	17	18	19	20	21	22	23	24	25	26	27	28	29	30
	3	31	32	33	34	35	36	37	38	39	40	41	42	43	44	45
	4	46	47	48	49	50	51	52	53	54	55	56	57	58	59	60
	5	61	62	63	64	65	66	67	68	69	70	71	72	73	74	75
	6	76	77	78	79	80	81	82	83	84	85	86	87	88	89	90
	7	91	92	93	94	95	96	97	98	99	100	101	102	103	104	105
	8	106	107	108	109	110	111	112	113	114	115	116	117	118	119	120
	9	121	122	123	124	125	126	127	128	129	130	131	132	133	134	135
	10	136	137	138	139	140	141	142	143	144	145	146	147	148	149	150
	11	151	152	153	154	155	156	157	158	159	160	161	162	163	164	165
	12	166	167	168	169	170	171	172	173	174	175	176	177	178	179	180

Table 10.6. Intersection table of Race 6 and Race 9

Look for 100, and there it is! At the intersection of Race 6, horse 7, and Race 9, horse 10. Which, as it happens, were indeed the winners that day.

Easy, once you know how.

Eleven: PEACE

In 1981, nearly a decade after my mass media attempt to know the unknowable future, I flew to Durham, North Carolina, where the late J.B. Rhine's ever changing research team had its headquarters across from Duke University. By then, however, it seemed that some parapsychologists were more interested in other topics (such as ghosts moving objects inside sealed boxes, and alleged survival after death) and had abandoned repeated guessing protocols. However, one psi researcher who retained a certain enthusiasm for that method kindly gave me xeroxed copies, clearly marked "Do Not Cite," on several typewritten papers laying out his own researches. This was psychotherapist Dr. James Carpenter, who more than 30 years later would publish an important monograph on the nature of psi, *First Sight: ESP and Parapsychology in Everyday Life* (2012). One of these early papers was from as long ago as 1968. In the recent book, Carpenter comments on attempts to devise effective psi applications using repeated guessing:

> In this approach, participants make several guesses at the same targets and the results are averaged in the hope of obtaining more reliable results. The idea of combining judgments of imperfect reliability in order to improve the correctness of the averaged judgments is a commonplace that is used to insure accurate information transfer between computers and is used routinely in psychology and other disciplines whenever measurements with imperfect reliability must be used... A single trial in an ESP test certainly represents a situation of imperfect reliability, even with the most talented performers on their best days. (p. 382)

But he warns against a common error, one we've noted previously:

> Those who have attempted to apply this intuitively appealing idea to increasing the reliability of ESP performance have not always understood that it will only work if overall scoring in the study is positive... Unsuccessful applications that have been reported

> (and probably not reported) have foundered on the pitiless logic of arithmetic. Averaged repeated trials will only enhance whatever scoring tendency is in the collection of individual trials to begin with. If there is overall negative scoring then averaged calls will score at a more strongly negative rate. If the dataset has an overall chance level of scoring, averages will be robustly at chance. This bootstrap offers no panacea unless high scoring can be independently predicted. (p. 382-83)

His recommended cure, other than searching for reliable high-scoring superstars, is preliminary sampling or indexing—Dr. Thouless's Index of Preference, where "the experimenter must know the identity of some of the targets that are being called, but not others. After some calling is done, the scores on the known targets are tallied. These serve as an *index* for the remaining trials in the set. If scoring on the index is above chance, above-chance scoring on the remainder is predicted. The opposite prediction is made when index trials score negatively." (p. 383)

And Carpenter is quick to note as well the lamentable problem with this remedy. Would-be psi percipients are liable to flip mode, at unconscious whim, from significant hitting to significant missing. There is no guarantee that scores on an index sequences will reflect or anticipate scores in the rest of the trials.

Even so, the documents Carpenter allowed me to read in 1981 (expanded in 1983 and 1991 into three valuable papers in the *Journal of Parapsychology*) revealed that his own experiments in this method had been quite strikingly successful. Those published papers share a common heading: "Prediction of Forced-Choice ESP Performance." The subtitle of the third was more specific: "Three Attempts to Retrieve Coded Information Using Mood Reports and a Repeated-Guessing Technique." These experiments went well beyond the simple use of redundant trials and majority votes on the result. Carpenter was looking for subtle cues that might tell him in advance how the mental state or mood of each of his participants (as measured by a mood adjective check list) was influencing any psi they manifested.

The outcome was positive, but somewhat dampening. Here (quoting *in extenso* with Dr. Carpenter's kind permission) is his summary:

> The results of the repeated-guessing analyses in the three studies reported here all tend to support the usefulness of this way of enhancing the reliability of an effort to acquire some piece of information using ESP. The work of a suitable group of subjects can be combined and rendered by using appropriate independent predictions, resulting in a level of reliability superior to that of the raw data of the whole sample. The additional steps of encoding ESP targets to represent verbal or numerical information apparently present no barrier to the procedure.
>
> Reflection makes it clear that the use of such repeated-guessing analyses is not limited to predictions based on mood items or the sheep-goat question. *Any ESP effect,* if reliable, and based on a predictor that is independent of the ESP data themselves, can be used in similar analyses, provided that targets are presented repeatedly and their identity preserved.
>
> There is an obvious caution, perhaps unnecessary. These efficiency-heightening procedures are only as good as the independent discriminations about performance that precede them. The problem of developing such discriminations (the "replicable phenomena" long sought by parapsychology) is still as much a problem as ever. In these studies, scales that worked well in earlier studies did not do so in later ones. This was not unexpected... but even the latest scales are only as good as replication proves them to be. Nor are there other discriminators that are nearly as reliable as we would wish. "Applied ESP" is not just around the corner. (*Journal of Parapsychology,* Vol. 55, September 1991, p. 274)

§

That can't really be denied. The world is not yet filled with psychic superstars (as far as we know—although if they exist they might be smart enough to keep their heads down). After all these decades, we are still at the parapsychological stage the Wright brothers reached when they skittered around a field in Kitty Hawk, North Carolina (a bit over 180 miles from the Rhine Research Center in Durham, as it happens). Still, it is intriguing and satisfying that the first of these tests by Dr. Carpenter was not only perfectly successful—it entailed the transmission and reception of the coded word "PEACE."

Wait, another caution: What seems a natural way to express psychic perception, as "transmission and reception," might be highly misleading. Today's theorists of psi tend to think that it is. One problem is that psi *can't* be due to electromagnetic waves flung outward from one place or person and detected by a sort of psychic radio by the "receiver." We know it can't be, precisely because one of the most remarkable yet well-demonstrated aspects of psi functioning is precognition. Since radio waves and other forms of electromagnetism are obliged by relativistic constraints to stay at the speed of light in vacuum (or slower, in denser media), there is no way messages can be transmitted faster than light, which seems needed if they are to go backward in time.

Some quantum effects notoriously skirt around the edges of such restrictions, or teleport right through the middle of them, but that doesn't help either. Quantum theory, as understood today, is forbidden to convey messages faster than light. Either all these fabulously well-attested theories are wrong (which is possible, but not the first resort to turn to), or something is missing and everyone is looking in the wrong place. Since psi *does* work (some of the time, with vexing inconsistency), we know some item of our current scientific worldview is in need of repair or extension. But it almost certainly won't bring back the "mental radio" model of psychic yesteryear.

Luckily, none of this should prevent experimenters from trying to get psi to work consistently and reliably. Yes, it would be nice to have a new renovated grand theory of physics ample enough to include psi (and it would surely speed up progress, providing precise focus), but in the meantime we can and must push ahead with the empirical end of the science. "Follow the facts," just as detectives and journalists are advised to "Follow the money" or *Cherché la femme*. And one key fact is that Carpenter's pioneering attempt to have the message PEACE detected via psi *worked,* using repeated guessing filtered by majority votes taken on the results.

§

Carpenter's goal was to discover advance screening devices that might allow him to determine if the calls of a given subject were likely to show psi-hitting or psi-missing (or, of course, no psi at all). The test of his conjectures would be, of course, the success or failure of his participants to replicate a secret message. Such messages are very simple — a single word or part of the word — translated into Morse code.

This formal work continued an elaborate series of experimental attempts to test the repeated guessing methodology. I won't test your patience by setting out the details of Carpenter's preliminary scaling questionnaires, which would probably cause your eyes to bleed again. Anyone interested in pursuing this protocol as a real paranormal application is advised to obtain Carpenter's papers and study them closely.

In essence, he looked at two characteristics or moderator variables that allowed the votes to be sorted in advance. One was the *mood* of the participant, as indicated by his or her response to a mood-adjective checklist. The other was the level of authoritarian tendencies, as measured by the California F Scale. The use of the second was simple: participants who were "high authoritarian" were simply excluded from further analysis, since other research had shown such persons to be unreliable in reporting their moods. The mood adjective questionnaire was established using what is called a "forward-stepping multiple regression procedure," and was intended to predict two things. One was the "modal trend," where participants were divided so that those in the numerically highest quartile were expected to hit, and those in the lowest quartile were expected to miss.

And the other characteristic predicted was *variance*: that is, in simple terms, how much the scores departed in *either direction* from chance expectation. High variance (extreme scores, such as 2 or 18 when chance is 10) was taken to imply an internally consistent employment of psi in one direction or the other (for whatever reason this intruded into psychic functioning), while low variance was thought to indicate an internal inconsistency in psychic functioning.

So perhaps counter-intuitively, given a result where with great consistency the guesses in a long sequence were almost exactly at the level of chance expectation, this could be taken as evidence of a blend of chance plus psi hitting *and* psi missing. Carpenter's First Sight theory has proposed that this is perhaps the mechanism that allows us generally to be unaware of psi in daily life.[10]

In the first of these three important exploratory experiments, as mentioned previously, Carpenter chose the word PEACE, translating it for binary reception into Morse code:

10. For further discussion of this last point, see Carpenter 1983, p. 211. I appreciate Dr. Carpenter's kind assistance in clarifying my account.

.- . / . / .- / -.-. / . /

Carpenter's percipients were 110 students at the University of North Carolina in Chapel Hill, some from his three psychology classes and the others students of his colleagues. They were not told about the repeated guessing aspect of this experiment, just that this was a test of possible relationships between mood and ESP performance. Participation was strictly voluntary, there would be no credit given, nor class evaluation. This in itself, it seems to me, probably helped filter out some of the goats while retaining the sheep. What's more, these psychic efforts should be undertaken outside of class, preferably in isolation. In several weeks' time, they were assured, after the testing was complete, they would be given their results.

In all, there were 424 sessions comprising 2120 runs. Before the moderator variables had been assessed and put to work, there were 25,573 hits, an excess beyond mean chance expectation of just 133 correct votes, hitting rate of 50.26 percent. But with the moderator variables in play, hitting rate rose to 52.1 percent — 4761 correct votes, by contrast to 4371 incorrect.

Decoded from the binary Morse form into English language letters, Carpenter' s message PEACE was correctly obtained.

§

This was a remarkable endorsement of the repeated guessing/majority vote approach to psi (although Carpenter candidly noted that it was due "partly to luck in the case of a couple of majorities that were extremely close." But it was encouraging, and led to two more experiments. Note that these were not precise replications, because Carpenter was more interested in fine-tuning his preliminary filters, sorting the student volunteers according to his advance discriminators.

In any event, as happens all too often, the ground shifted under the experimenter's feet. In the second text, the target word was INFO (derived, of course, from INFORMATION), and only the first three letters were replicated correctly, with 5043 post-screening votes correct and 4692 wrong, for an overall hit rate of 51.9 percent. The chance probability of this result was calculated as 0.0002—that is, about one chance in 5000.

The third test differed from the first two, most notably because the investigator was not Carpenter but Dr. Richard Broughton, then at Rhine's establishment in Durham. (Broughton went on to be twice president and long-time Board member of the Parapsychological Association.) The target was no longer coded words with their friendly and perhaps nerdish flavor, but rather a randomly selected

> octal number between 0000 and 7,777 (equivalent to 0 to 4,095, the decimal numbers), which had the advantage of being easily represented by the 12 binary units. Each octal digit was to be converted to three binary digits (ranging from 000 to 111). Then, the binary '0' was set as equivalent to the target symbol '0,' and the binary '1' was set as equivalent to the symbol '+.' Thus, a series of 12 +'s and 0's was to be determined, arranged in four sets of three digits each.

In 600 runs comprising 3000 sessions, there were just 33,883 correct matches, 117 fewer than chance expectation. This negative score of 49.84 percent is not even large enough to suggest overall psi-missing. When the various discriminator scales were applied, some familiar from Carpenter's earlier work, some new and expected to work better—the results were mixed. The variance scales did not succeed in predicted performance, nor in helping generate accurate target predictions. The scales intended to predict directional tendency (above or below chance overall performance) did succeed in predicting performance, and did contribute to good prediction. Looking only at the scales most expected to work well, the hitting rate on the adjusted trials rose to about the level found earlier: 51.7 percent. However, the distribution of the hitting across the targets (probably a random phenomenon) was such that, as he said,

> In spite of the relatively high hitting rate, votes happened to be distributed such that only seven majorities were correct, four were incorrect, and one was indeterminate. These seven binary hits were themselves distributed such that none of the four octal digits was retrieved correctly.

§

Elsewhere, and not pertaining directly to this research, Carpenter wondered if using numerous volunteers was too confusing to work reliably, suggesting instead that self-testing, either forced-choice or free-response, by a single psi explorer might prove more effective and efficient. His argument:

> This difference in reliability between group and individual testing, if generally true, is itself a potentially important phenomenon that has not been explicitly studied and is not really understood. One can speculate, however, that the distractions inherent in group testing may preclude the states of mind most conducive to the expression of ESP, and the anonymity of functioning as part of a mass of people may make individual difference variables (traits, moods, etc.) unlikely to be expressed in performance.

Some of these problems can be avoidable by adopting test formats that force differential effects—like those I used in my own quite primitive newspaper experiment, with words and figures interleaved, and perhaps other ways to distinguish likely *phi*-mode people from their inverse *mu*-mode friends (and perhaps spouses). Another is to partition calls into Sample (or Index) and Application, but as Carpenter has noted this cannot be counted upon to give a reliable prediction:

> Index sampling by itself requires that another key assumption be met by the data to be sampled and averaged. This is the requirement that sets of the ESP data (like the runs in standard forced-choice testing) be internally consistent in scoring direction. As Schmeidler (1960) pointed out, and many others have observed, this assumption generally does not hold true for ESP data. Early attempts to find internal consistency, such as split-half reliability with ESP runs, have usually failed. Because of this, the scoring directions of index samples and remaining data are as often opposite as they are the same. (Carpenter 2010, p. 671)

The recent paper cited above, which looks at two further small studies, provides a detailed account of other methods that can enhance or pre-sort results using estimates of variance effects, mood and attitude to detect the presence and direction of psi in data that have not yet been examined closely. As noted already, the key proviso is the need for at least some small psi capability in the participants: “a critical requirement is the above-chance rate of overall scoring.” You can’t amplify what isn’t there, even by turning to subtle methods such as the sequential analysis used in a majority vote project by Dean Radin, perhaps including as well a “bit-rating scheme” (Radin, 1990-91). It’s quite clear that some of the most careful and inventive applications using repeated guessing and majority vote have been successful. What remains is to learn from many more attempts just why the ones that worked did so, and why some failed, or didn’t quite come together at the end.

§

Psi is a peculiarly frustrating phenomenon. It comes and goes in a haphazard way that electricity and radio broadcasts and love for one’s spouse and children generally don’t, even though these can be interrupted by solar or emotional storms, say. There’s that long history of observations suggesting that a U-shaped decline effect is common—performance at a psi task starting well with extra-chance results, then fading, tending to worsen with repetition of the task, but finally starting to recover. But sometimes it’s worse even than that, with scoring going negative, creating mathematically significant degrees of *wrong* answers. So we shouldn’t be surprised to find these galling evasions and whimsical episodes reducing or even spoiling attempts at repeated trials judged by majority vote.

In an important paper delivered in 2004 at the Parapsychological Association Convention, ten French researchers (Bernard M. Auriol, Frédérick Garcia, Laetitia Puech, Sylvie Lagrange, Corinne Morer, Myriam Campardon, Olivier Rabat, Sophie Valentin, Olivier Perrin and Eve Leconte) addressed this history. Their own long attempt to investigate the majority vote approach and get it to work reliably proved to be a failure. They commented: “Over the course of seven years, participants contributed a total of 240 sessions, involving 27,845 collective trials, which represent over 250,000 individual trials. The Overall hit rate was at chance, both for individual trials and for collective (majority vote) trials” (“Agapè: Group Telepathy. A Long-Term Experimental Series”). One interesting point, noted as well by other experimenters, is that “We especially noticed that, unlike what we expected, strong majorities didn’t get better results than weak ones” (p. 339) They admitted that “Some interesting variance results are noted, though their interpretation remains ambiguous" (p. 325). This is not sheer chance randomness—but it isn't like the dog showing up reliably at the same time every evening for dinner, either.

Here is their thumbnail history of work in this realm. Some of it we have covered already in this book; some we've passed over in silence:

> Osty (1932) and Barker et al. (1975) reviewing the existing literature noticed that the tests involving groups generally tend to produce "psi-missing," or even purely random results. Haight et al.(1978) attempted to design a method that would be a compromise between an individual approach and a group approach but they were not able to get any significant effect. Milton's meta-analysis (1994) of eight studies (ESP in forced choice), gathering more than one and a half million of individual trials, comes to the same conclusion: The mean effect size was very small, and negative; the overall cumulative outcome of the studies was nonsignificant. [...]
>
> On the other hand several other protocols got positive results: For instance, Barker et al. (1975) and Dalkvist & Westerlund (1998). Similarly, Musso and Granero, (1981) got very significant results and vote success was more impressive than individual rate. Carpenter (1988, 1995) used an ingenious protocol to get Psi information from group interactions. He also got significant results. (pp. 325-26)

Their own failed attempt, detailed in the paper, is attributed, with a certain air of surprise, to the stacking effect—"we are most probably facing a stacking effect"—precisely that tendency of a group of people sharing much the same history and ingrained human regularities to vote in a similar way without any overt collusion. That's what Goodfellow found more than two generations earlier marking the Zenith data, just as such biases and population preferences emerge in all such experiments. The methods described in this book, not only to circumvent stacking but even to turn it to advantage, should make it easier for future psi applications to beat the odds without falling foul of that hazard.

The cost, of course, is that so many guesses in a large-scale majority vote program are wasted in blindly following these subliminal urgings. Still, it can be hoped that the comparison of each option "*When Target, compared with When Not Target*" can allow a small proportion of psi to sneak through. And that is where the repeated guessing paradigm plays its part. The true success story will be to minimize the sometimes dreadful tedium of making one guess after another hundreds or thousands of times, perhaps ideally in a state of meditative calm, ego-less flow, open to whisperings at the very edge of detection.

§

Dr. Carpenter was obviously right in warning that " 'Applied ESP' is not just around the corner." But it might be only a few blocks away. In 2012, the *Journal of Parapsychology* (Volume *76*, Number *2*) published a detailed report of what amounts to a protracted and successful repeated guessing endeavor using computerized protocols and a focused, industrious self-experimenter, Greg Kolodziejzyk.[11] (His family name is pronounced Call-a-Jes-sick.)

Born in 1961, this world-record winning Canadian cyclist, Ironman competitor and adventurer was trained as an engineer and has been a graphic designer and millionaire businessman. Between May 11, 1998 and September 26, 2011, he made 5677 binary trials at future binary outcomes, which themselves were coded to 285 majority vote decisions. This long drawn-out and disciplined approach resulted in an excess of 2.65% of successful calls above the 50% expected by chance coincidence.

As we've seen in almost all the studies presented earlier, while this meager success rate is only just about the noise level, it's both significantly improbable and capable of being concentrated into a profitable series of bets or investments. Kolodziejzyk used the majority vote method to distil these guesses, made via a compressed or abbreviated associative remote viewing technique (ARV), into a rewarding real-world venture. "One hundred eighty-one project questions resulted in actual futures trades where capital was risked." Of these, 60.3% of the trades (with a z score of 3.49, and a chance probability of only 1 in 4299) were profitable, amounting to some $146,587. The capital in his trading account was "generally around $50,000."

Here's his own simplified account of the method he used:

> I figured out a way to *leverage* the small effect size by using consensus from multiple ESP trials to increase the success per prediction to a level that I felt would be worth risking capital

11. Conveniently linked at http://www.remote-viewing.com/indexmain.html

> on. And, I figured out a way to *hide* what I was trying to predict from my conscious mind, in order to produce a true ESP intuitive impression about the future event.
>
> ...I later discovered that someone had already invented that same protocol about a dozen years before I thought of it! It already had a name, and it was called "Associative Remote Viewing."
>
> And so this was 1998, and thus began my 13 year experiment in which I used my ARV method to predict the outcome of random futures markets over random periods of time, where I actually risked my own capital on those predictions.[12]

The details of how Greg Kolodziejzyk used ARV can be found in the paper cited above, and differ little from those used in now-conventional remote viewing methods, adapted for associational coding. You, as viewer, attempt to describe features or aspects of a target that will be chosen in the near future from two candidate images drawn from a large array. These differ from each other, perhaps (to borrow his example) showing either a starfish or an egg. Minutes or even weeks after the remote viewing exercise has yielded its notations and sketchy images or icons, a question will be posed: will the market for a particular commodity close up or down by the close of trading? (Trades used by Kolodziejzyk in this coded precognition task were from "a basket of a dozen different futures and commodities like Corn, Wheat, S&P 500, Bonds, Oil, Gold, and a few currencies.") If the answer is YES (that is, whatever it is you are coding will have *risen* in value), the target will be the image of a STARFISH, so you should BUY. If the future value has *fallen*, the answer will be NO, coded as the image of an EGG.

To emphasize this point: which card is coded for which outcome is arbitrary, so the images have no intrinsic resemblance to either the YES/UP/BUY possible future outcome or the NO/DOWN/SELL outcome.

At a predetermined time in the future, then, the choice of target image will be governed by what actually happened in the market. Your computer will display one of these two potential images, reflecting the state of trading. This, then, is the target you were trying to identify in advance.

At this point, the repeated guessing/majority vote element kicks in. We know that psi is feeble and jittery, so most guesses will lack its benefit.

12. Summary of *JPara* paper, at http://www.remote-viewing.com/indexmain.html

They will have, in short, only a chance correspondence to the future target. But a few times in every hundred guesses, psi will modify this quasi-random guessing process. Like a face seen clearly for a moment as fog clears, or a single voice cuts through the babble of a party when everyone else happens to fall silent, a brief burst of information from the future can skew your call in the right direction.

You almost certainly won't recognize this golden moment or be able to tell it from all the others, but if you continue this regime of guessing eventually the excess of correct answers will accumulate and tip the balance. A majority vote can then show a small deviation in the direction of the right answer. Kolodziejzyk writes: "This method 'nests' many sequential, brief-duration individual free response remote viewing trials to form a single consensus-vote about the event to be predicted." What's more, "The percipient assigns a confidence score from .1 to 4 with .1 indicating that there were no similarities between the sketch and either image, and 4 indicating a high confidence that there were likely nonrandom similarities between the image selected and the sketch..." (These confidence calls would later prove to be valuable indicators of the validity of a call, although this has not always been the case with other experimenters.)

Of course, in many trials sheer random factors will swamp such psi-mediated calls—but given enough dedication and endurance, majority vote compression can turn a small psi factor (say, Kolodziejzyk's extra 2.65% correct) into a more robust distillate (his 10.3% above the average of 50%).

So far, then, Kolodziejzyk had rediscovered what West, Ryzl, Targ and Puthoff, Carpenter—and I, independently, in the early 1970s—had realized about intensifying and clarifying a faint psi signal. ("Signal," as stressed previously, might be a misleading metaphor from information theory, itself derived from telecommunications, but it remains a handy way to point to whatever is happening when we respond to distant or future events.)

What is new in his approach was the clever use of computer apps that randomly selected one of the possible trades, set a future date for his decision whether to buy or sell, and did all this without disclosing to him the nature of the commodity. This step removed any chance that his own preferences and biases could contaminate and thus skew his responses.

Because this is a majority vote approach winnowing many repeated trials (but in this case with each trial having a different pair of images to choose from), every trade is based on trials ranging from a few to a couple of hundred different guesses, taking 20 to 30 minutes to record 10 sets of impressions. Kolodziejzyk notes:

> I use a custom computer program to manage the entire process which uses digital stock images rather than paper photos, and I repeat the above ARV trial many, many times in order to develop a consensus prediction before capital is risked on a single prediction. In fact, some trades have consisted of over 200 trials! That would have taken me nearly a month of perceiving images and recording my perceptions, and comparing the drawings to computer photos, etc, then having the computer program calculate the consensus and make the trade.

In his *J. Parapsychology* paper, he elaborated on this:

> After all trials had been remote viewed and analysed, the ARV application calculated the sum of all confidence scores for outcome A and the sum of all confidence scores for the outcome B. The outcome with the highest resulting sum was the final prediction for the project question. If actual capital was to be risked on a trade, then the difference between these two sums was a consideration, with a larger differential resulting in larger effect size...

A key innovation (which somewhat resembles old-fashioned rapid forced choices of the kind Ryzl imposed on Stepanek, but differs in its RV complexion) was the way these many different images coding a single outcome were stacked, so to speak, to be displayed a minute apart in the future. This rapidity is unorthodox in parapsychology, and might be expected to blur subsequent images together (although displayed photos were not reused, unlike the Star, Cross, Square etc of classic Zener cards). But that confusion did not happen. He comments:

> My method of conducting many "rapid-fire" free-response trials naturally entails that an equally "rapid fire" series of multiple feedback images be presented in the future to the viewer in the same order they were viewed, with a short rest period (a minute or more in duration) interleaved between the presentation of each feedback image... if my intention is to perceive elements of a

> photo that I will view tomorrow at 10:00 a.m., my perceptions of that feedback event will not be intruded upon by elements of a different photo from, say, the one to be presented at 10:05 a.m.

Perhaps this fortunate absence of displacement problems is a special benefit of Kolodziejzyk's iron determination and character, so it is not yet clear from replication attempts if this will work for everyone. My guess is that it might not. But it is certainly worth trying.

§

It's worth noting one caution expressed in April, 2015, in rather strong terms, by perhaps the world's best and most consistent remote viewer, Joe McMoneagle. He has given me permission to cite him: "Good remote viewers wouldn't comply with such a tasking—twenty-five RV's in an hour! And then Pigs will fly!" He followed this with the emoticon for a wink, but he's serious. His point is that for true RV to function optimally, a somewhat time-consuming protocol is need. McMoneagle sketched his reality this way: "I spent one week a year in Vegas for the past three years ... doing nothing but ARV, and I've personally hit nine bets in a row; however, those I work with have never gone beyond what is probably the norm—three hits, before failure. I've not seen anyone make any fortune doing ARV."

One aspect of using ARV that's shared by Kolodziejzyk is Joe McMoneagle's insistence upon "Practice, practice, practice, and when you are totally sick of it, more practice till it bores you to death, then more. It puts the ego to sleep. However, plan on being at war with your ego for a lifetime, since you can't fully eliminate it from the process. You also have to do a remote viewing every day whether you want to or not."

§

A final practical discovery Greg made was a correlation between psi accuracy and an effect of the Sun's impact on the Earth at the time. Gales of particles somewhat inconstantly gust from the Sun at an average million miles an hour, or 400 kms per second. We and the entire biosphere are shielded from most of this torrent of electrons and protons by a natural magnetic shield blanketing our planet. Still, when the Sun's wind rises, psi effectiveness tends to fall. Kolodziejzyk reported an impressive link (which, though, like most of the findings in this book, must be regarded as exploratory, as it has not yet been tested, let alone confirmed, by multiple replications in independent labs):

> In the ARV database, there is a statistically significant negative correlation between effect size and solar wind speed. By filtering out all trials where the remote viewing was conducted during active solar conditions with solar wind speeds greater than 450 km/s, the trial success rate jumps from 52.6% to 54.2%, resulting in a significant z = 5.0. Using this [solar wind speed] filter with a minimum 20-trial project question and a minimum of 4 point score sum spread, results in 94% correct project questions and a significant $z = 5.3$.

Is this correlation related somehow to the Local Sidereal Time (LST) effect discovered by James Spottiswoode, where certain slowly shifting times of the day (as calibrated by the stars rather than the Sun) apparently augment or suppress psi effectiveness? At about 13.5 hours LST, psi has been charted as up to 400 percent more effective than at other times, while at 18 hours LST it sags noticeably before recovering.

Spottiswoode and May suggested one way in which the solar phenomena might have an impact on this fluctuation in psi:

> The solar wind plasma is a near perfect conductor and as such cannot cross the field lines of the GMF [geomagnetic field]. The pressure of the wind therefore distorts the earth's field and a dynamic pressure balance is maintained between the two. During times of increased solar activity the solar wind speed can increase, further compressing the earth's field and leading to GMF strength changes at the earth's surface, which are reflected in the GMF indices....

What's more, Spottiswoode and May noted:

> The correlation between AC and *ap* geomagnetic index turns out to be strongly dependent on the region of sidereal time considered and there exists substantial correlation near the 13 h point where the maximum effect size was found. The maximum magnitude correlation of -0.33 ($N = 134$, $p = 0.0001$) occurs at 12.9 h, in

approximate agreement with the maximum of effect size for this data at 13.3 h. Elsewhere in LST space there is little correlation.[13]

These correlations suggest the impact upon our subtlest and most evasive mental capacities from our planetary environment, and its extraterrestrial surround, mediated via constantly volatile global geomagnetic conditions.[14]

We might wonder whether the solar wind conditions in the future (when each UP or DOWN / BUY or SELL question is answered) *also* correlate with success or failure? For example, if precognition happens when one's nervous system becomes "entangled" with its state at a certain time in the future, could this happen more readily when both the trial and the future target presentation take place in times of a temporarily quiet Sun? If so, we might expect that attempting to foresee a month or a year hence would be less effective, overall, than precognizing tomorrow or a week from now.

It turns out this is not the case, at least in Kolodziejzyk's ARV records. He tells me (email, 21 December, 2014): "I have looked at that, as I do keep all of the exact feedback times for every trial. There did not seem to be any significant correlation between solar wind speed at time of feedback and success compared to solar wind speed at time of mentation and success." However, unexpectedly, his data shows a surprising drop in his psi effectiveness at the New Moon, a peak at Full Moon, and lesser peaks at the two quarter Moons. Remarkable, his psi effectiveness

13. S. James P. Spottiswoode and Edwin C. May, "Anomalous Cognition Effect Size: Dependence on Sidereal Time and Solar Wind Parameters." Proceedings of the Parapsychological Association 40th Annual Convention, Brighton, England, 1997. See also Ryan, A., "Variation of ESP by Season, Local Sidereal Time and Geomagnetic Activity." In May, E. C., & S. B. Marwaha (Eds.), *Extrasensory Perception: Support, Skepticism, and Science. Vol. 2: Theories and the Future of the Field.* Praeger, CT: Westport, 2015.
14. See also Zilberman, 1995. From the Abstract: "A comparison of the True Predictions Density in the public numerical lotteries of France and the USSR with day-by-day planetary indices of Geomagnetic Activity from 1980-89 showed that: a) On days of low geomagnetic activity the true predictions density differs significantly from its density on days of high geomagnetic activity (p <0.002); b) On days of low geomagnetic activity the true predictions density significantly exceeds chance expectation (p <0.003); c) The true predictions density correlates significantly with geomagnetic activity on the draw days but not on the days before and after (p <0.005).

also rises sharply just prior to, and at, the far Northern hemisphere Summer Solstice, while dipping dramatically at the Spring and Autumn Equinoxes, recovering somewhat at the Winter Solstice.

Is this equinoctial and solstitial cycle reversed in the Southern hemisphere? As far as I know, that hasn't been explored yet, but could make an important contribution to our understanding of psi and its environmental correlates. Complicating matters even more, effects on the Earth's geomagnetic field can't always be disentangled reliably, or attributed confidently to either lunar or solar influences, since both the Sun and Moon show similar but not identical cycles: the Sun's equatorial rotation is roughly 27 days long, with variations at other latitudes, while Full Moons come every 29 and a half days.[15]

With heroic self-experimenters like Greg Kolodziejzyk, we have to be cautious in interpreting the accumulating results. Psi manifests itself through subtle and usually unconscious tweaks in our neurophysiology, and it's obvious from his records as a sports record-winner that Kolodziejzyk is in a class of his own. What's more, he did his ARV trials in Calgary, Canada, far up the globe at 51 degrees North. Parapsychology researcher Adrian Ryan, a specialist in the links between psi and geomagnetic effects, cautions that "patterns of effect size by solar wind speed may not hold at other latitudes" (email, 22 December 2014).

§

In the next chapter, we will look more closely at the question everyone asks: "If psi is real, why haven't you guys won the lottery? And not just once, but every week?" Finally, in an Appendix, I will present in outline a scheme for using repeated guessing and majority vote to predict future unknown events—perhaps even lotteries. It is closer to Jim Carpenter's approach than to Greg Kolodziejzyk's, but inventive explorers will no doubt find the most efficient ways to fuse the two methods. If so, we really are on the verge of creating a technology of psi with all that this will bring for human benefit and risk.

15. Ryan, A., "Physical Correlates of Psi," in Cardeña, E., J. Palmer, & D. Marcusson-Clavertz (Eds.), *Parapsychology: A Handbook for the 21st Century*. Jefferson, NC: McFarland (2015).

Twelve: Lottery

Let's start by summarizing the evidence offered in this book for a possible psi technology, using repeated guessing evaluated by (normalized) majority vote.

The first thing we found, going back to the 1930s and forward to today, was that unconscious preferences for some numbers, words, patterns, etc, always play a significant role in any redundant series of psychic trials at unknown targets. Psychologists have known about these biases for decades, and provided a catalogue of the most common.

Ask 1000 people independently to choose one number in the range 1-10, and a majority will almost always choose 3. So "majority vote" has to be pre-filtered to rid our data base of as much recurrent bias as possible.

An easy and effective way to do this for many preference factors is to normalize the collective or aggregated votes for each option. If a highly favored number gets a preponderance of votes or guesses, while a generally disdained number gets far fewer votes, we have to compensate by representing the guesses at each option as a proportion of its expected bias-skewed score.

Recall again how this works (discussed above in chapters 3 and 6, especially). Instead of staying with the raw votes, each possible target's tally of guesses is rescaled or normalized to its proportion of the vote expected overall by that target.

To simplify the benefits of this step: if number 3 is usually called about 700 times out of 1000, while number 8 is called only 40 times, we might find in a particular application that 3 was called 680 times while 8 scored 50 calls. Thus 3's adjusted aggregate vote will be 97.14 percent (of its expected vote), while 8's normalized vote will be 125 percent. That makes choice number 8 the clear winner over 3 (and, let's assume, over the other eight contenders). Using this approach, 50 calls for number 8 can be regarded as the true "majority vote" rather than 680. Granted, this tortures ordinary language somewhat, but the principle should be plain enough.

So to test this hypothesis, we need many, many double-blind guesses (where neither the experimenters nor the percipients know by ordinary means what the target is in each trial). This can be arranged either by having one intensely dedicated and persistent guesser such as Stepanek or Kolodziejzyk, or by using thousands or millions of percipients scattered widely so they don't influence each other directly.

The latter approach in particular is very different from remote viewing or Ganzfeld, even when aspects of RV or GF are included. The idea is to poll as many people as show interest in the task, without spending a costly and exhausting time pre-testing them one by one in order to winnow down to a handful of the "psi-talented." True, selecting superstar candidates is ideal, and was used originally in the Star Gate program when viewers such as Joe McMoneagle did extraordinarily well—if never with perfect reliability call after call. Repeated guessing with majority (normalized) vote could never achieve the degree of sustained individual success from an expert remote viewer. Our hope has to be that, done right, the accumulated faint traces of psi will peer over the top of the inevitable storm of noise and shifting preferences.

And what is (in principle, anyway) the most likely blend of millions of highly motivated guessers at a future event, with an incentive to look for feedback on the correct targets, recording their guesses in searchable electronic form proof against tampering? Why, of course, a lottery—the sort where you get to nominate your own choice of winning numbers, with the prospect of a huge payoff if you correctly precognize all of the target numbers.

§

Luckily, I had the chance to get hold of 848,051,814 guesses comprising 141,341,969 entries from 23 consecutive draws of an Australian lottery called Tattslotto (with the company's kind permission, of course, and their assistance). It's very similar to the US lottery Powerball. There are 45 numbers, 1-45, shown on a ticket with eight columns (starting 1, 2, 3, 4, 5, 6, 7, 8) and six rows (in which the last contains only the choices 41, 42, 43, 44, 45). To win first prize, you need to mark all six of the next draw's winning numbers with a clear X or electronic equivalent.

In short, this is a sort of vast natural or wild experiment, repeated several times a week, in applied precognition.

There are lesser prizes for getting fewer number right, and two Supplementary numbers also allow for alternative prizes. You can check these numbers by individual choice, or allow a random number generator at the point of ticket sale to machine-choose for you; these latter "quickpick" entries were removed from the data in advance of my study, because I was looking for human choices open to psi guidance.

I published my findings in *The Lotto Effect* in 1992, and the data are there (both raw and normalized) for everyone to examine, check my analysis, and see some of the complications and promise in the redundant guessing technique. The most obvious finding is the typical number preferences. Most liked numbers are 13 (strangely not condemned as an "unlucky" number), 7 and 30, which tend to be liked by 20 to 25 percent more than average.

Least liked are 41 and 42, tucked away in the bottom left-hand corner. In general, edges of the coupon are disliked, and for the obvious reason votes for numbers 32-45 tend not to be preferred either. (Because they're not birthdays, you see.) In addition, it's known to be the case that many people are attracted to bold patterns, especially crosses (+) and tilted crosses (X).

Other temptations were reported in 2010 by a Canadian psychologist of gaming and addiction, Dr. Nigel E. Turner. He found certain adorable quirks, such as a taste in some players for numbers that end with the same numeral (10, 20, 30, 40, with the other two then selected for other motives) and strings of consecutive numbers (40, 41, 42, 43, 44, 45, which to a small extent offsets the dislike for the larger numbers, even those at an edge of the coupon.)

Here, though, I'll leave aside a lot of the fine-grain detail so we can get a quick general feel for how this looks in the real world—and whether it offers insiders (the owners or operators of the lottery, for example) a psi lead on next draw's winning numbers. To give you a sense of what the raw vote tallies look like, **Table 12.1** shows the actual numbers of guesses in the first four Saturday draws provided to me by the Lotto organization. These are Saturday draws No. 997, 999, 1001, 1003; see how these raw tallies of votes look, on pages 225-228, when they are normalized to percentages in **Table 12.4**. Note that the third set, plumped up with hundreds of thousands of extra votes, is a jackpot draw.

In the Tables of data below, each number's vote is normalized to 100 percent of mean chance expectation, which is calculated by reference to its column's total divided by 45. The winners have an asterisk (*) placed after them. You can see that normalizing the data has removed the bulge in jackpot draw 1001, making its votes more directly comparable to the other Lotto draws.

	Draw 997	Draw 999	Draw 1001	Draw 1003
1	1162572	1167736	1486973	1136556
2	1263090	1271630	1641900	1241682
3	1353445	1358637	1769640	1335570
4	1318749	1339203	1724479	1304018
5	1374645	1390082	1795989	1354209
6	1271508	1274722	1649379	1248432
7	1574496	1564162	2002405	1521504
8	1340856	1347938	1750584	1318072
9	1300274	1303093	1659041	1272148
10	1485755	1498494	1957629	1471367
11	1544334	1562292	2032074	1517035
12	1446903	1452026	1905269	1424076
13	1564392	1576512	2045337	1540846
14	1267285	1290645	1677423	1255952
15	1294608	1315623	1700064	1267953
16	1215894	1225059	1553746	1186313
17	1303089	1314546	1671300	1273051
18	1434662	1445169	1862203	1402215
19	1569658	1606040	2089129	1564835
20	1601798	1628434	2130713	1583424
21	1464726	1489906	1930084	1429215
22	1346668	1360675	1787447	1322837
23	1346843	1349980	1768846	1321566
24	1174756	1178607	1505822	1152314
25	1264991	1276632	1632517	1247179
26	1332128	1337706	1737804	1297599
27	1531800	1539930	2006954	1487805
28	1487852	1496482	1977740	1458483
29	1382858	1401042	1841438	1352512
30	1430302	1432765	1867255	1394250
31	1227272	1240359	1600936	1209941
32	1054380	1043154	1332096	1014981
33	1122991	1133958	1449541	1097025
34	1194937	1208477	1568578	1164367
35	1299758	1309341	1727836	1269889
36	1306096	1324736	1748877	1286743
37	1248649	1258402	1662033	1225923
38	1123961	1145734	1483212	1100426
39	1079271	1090465	1401021	1046815
40	1201223	1198201	1514671	1159244
41	896145	904075	1181969	868127
42	963186	963530	1285337	933151
43	1036134	1041475	1378226	998305
44	1007458	1021393	1362083	980908
45	1061024	1077834	1426070	1039137

Table 12.1
Raw numbers of guesses for each option 1-45 in four Saturday draws, 997-1003.

	998	1000	1002	1004	1006	1008
1	88.53	89.43	89.56	89.57	88.79*	88.64
2	96.84	98.05	98.26	97.61	97.00*	95.87
3	106.37*	105.66*	105.97	106.61	106.45	107.18
4	101.72	102.37	102.61	102.64	102.44	102.77
5	108.64	108.79	108.74	109.01	108.47	108.63
6	96.64	97.40	97.66	98.64	98.01	98.52
7	121.74	121.95*	122.38	122.28*	122.18	122.65
8	102.60	103.35	103.62	103.76	103.11*	102.49
9	101.24	101.37	101.77	101.48	102.03	102.57
10	114.50	115.22	115.63	114.74	114.13	114.54
11	120.70	121.16	120.87	120.46	120.51	121.01
12	111.56	111.50	112.43	112.70	112.64	112.45
13	125.73	124.71*	125.08*	124.99	127.01	125.77
14	98.30	98.15*	97.99	98.26	98.31	98.37
15	99.71	99.98	99.44*	99.26	99.91	99.61*
16	90.37*	90.05	90.27	90.34	90.55	90.17*
17	98.70	99.41	99.91*	98.24	98.36	98.54
18	108.10	107.31	107.43	107.60	107.67	107.79
19	125.50*	125.83	126.39	126.54	126.56	126.80
20	124.57	125.22*	123.63*	124.30*	124.60	125.23
21	112.36	111.76*	112.12	111.84	111.88	112.17
22	103.94	103.93	104.10	104.07	104.10	104.49
23	103.56	103.39	103.75	103.57	104.08	103.97
24	86.46*	86.47	86.65	86.61	86.73	86.82
25	94.90	94.57	94.26	94.83	94.20	94.29
26	99.21	98.73	98.77	99.28	99.14	98.86*
27	119.04	119.06	119.97	119.19*	119.18	118.78
28	116.02	115.86	116.44	116.32	116.02	115.82
29	109.01	108.46	107.97	108.11	109.01	108.73
30	110.17	109.28	109.48	109.12	109.91	109.48
31	92.35	92.12	92.49	92.32	92.16*	91.58
32	74.15	74.10	74.46	74.24	74.56	74.97
33	83.45	83.12	83.21	83.45	83.54	83.69
34	89.41	89.23	88.89*	89.34	89.33	89.23
35	99.62	99.54	98.95	98.79	98.60	98.68
36	101.35	101.11	100.79	100.26	100.06	100.44
37	96.78*	96.51	96.21	96.28*	96.86*	96.91*
38	86.06	85.70	85.38	85.62*	85.17	85.05
39	82.33	82.18	81.70	81.54	81.69	81.75*
40	89.07	89.11	88.56	88.95	89.35*	87.39
41	71.13	70.92	70.84	71.09	70.96	71.01
42	77.59*	77.83	77.24	77.60	77.62	78.12
43	87.93	87.76	87.03	87.30	87.17	87.82*
44	82.50	82.65	82.05*	81.56	81.50	81.72
45	89.54	89.70	89.04	89.67*	88.46	88.65
Million guesses	13.129	13.255	12.912	12.599	12.519	12.641

Table 12.2: Normalized comparison of single-entry Midweek Lotto data draws 998-1008

	1010	**1012**	**1014**	**1016**	**1018**
1	88.79	88.66*	89.91	90.54	90.23
2	95.97*	96.78	97.95	97.53	97.69
3	107.47	108.19	107.44	106.76	107.14
4	102.47	103.15	104.91	104.45*	103.82
5	108.22	107.49	104.90*	109.09	109.25
6	98.61	98.04	98.99	98.99	98.99
7	122.73	121.96	122.29*	122.82	123.11*
8	102.62	102.10	99.99	103.18	102.93
9	102.06	100.88*	97.03*	102.07	101.49
10	114.67	114.11*	113.33	114.04	114.09
11	120.77	121.00	123.00	121.58	121.69*
12	112.42	112.52	112.61	110.39	110.12
13	125.70	125.55	124.88	126.11*	125.84*
14	98.64	99.06	97.31	99.15	98.91
15	99.56	100.12*	97.83	101.17	101.22
16	89.76	90.68	91.80*	91.72	91.24
17	98.91	97.51	94.90	100.06	99.44
18	107.55	107.17*	107.83	106.50	106.19
19	126.70	126.85	128.33	127.47	127.14
20	124.17	124.49	122.49	124.25	124.98
21	111.95*	114.06	111.84	113.06*	113.64
22	104.79	105.30	107.01	104.47*	103.31
23	103.51*	103.12	100.33	103.39	103.07
24	87.23	86.17	86.68*	86.31	87.04*
25	94.77	93.43	93.69	94.41	94.70
26	99.66*	100.92	100.07	100.52	100.27
27	120.05	119.63	121.34	119.01	119.15*
28	116.56	116.40	118.51	115.54	115.57
29	108.92	109.20	108.16	108.34	108.22
30	109.42	109.24	107.01	108.74	108.35
31	92.48	93.79	94.47	92.79	92.19
32	75.34	74.73	75.93	74.88	74.92
33	82.03*	81.76	82.45	81.48	81.75
34	89.79	89.64	91.74	88.86	89.01
35	98.27	99.08	101.33	98.02*	97.17
36	100.93	101.38	104.21	100.14*	99.17
37	97.47*	98.59	97.25	97.12	97.93
38	85.72	85.54	88.45	84.58	85.46
39	81.79	81.56*	79.51	81.60	82.00
40	86.98	85.63	82.97	86.34	86.84
41	71.09	70.96	69.98	71.00	71.09
42	78.09	77.66	79.79	77.50	78.18
43	84.71	84.73	87.31	84.26	84.42
44	81.97	82.61	81.70*	81.48	82.43
45	88.71	88.58	90.54	88.30	88.57*
Million guesses	12.741	16.165	21.812	13.447	13.404

Table 12.3: Normalized comparison of single-entry Midweek Lotto data draws 1010-1018

	997	999	1001	1003	1005	1007
1	89.78	89.43	87.72*	89.61*	89.69	90.09
2	97.54	97.39*	96.86	97.89	97.88	97.45
3	104.52	104.05	104.39	105.30	105.68	105.96
4	101.84	102.57	101.73	102.81	102.81	102.96
5	106.15	106.46	105.95	106.77	107.03	106.85*
6	98.19	97.63	97.30	98.43	98.75	99.05
7	121.59	119.79	118.12	119.95	120.51	120.83
8	103.54	103.23	103.27	103.92	104.53*	103.42
9	100.41	99.80*	97.87	100.30*	100.85	101.06
10	114.73	114.76	115.48	116.00*	115.13	115.37
11	119.26	119.65	119.87*	119.60	119.78	119.95
12	111.73	111.21	112.39	112.27	112.38	112.01
13	120.81	120.74	120.66	121.48	121.53	121.67
14	97.86	98.85*	98.95	99.02	99.04*	99.06
15	99.97	100.76	100.29*	99.96	99.88	99.99
16	93.89	93.82	91.66*	93.53	93.50	94.21
17	100.63	100.68	98.59	100.37	100.07	100.53
18	110.79	110.68	109.85	110.55	110.52	110.43
19	121.21	123.00	123.24	123.37	123.17*	122.88*
20	123.69*	124.72	125.69	124.84	124.95	124.85
21	113.11	114.11*	113.86	112.68	112.64	112.51*
22	103.99*	104.21	105.44*	104.29	104.31	104.11
23	104.01	103.39	104.34	104.19	104.13	104.00
24	90.72	90.27	88.83	90.85	90.68	90.97
25	97.69	97.77	96.30	98.33	98.33	98.53
26	102.87	102.45*	102.51	102.30	102.25*	102.33
27	118.29*	117.94	118.39	117.30	117.23	117.42
28	114.90	114.61	116.67	114.99	114.85*	114.09
29	106.79	107.30	108.63	106.63	106.65	106.95
30	110.45	109.73	110.15	109.92	109.64	110.04
31	94.77	95.00	94.44	95.39	95.25	94.93*
32	81.42*	79.89	78.58*	80.02	80.02	80.26
33	86.72	86.85	85.51	86.49	86.52	86.51
34	92.28	92.55	92.53	91.80	91.75	91.82
35	100.37	100.28	101.93	100.12*	99.68	99.60
36	100.86	101.46	103.17	101.45*	101.03	100.95
37	96.42*	96.38	98.04	96.65*	96.48	96.66
38	86.79	87.75	87.50	86.76	86.75	86.85
39	83.34	83.52	82.65	82.53	82.81*	81.84
40	92.76*	91.77	89.35	91.39	91.46	91.34
41	69.20	69.24*	69.72	68.44	68.47	68.45*
42	74.38	73.79	75.82	73.57	73.54	73.49
43	80.01	79.76	81.30	78.71	78.91	78.75
44	77.80	78.23	80.35	77.33	77.36	77.30
45	81.93	82.55	84.12	81.93	81.62	81.69*
Million guesses	58.273	58.757	76.284	57.078	56.109	55.769

Table 12.4: Normalized comparison of single-entry Saturday Lotto data draws 997-1007

	1009	1011	1013	1015	1017	1019
1	90.13	90.51*	90.78	90.68*	91.00	91.44
2	97.45*	97.55*	97.95	98.11	98.50*	98.60
3	105.94	106.15	106.19*	105.54	105.81	105.77
4	102.98*	102.75	103.56	103.79	103.68	103.77*
5	106.38	106.58	106.84	106.98*	107.14*	107.45
6	99.28	99.00	98.70	98.58	98.68	98.66
7	120.81	120.87	121.26	121.21	121.36	121.47
8	103.50	103.73	104.19	103.95	103.74	104.16
9	101.03	101.13	101.15	101.17	101.47	101.64
10	115.13	115.17	114.97	115.30	115.12	115.51
11	119.77	120.08	120.36	120.53	120.57	120.25
12	112.15	112.02	111.85	111.58*	110.81*	110.61
13	121.51	121.31*	121.52	122.06	121.80	122.04
14	99.29	99.32	99.39	99.50	99.58	99.25
15	100.00	100.14	100.31	100.50*	100.51	100.73
16	93.56*	93.66*	94.34	94.41	94.46	94.62
17	100.46	100.52	100.43	100.43	100.76	100.74
18	110.73	110.40	110.31	110.10	110.45	110.10
19	122.85	123.40	123.35*	123.36*	124.11	124.21
20	124.95	124.86	124.86	124.78	125.24	124.58
21	112.57	112.59*	113.15	113.21	113.31	113.46
22	104.24	104.37	104.27	104.21	103.92	103.72
23	104.57*	103.76	103.93	103.93	103.77	103.52
24	91.00	91.22	90.86	90.58*	90.24	90.26
25	98.53	98.48	98.44	98.12	98.44	98.39
26	102.49	102.63	102.80*	103.02	103.06	103.14
27	117.46*	117.24	117.09	117.36	117.47	117.57
28	114.14	114.18	113.97	114.07	113.96	113.78*
29	106.91	106.93	106.62*	106.22	106.35	106.36
30	109.47	109.81	109.17	109.28	109.07	108.76
31	94.95*	95.59*	95.87	95.82	95.90	95.89
32	80.45	80.40	80.18	80.08	80.15	80.04
33	86.33	86.01	85.83	85.63	85.84	85.78
34	91.96	91.93	91.61	91.58	91.53	91.21
35	99.60	99.58	99.53	99.60	99.14	99.09
36	101.14	100.98	100.76*	100.86	100.74	100.44
37	96.80	96.96	96.90	96.96	96.87*	96.68*
38	86.84	86.64	86.53	86.58	86.41	86.56
39	82.03	82.23	81.91	81.83	82.03	81.89
40	91.50	91.25	91.12	90.94	90.93	90.95
41	68.08	68.23	68.06	68.25	68.03*	67.84*
42	73.90	73.39	73.39	73.64	73.40	73.52*
43	78.56	78.22	77.87	77.57	77.15	77.22
44	77.72	77.39	77.19	77.47	77.16	77.53
45	80.84	80.84	80.61*	80.66	80.32*	80.79*
Million guesses	55.304	54.967	55.450	55.840	54.871	54.727

Table 12.5: Normalized comparison of single-entry Saturday Lotto data draws 1009-1019

§

The first thing to notice in **Tables 12.1-5** is that the data falls naturally not to a single homogenized group of bettors, but to two groups (in which many of the same players will participate, but obviously not all). The Saturday draws were the odd numbered 997-1019, while the Midweek draws were the even numbered 998-1018. The Saturday draws attracted many more bettors, with entrants ranging from 54.727 million to 76.284 (although most hovered in the mid 50 millions). The Midweek draws ranged from 12.519 to 21.812, with most around the 13 million zone. So on the whole Midweek draws pulled in only about a quarter of the weekend population of players. That's an *a priori* reason to consider treating the two sets of data separately.

But is there any way to check the two populations to see if they actually embody different preference patterns? In **Chart 12.1**, I've charted all the aggregated votes in the first eight draws for which I had data—four from the Midweek draws, together with four from Saturday draws. Three features are instantly and rather amazingly apparent, and explain why we can't just use the raw data to estimate the presence or absence of psi.

From **Chart 12.1** (on following page) we can see immediately that biased preferences retain a sharp and evident stability from draw to draw (at least over such a short time as this). Equally, we cannot compare the raw voting for each number *When it is a winning target* and *When it is not a winner*, because the numbers of players vary so widely (as seen in the sample at **Table 12.1**). That's why we need to normalize the votes, measuring them against a mean chance expectation of 100 percent.

Even so, might we expect to gain any useful guidance in predicting the winning numbers? A simpler test might be to compare the ways in which the normalized voting for each candidate numbers agrees or varies depending on the population making the guesses. For example, look at the Midweek normalized votes for box number 1, the top leftmost option on the entry coupon:

88.53 89.43 89.56 89.57 88.79 88.64 88.79 88.66 89.91 90.54 90.23

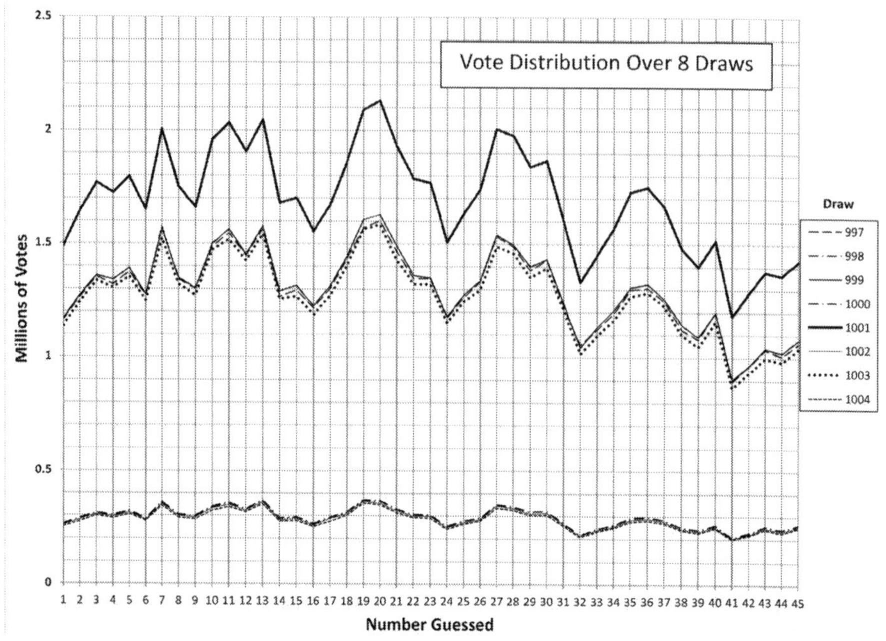

Chart 12.1: Comparing the influence of number and position preference factors in eight Lotto draws.

The *x* (or horizontal) axis marks the 45 possible numbers on each coupon, of which 6 are selected by player. The *y* (or vertical) axis shows the number of guesses in these draws.

The lowest jagged curve tracks the four overlaid Midweek votes. These draws attracted roughly the same number of entrants, and their guesses were strikingly similar.

The central curve maps three of the four Saturday draws, each more numerous than any Midweek draw but comparable to each other.

The single line at the top shows the guesses recorded in draw number 1001, where a jackpot enhanced the prize money and attracted additional bettors. While this numeric superiority pushes that line higher on the graph, its shape remains consistent with the others.

Compare this sequence with the equivalent votes in Saturday draws, with one extra draw at the start:

89.78 89.43 87.72 89.61 89.69 90.09 90.13 90.51 89.91 90.68 91.00 91.44

The general preference *against* number 1 is strong, and surprisingly consistent, but there's an average 0.74 percent difference between the Midweek and Saturday groups. This suggests that they should be treated separately.

So the question's this:

Is there enough stability from draw to draw, even when the data is compartmentalized into Midweek and Saturday draws, to allow a small weak psi signal to peep over the top?

The answer, alas, from simple inspection, is *No.* Not with this kind of data, drawn from so many unfiltered participants—that, for people not selected in advance for any significant amount of psi competence. It is interesting indeed, though, to find this background stability of bias for and against each number. This is evidence that even for people with a powerful incentive to win a million dollars or more, their submission to preference factors and chance fluctuations is enough to overcome any gusts of change from small psi effects that also might be at work.

But does this also prove that the skeptics are right, that there is no psi contribution to this tumble of nearly a billion guesses? Again, *Not necessarily.* Why? Because we can test the entire database, treated as a single entity, and ask if the winning numbers in toto vary interestingly from their competitors. Luckily, the Tattslotto programmers included an exact count of the votes for all winning numbers in the 23 draws, and calculated the frequency of their appearance.

Draw	Frequency percentage
997	13.702
998	12.957
999	12.930
1000	15.277
1001	12.968
1002	13.756
1003	13.425
1004	14.163
1005	13.925
1006	12.606
1007	13.051
1008	12.336
1009	13.577
1010	13.124
1011	13.582
1012	13.167
1013	13.785
1014	12.987
1015	13.859
1016	14.361
1017	12.482
1018	14.787
1019	11.920
Mean	13.423

Table 12.6:
Frequencies of calls (as percentages) for winning numbers in all 23 draws studied, showing slightly larger-than-chance mean of all draws taken together.

By sheer, unbiased chance, the six numbers in each draw would have totaled 13.332 percent of the raw vote—that is, 2.222 percent (100 percent divided by 45) multiplied by 6. In fact, as shown in **Table 12.6**, above, the observed winning votes across all 23 draws comprised 13.423 percent. This is a small excess of +0.09 percent gained by all winners taken together—and an even smaller +0.015 percent per individual target.

Yes, that's tiny, even though it is extracted from nearly a billion votes—but it's roughly in line with the PEAR experiments using non-selected or non-psi-gifted participants. (The PEAR site notes that "The observed effects were usually quite small, of the order of a few parts in ten thousand on average, but they compounded to highly significant statistical deviations from chance expectations."[16])

However, we have to be extra cautious here. These are raw votes, so a lucky hit or unlucky miss in a draw with unusual large numbers of players will disturb the contrasts we are looking for. This is one reason for normalizing the votes to a percentage of their total per draw. Using the normalized numbers, Italian scientist and parapsychologist Patrizio E. Tressoldi, PhD, of the Dipartimento di Psicologia Generale, Università di Padova, ran such a comparison for me. He found that the mean normalized result for the *winning* or target numbers is 100.98 percent, while that for the *non-winning* or non-target numbers in all these concatenated draws is 99.89 percent. That is, winning numbers, overall, attracted an average excess of +1.09 percent.

But recall again that each number actually has a mean chance expectation of 2.22 percent. So the average *actual* deviation from chance for each target is an excess of 1.09 percent divided by 45, or +0.024 percent. Slightly improved over the +0.015 percent raw vote for individual targets.

§

Approaching the problem from a different direction: in a Monte Carlo randomized permutation test under the direction of Ben Goertzel, PhD (my co-editor of *Evidence for Psi*), 1000 different selections of six random numbers were generated. If nothing but chance were displayed by the numbers in these imaginary draws, the expected test outcome would have been 0.5 (that is, half the time the arbitrary "winning numbers" would have done better than chance, and half the time they'd have done worse than chance). In fact, it turned out that players could only have scored better by selecting six numbers from a reduced 48 percent of the "random winning number" trials, rather than the 50 percent expected by chance.

This seems a seriously impressive result because, even with preference biases operating, the permutation test compensates for such

16. http://www.princeton.edu/~pear/experiments.html

skews. Granted, the requirement in statistical analysis for independence of each guess is violated by preference factors—but the Monte Carlo resampling shows that even with these deformations in play the results here are more accurate than they should be by chance alone. Could there be some other non-psi factor in play here?

Well, perhaps. A final hazard remains to be taken into account. Although we have more than 800 million guesses in this vast data dump, together they only constitute 23 trials of six guesses each, aimed at a total of a mere 138 targets. If, instead, a million targets had been randomly generated, or even a thousand, chance would have plucked them equally randomly from the entire range of 45 candidates. But with so few candidate options in play here, we have to ask: what would happen if numbers favored by preference biases just happened to fall into regions of the coupon where bettors were more likely to place their bets?

One test of this possibility is to check whether the numbers 1-31 (the somewhat favored "birthday" numbers) came up by chance disproportionately often. Well, in fact they did. Of the 138 winning numbers, 99 were scattered into that large upper portion of the coupon, while only 39 appeared in the range 32-45. That's a serious imbalance—an average per option of 3.2 winners in the more favored region, compared with 2.8 for the less preferred numbers. (A psychokinetic effect? No—examining a very much longer string of results shows that all 45 numbers have been fairly represented as winners.[17])

There are other bias factors, of course, and to a large extent they remain unplumbed and unspecified. The only way to learn if the small excess of correct votes was due to precognition rather than mere chance is to repeat the experiment with a much larger array of lottery data. *If* scientists can find anyone in the lottery business to permit them access...

§

Bear in mind, though, that a coarse search of this kind for psi anomalies in the available Lotto data does not directly address the key idea presented in this book.

What we are asking, always, is whether a certain target option (say the number 7) gains extra votes *when it's going to be randomly selected*

17. See https://tatts.com/tattersalls/results/number-frequencies . As of June 13, 2015, there were 8632 winners in the range 1-31 (averaging 278.45) and 3872 in the range 32-45, averaging 276.57, not a significant difference.

as a winning number compared to *when it is not.* It doesn't matter if 7 always tends to attract more guesses than its fair share (just because the superstitious regard it as a "lucky" number, and because it's in the more preferred zone of the coupon).

We can see easily from the normalized data that in our Midweek draws, number 7 gained between 121.74 and 123.11 percent of the expected chance vote, while 20 gained between 123.63 and 125.23 percent, and 45 got only between 88.46 and 90.54 percent. The question is not "Did option Number 45 obtain more votes than option 20 did?" We know that will never happen. All that matters is whether ball 45 held proportionately more votes than usual when it came out of the spinning barrel. As it turns out, in these 23 draws it didn't. For a discussion of some other bothersome factors (like slow, visible fluctuations in the popularity of each number, week after week), you'll have to consult *The Lotto Effect.*

§

Bottom line: the results from this kind of mass exploration could help test the reality of psi as an anomaly (if it stands up to further scrutiny) but useful *psi applications* probably need a different approach, perhaps combining redundant guessing (or perception) with aspects of remote viewing, ideally by trained super-psi stars. And this is precisely what Greg Kolodziejzyk did successfully in his trading tasks, serving as his own star percipient.

Can any carefully designed methodology using repeated efforts and combined consensus vote reliably (or even occasionally) help you win the lottery?

Well, James Spottiswoode came very close to doing so in 1995, when he designed a rather complicated Associative Remote Viewing project aimed at winning the California State Lottery's Fantasy 5 jackpot. The chance of winning was one in 575,757, by picking the correct five numbers out of 39.

His method combined precognitive reports from seventeen remote viewers who each had a track record of significant successes. These multiple viewers did not share the same targets, which would have brought the attendant risk of stacking effects that amplify preference biases. His sub trials were combined according to a predefined algorithm and a forecast given only if and when a threshold was exceeded.

Together, by a kind of majority vote consensus, the viewers

pinpointed the winning numbers—but failed to win the prize, because, alas, James miscalculated how long it would take to print out and return the $2000 worth of overlapping coupons required by his sophisticated method (Dossey 2009, p. 56). Why leave the printing and purchasing so late to meet the deadline? Because he wanted to reduce to a minimum the interval between remote viewing, analysis and feedback (once the winning numbers were drawn). The two hours he'd allocated proved not to be long enough (private communication, June 8, 2015).

It's like one of those reproving parables advising the ambitious not to dabble in magic—you always end up with a sausage stuck to the end of your nose, or dancing brooms multiplying disastrously even as you try to chop them back. In this case, nothing so dire happened, nor was the fault irreparable, in principle. So why did James Spottiswoode decide not to replicate the experiment? Too much hassle and effort, perhaps, too many cats to herd? Other more pressing demands and interests getting in the way? Theoretical arguments asserting that something will always go wrong when retrotemporal causality is messed with? (A case advanced by Dr. Harald Walach and others [Walach, 2014].) At least some of the above, I suspect. But someday somebody is going to pull this off, perhaps a number of times in a row, and the world will be changed forever.

Stephan Schwartz, inventor of the ARV (associative remote viewing) method using consensus to combine reports from a number of psi-gifted individuals, turned his attention to a kind of psychic archeology rather than massively lucrative lotteries (Schwartz, 2001, 2005). Why no stock market investments or lottery wins? Here is his explanation:

> The first investment ARV was a horse race in 1977. Six Trotters at Hollywood Park. Two viewers, a naive, Neddie Pena, who had never done an RV, and Hella Hammid. Two teams: Ed May and Hella Hammid, and myself and Neddie. There was consensus and we correctly selected the winner of the 6th race. Bet $2, won $14. I ran a 42 week, once a week, ARV, beginning with $5,000 that got to $150,000. I quit because it was literally eating the lab alive. I could not get people to concentrate on anything else. All anyone could focus on was the Thursday viewing, for an S&P 500 Friday call. The protocol called for seven viewers to independently view a photo target, each one getting a separate target. The protocol was market up, market down, pass. If there was a consensus we called. If not we passed. These were all highly experienced viewers:

> Hella Hammid, Alan Vaughan, Judith Orloff, George McMullen, Ben Moses, Andre Vallaincourt.
>
> It is worth noting that in one seven week run we got six right and one wrong, and actually lost money. On the six right the market move was small each time. On the seventh the market moved to the stops. The net-net was that the seventh wiped out the preceding six, plus a few hundred dollars. (private communication, 2015)

Perhaps this difficulty can be overcome, though, since it looks like a group psychological obstacle rather than something intrinsic to the psi process (whatever that is).

§

Well, if so, how soon can we expect strong evidence of this kind via, say, a psi application method able to win a major lottery several times in a row? It's hard to predict (insert sardonic joke here if you wish), but if the parapsychology labs don't do it one or more of the private enthusiast groups might managed it.

In something like the way spiritualist churches and séance groups proliferated at the end of the 19th century, remote viewing clubs and associations have started to blossom across the USA and probably other nations as well. To date, as far as I can tell, none of them has carried off a Lotto-type or Powerball coup. Some seem to be offshoots of individuals or companies who charge considerable fees to those eager to learn how to use psi for fun and profit, although in many cases the profit appears to be made by the instructors. Teachers frequently claim to have been associated with the Star Gate program, or other long-classified research and operational entities funded by Congress and the military. A few actually are, but generally they magnify their importance and success rate.

Other groups cropping up like mushrooms make no such extravagant claims, but I get the impression that there is a considerable amount of self-deception and confirmation bias at work. That is, these groups are not fraudulent or extortionate; often their fees are minimal. Many are linked into IRVA, the International Remote Viewing Association, which holds annual conferences, usually in Las Vegas (the world headquarters of gambling, suitably enough). Experts in the field give learned addresses and run teaching sessions. In 2002, for example, guest speakers included Russell Targ, Ingo Swann, Stephan Schwartz and Hal Puthoff. In June

2015, the IRVA conference took place over three days in the Hyatt French Quarter, New Orleans. The conference bills itself as seeking to accomplish these goals (not forgetting excited spoon-bending parties):

- To provide a stimulating environment for education, understanding, and expanded awareness in the rapidly growing remote viewing community.
- To bring together a wide range of remote viewing practitioners, trainers, and researchers to share their experiences and knowledge in a friendly and supportive group setting.
- To foster cooperation, expand friendships, and facilitate intellectual cross-pollination among those wishing to help expand the boundaries of human consciousness.
- To provide an accurate and responsible picture of remote viewing history and state-of-the-art.[18]

One of the hotbeds of remote viewing activity is Hawaii, where groups such as Glenn Wheaton's Hawaii Remote Viewing Guild, and Marty Rosenblatt's Physics Intuition Applications, bring together enthusiasts for mutual support and experimentation. While this is not to be confused with rigorous scientific empirical and theoretical investigation of psi, it would not be entirely surprising if some of these enthusiasts actually get psi to work. I can't vouch for what follows, but Rosenblatt's P.I.A. reports the following:

We recently facilitated a workshop at the [10th] IRVA Conference in Las Vegas. The workshop was called, "10-Choice Associative Remote Viewing (ARV)".... This presentation followed a 4-day workshop with Stephan Schwartz called, "Remote Viewing and Applied Intuition." The two workshops resulted in a string of four successful predictions, with wagering on the first three:

- Black/Red bet at the roulette wheel
- an Up/Down financial wager on S&P 500 futures
- betting on the Winning Horse in an evening horse race
- a non-wagering roll of the dice at the conference which was successfully predicted by the conference participants as a group

18. http://www.irva.org/conferences/

With rather innocent candor, Rosenblatt admits:

> There was a second roll of the dice which was not predicted correctly—there was an error by the facilitator (me) which probably influenced this negative outcome. The odds of our success up to the second dice roll were about 400 to 1 versus chance. In fact, it was the prospect of having the astonishing result of odds of 4,000 to 1 being lived in real time that through [sic] me off my planned protocol... interesting lesson for me, and hopefully for the audience as well.[19]

What I find significant about these approaches is the way the best of them combine associative remote viewing with consensus or majority voting. This blend of methods might well prove to be the most efficient way to get a working psi technology. But there will be, inevitably, some problems. Amateur groups are far more prey to amateur blunders with procedure, safeguards and strict analysis. And enthusiasm can blind proponents to errors. James Spottiswoode expressed his own increasing skepticism toward the claims. Associative remote viewing, he notes, has "bias built in, as there is no fixed protocol and a huge bias on the part of the experimenter to either make it work or appear to do so. Even to themselves" (private communication, June 8, 2015).

In 2015, an ambitious psi application program (looking for a "future-prediction tool") was proposed by neuroscientist Dr. Julia Mossbridge, a PhD from Northwestern, and Stanford and Harvard educated Dr. Garret Moddel, University of Colorado Professor of Electrical, Computer and Electrical Engineering, an expert in nanostructures, optics and photonics. Their hope was to crowd-fund this project for a year or 120 trials, whichever came first, testing and comparing three different methods of precognitive stock market investments. Without denying the key psi aspect of these trials, they presented it as a scientific exploration of "non-conscious processing correlates with future events."[20] The initial crowd-funding bid for $50,000 (via experiment.com) was lowered by half, and $25,000 has been pledged.

19. "Wagering with Remote Viewing":
http://p-i-a.com/Magazine/Issue33/Connections_33.html
20. Nicely described in
https://www.youtube.com/watch?v=AntWJscu-nE
https://www.youtube.com/watch?v=NNcgqoJ5mXI
https://www.youtube.com/watch?v=T9q6rfJQSEo

To test the working assumption that dreaming is a better gateway to precognition, they planned to try three approaches. The first would use a trained, gifted precognitive dreamer hoping to tap into unconscious processes. The second and third would use associative remote viewing "by both a single trained ARVer and a group of untrained ARVers" who, it is hoped, "will all produce accurate stock market predictions at a rate that is significantly above chance." This third approach blends majority vote/multiple attempts with remote viewing of a future choice between two coded images as unlike each other as possible, one coded for a rise in stock value and the other for a fall (without either the viewers or the tasker knowing the details).

Successful earlier tests of this kind, without the dreamers, were conducted as part of a course in parapsychology and critical thinking run by Moddel at the University of Colorado, Boulder, under the auspices of the College of Arts and Sciences. In one, published in the peer-reviewed *Journal of the Society for Scientific Exploration* (Smith, et al., 2014), inexperienced students served as participants during class, sketching what they guessed (or remote viewed) would be displayed at the next class, a day or three later. In an interview, Moddel describes this succinctly: "They're simply told, 'Draw what I'm going to show you at the end of the day tomorrow.' So they just sit down and we spent five minutes at the beginning of each class with each student drawing pictures. Then those pictures were sent off to the person who acted as a judge, and the judge decided did each picture look more like the rabbit or more like the bowling ball... the images were changed each time we did this. And so from that we predicted whether the stock market was going to go up or go down. In fact, a couple of us invested in the market using stock options to amplify the effect. So we carried this out seven times until the end of the semester, with the entire class doing the remote viewing. We got it right seven times."[21]

Such attempted precognitive applications, as we've seen, have been successful before. The frustrating aspect to this experiment was what happened when it continued informally. Moddel: "You now ask the question can you use this in order to get rich? My initial answer is no, because I continued using this effect with a few of us afterwards, and we found that as we continued to do it, a little less formally than we had done it with the class, that the effect started going haywire."

---

21. http://www.skeptiko.com/garret-moddel-brings-psi-to-colorado/

Why would this decline occur? It's an effect familiar to parapsychologists, and not simply explained as "regression to the mean" or other well-known statistical quirks. Moddel hazarded: "It may be, as [former Star Gate military viewer] Paul Smith would say, because some of the remote viewers were also some of the investors, so they were too literally invested in the outcome of the remote viewing. Or it may be that these phenomena really work initially when you're excited about it and a little bit naïve about it. For psychological and intention based reasons, they break down after a while."

There are problems with this kind of ARV method, even buttressed by consensus elements. No attention seems to have been paid to defeating preference effects—although perhaps these are less important given the immense diversity of possible real-world targets, compared with, say, the Zener circle-cross-wavy lines-square-star, or one-digit number targets. Even so, there's a fairly limited quantity of basic schemata or shapes that most of us draw on when trying to imagine an unseen target, and I suspect this needs to be calibrated somewhat to get best results. Perhaps it would help to include Carpenter-style psi-mode detection using variance and mood scales. Still, if this interesting experiment gets funding, perhaps from a well-heeled private source, it will tell us a lot about not just the reality and reliability (or its absence) of psi, but how to aggregate such premonitory experiences into a useful and profitable future-telling tool.

In the Appendix that follows, I do not stress variance or mood scales, either, which add to the burden without necessarily providing a strong benefit. Still, the rough-and-ready recipe given below is undoubtedly complex and time-consuming, although a lot of the hassle can be reduced by recasting these points into a computer algorithm.

Can applied psi be worth all this elaborate activity?

It depends what drives you. As a matter of pure research, this seems an excellent way to grapple with the usefulness of psi, not just as a phenomenon in our world of experience but as a technology. Once that's been established, scientists in great numbers might flock to parapsychology labs in search of explanations for these puzzling anomalies. More likely, alas, they will publish their own belated results in approved mainstream journals like *Nature* and *Science* and be hailed as geniuses for opening up an entire new unprecedented realm of knowledge, instantly writing the parapsychologists out of history. Either way, perhaps a whole new paradigm will burst upon us.

§

In the millions of years that lie ahead of our species, beyond the lethal hazards of our present troubled age, humankind has a prospect of boundless fulfillment. Lyrical visions of the future are unfashionable these days, faced as we are by frightening prospects of global climate change, financial chicanery on the most outrageous scale, overpopulation, energy crises, disease pandemics and mass hunger and thirst in some corners of the planet. It is hardly comforting to surmise that in some remote century our offspring will bask in the light of alien galaxies.

At root, our current problems are the old, classic recipes for war, terror and grief: too little food, inadequate space, not enough known resources to go around, insecurity. All our political and personal freedoms depend on a surplus of necessities, and our surplus is running out. Political solutions, and "change of consciousness," can do very little unless we first obtain the technical means to multiply the world's goods faster than we reproduce their users, and to reduce our potentially lethal impacts on the biosphere.

There is a more optimistic perspective. In the long run, there is no doubt that science will be capable of giving us all we need, and more. Within several hundred years at the very most—unless we blast, breed or pollute ourselves back to the Stone Age—medical research will surely find not only a cure for cancer and heart disease, but for aging and death itself. Our immortal descendents will have unlimited power, not from the Sun or the atom but in the furious energy storms of stellar black holes, collapsed stars of immense gravitational potency. Far from competing with computers for jobs, our offspring will link their minds to machines operating at the speed of light, exploding consciousness into a new realm of ultimate expansion: the Singularity, or Spike.[22]

Granted, such optimism rings hollow. We, today, apparently don't even have time to create the scientific breakthroughs needed to arrest a downhill slide into a late 21st century of world poverty and misery. There seems no way to speed the process up. Science must proceed by its own dogged rules, learning step by step, however accelerated those steps become as we approach a technological singularity, adding to knowledge not by magical incantation but by stolid experiment and brilliant theory.

---

22. See my book *The Spike*, 2001. Many of the predictions in that book have already occurred.

The exploratory trip might require not astronauts or cosmonauts (as in the movie *Interstellar*), but experts in psi. Specialists in knowing the apparent unknowable.

Appendix: Do It Yourself psi applications

Let's list the considerations needed for...

BASIC DO-IT-YOURSELF PSI FORECASTING

- If possible, obtain the services of one or more participants pre-tested for successful psi performance of a statistically significant level.

- Number of elements in the message string, and format of targets, are governed by the complexity of the message and likely response-biases and preferences. Binary coding such as the choice "red or black" or "green or white" is statistically convenient, but tediously boring in any extended guessing session. Alas, choosing directly from the range of Powerball's 59 white numbers and 35 red balls, or from a standard deck of playing cards (which will encode 52 possibilities) opens the gate to savage psychological prejudices, pattern-making and other biases that are not easy to counter.

- Many parapsychology experiments have found that alternation of psi-hitting and psi-missing behavior can be "forced" in a single subject by the use of strongly differentiated classes of targets. In the 1960s, John A. Freeman (see chapter Eight) investigated the use, within a single test, of both Verbal and Spatial targets—a notion based to some extent on American school psychological testing that revealed broad female superiority on Verbal tasks, male superiority on Spatial tasks. Feminist hostility to the supposed genetic sources of sex-marked mental ability differences (if they do exist) has perhaps done as much to cast doubt on these parapsychological findings as any assaults by anti-psi skeptics. It might be, of course, that the observed differences were instilled by cultural deformations of child-rearing patterns or by a bigoted education system, and are now harder to find or gone entirely. Still, some differential effects do exist, so it seems a good line to pursue.

- Decide the basic message parameters—say, a string of 6 binary choices to encode a single winning Powerball number ($2^6=64$). Six modules can be added to retrieve all six numbers in 36 binary choices.

(To win Powerball with a single ticket or set of 6 numbers is 1 chance in 175,223,510. A single string of 28 binary choices can encode the whole lot in one hit with room to spare—2^{28} equals 268,435,456—if it's done carefully, though a single erroneous bit will spoil all six predictions.)

- Add or interleave the inverse of the message sequence (001010, for example, if the message is 110101). This is a partial cure for response bias—and at no great cost, since psi can still operate to your advantage on these data bits.

- Add an index bit or sequence. This sample can be decoded in advance of the main message string, permitting a preliminary test of the presence of psi, and its mode if it's detectable.

- "Null" or meaningless bits can be added if desired, to track shifts in preference over time. This is probably only necessary if a single choice, such as "yellow or blue," is repeated *ad nauseam*.

- Make repeated trials at the targets, either by yourself or with a number of collaborators. If the goal of the exercise is to predict next week's lottery results, a many-participant program might split the task six ways, each operator taking one of the six winning numbers as her or his goal. For safety, it might be best to have two or more people cover each individual number. If they come up with the same answer, the prediction can be accepted with greater confidence.

- Most such psi applications will be computerized. The program would keep a tally of entries as they are made, inverting the reverse sequence and adding its guesses to the basic sequence, normalizing the consolidated votes according to its on-going estimate of bias, stacking effects and preference skews, and performing a running statistical assessment of results to date. Ideally, deviations should be measured from empirical rather than theoretical baselines. The ultimate test applied by the program should be this: *The vote gained by each option will be* significantly *higher or lower when it is the target rather than when it isn't.* Usually this will not be as simple as finding a clear majority-vote. For example, if the third bit in the string is determined by the choice "half-peeled banana" or "roaring lion," it would be prudent to discover the weights associated with each option. It might be that most percipients will always tend to vote more than 60 percent of the time in favor of "roaring lion." Thus, the program should estimate any such bias and control for it, perhaps by an Index of Preference (which divides all scores for a given option by the mean vote for that option).

- Two termination procedures are possible. In one, a predetermined number of trials should be set (anywhere from 5 to 10,000 guesses per bit). Once this designated tally has been accrued, index or sample bits should be examined first for any significant difference from chance expectation. If the index reveals voting close to chance, the message votes may be abandoned as unreliable. If index options do suggest significant psi is present, preliminary decoding of their known targets will give an estimate of psi-hitting or psi-missing mode (perhaps aided by variance tests), and the main message string will be decoded accordingly. (Which might mean, vexingly, in the *contrary* mode to the index outcome—a factor that only experience with the participants and experimenter can establish.)

- A different termination procedure permits each bit in the message string to be repeated as often as possible, until a significant vote is gained by one of the alternatives (one of the two, in the binary case; one of the 52, if playing cards are used). Again, if an index of preference has indicated that marked bias is disturbing the *a priori* probabilities associated with the options, the option chosen will not necessarily be the one with a simple majority, but the one with the outstanding normalized score.

- In a precognition application, the actual string at which the operators have been directing their trials will be encoded only *after* all the data is collected, and using the same protocols. This target will derive from some real-world random event such as a future lottery draw, stock market movement, or extreme weather event. What is then done with this target message-string depends on one's favorite theory of psi. Studies of the value of feedback suggest that operators should later see and interact with this coded target string, perhaps in the form of a computer monitor display similar to the graphics used to solicit their guesses. So if the choice for the third bit was coded as "bananas" or "lion," and "bananas" was the answer, the monitor screen might display the original pair of choices and then flash the correct answer several times—in addition, asking the operator to confirm recognition of this target by entering it once more (and maybe eating the piece of fruit in question!).

Bibliography and Related Reading

Alcock, James E., "Parapsychology: Science of the anomalous or search for the soul?" in "Parapsychology Debate," below.

——— "A Comprehensive Review of the Major Empirical Studies in Parapsychology Involving Random Event Generators or Remote Viewing," Commissioned by National Research Council.

——— and Burns, Jean E., & Anthony Freeman, *Psi Wars: Getting to Grips with the Paranormal*, Imprint Academic, 2003.

Auriol, Bernard M., Frédérick Garcia, Laetitia Puech, Sylvie Lagrange, Corinne Morer, Myriam Campardon, Olivier Rabat, Sophie Valentin, Olivier Perrin and Eve Leconte, "Agapè: Group Telepathy. A Long-Term Experimental Series," Parapsychological Association Convention 2004, pp. 325-39. *archived.parapsych.org/papers/36.pdf*

Barker, P.L. Messer E. and Drucker S.A. (1975). "Internally-Deployed Attention States: Relaxation. A Group Majority Vote Procedure with Percipient Optimization," *Research in Parapsychology, Abstracts and Papers from the Sixteenth Annual Convention of the Parapsychological Association*, 1975, pp. 165-167.

Bierman, D.J. "Exploring correlations between local emotional and global emotional events and the behaviour of a Random Number Generator," *Journal of Scientific Exploration,*10, 3, pp. 363-373, 1996.

Blackmore, Susan, "The Elusive Open Mind: Ten Years of Negative Research in Parapsychology," *The Skeptical Inquirer*, Vol. XI, No. 3, Spring, 1987.

——— "The lure of the paranormal," *New Scientist*, 22 September, 1990.

Brier, Robert M., "A Mass School Test of Precognition," *Journal of Parapsychology*, 1969.

——— and Walter V. Tyminski, "Psi Application: Part I. A Preliminary Attempt," and "Psi Application: Part II. The Majority-Vote Technique—Analyses and Observations," *Journal of Parapsychology*, Vol 34, March, 1970.

Broderick, Damien, *The Architecture of Babel: Discourses of Literature and Science*, Melbourne University Press, 1994.

——— *The Lotto Effect*, Hudson: Hawthorn, Australia, 1992.

——— *Theory and Its Discontents*, Deakin University Press, April 1997.

——— *Outside the Gates of Science: Why It's Time for the Paranormal to Come In from the Cold*, Thunder's Mouth Press, 2007.

——— and Ben Goertzel (eds), *Evidence for Psi: Thirteen Empirical Research Reports,* McFarland, 2015.

Burdick, Donald S., "Analyzing Binary Data in the Presence of the Stacking Effect. A Technical Note," *Journal of Parapsychology*, Vol 47, 1983.

Cadoret, R. J., "The Reliable Application of ESP," *Journal of Parapsychology*, Vol., 19, 1955.

——— "Some Applications of Information Theory to Card-Calling Performance in ESP," *Journal of General Psychology*, Vol. 65, 1961.

Carpenter, J., "The Facilitation of Psi Communication by the use of Run Score Variance Effects, Index Sampling, and the Repeated Guessing Technique," *Proceedings of the Parapsychology Association 1970,* W. G. Roll, R. L. Morris & J. D. Morris (Eds.), The Parapsychological Association, 1972, 13-14.

——— "An elaboration of the repeated guessing technique for enhancing ESP information efficiency," *Research in Parapsychology*, W. G. Roll, R. L. Morris & J. D. Morris (Eds.), 1982, 78-85.

Carpenter, J., "Prediction of Forced-Choice ESP Performance. Part I. A Mood-Adjective Scale for Predicting the Variance of ESP Run Scores; Part II. Application of a Mood Scale to a Repeated-Guessing Technique," *Journal of Parapsychology*, Vol 47, 1983.

——— "Prediction of Forced-Choice ESP Performance, Part III: Three Attempts to Retrieve Coded Information Using Mood Reports and a Repeated-Guessing Technique," *Journal of Parapsychology*, Vol. 55, September 1991.

——— "Laboratory Psi Effects May Be Put to Practical Use: Two Pilot Studies," *Journal of Scientific Exploration,* Vol. 24, No. 4, pp. 667–690, 2010.

——— *First Sight: ESP and Parapsychology in Everyday Life*, Rowman & Littlefield, 2012.

Clark, W. H., "A Practical Application of Precognition," *Journal of Parapsychology*, Vol. 22, 1958.

Collins, H. M., and T. J. Pinch, *Frames of Meaning. The social construction of extraordinary science*, Routledge & Kegan Paul, 1982.

Dossey, Larry, *The Power of Premonitions: How Knowing the Future can Shape our Lives*, Dutton, 2009.

Druckman, Daniel, and John A. Swets, eds, *Enhancing Human Performance: Issues, Theories, and Techniques*, National Academy Press, 1987.

Duncan, David, *Occam's Razor*, New York: Ballantine, 1957.

Dunne, B. J., "Co-Operator Experiments with an REG Device," Technical Note PEAR 91005, Princeton University School of Engineering and Applied Science, December, 1991.

——— and R. G. Jahn, "Experiments in Remote Human/Machine Interaction," Technical Note PEAR 91003, Princeton University School of Engineering and Applied Science, November, 1991.

Dunne, B. J., and R. D. Nelson, Y. H. Dobyns, and R. G. Jahn, "Individual Operator Contributions in Large Data Base Anomalies Experiments," Technical Note PEAR 88002, Princeton University School of Engineering and Applied Science, July, 1988.

——— and Roger D. Nelson, Robert G. Jahn, "Operator-Related Anomalies in a Random Mechanical Cascade," *Journal of Scientific Exploration*, Vol. 2, No. 2, 1988, pp. 155-79.

Eysenck, Hans J., and Carl Sargent, *Explaining the Unexplained. Mysteries of the Paranormal*, Weidenfeld and Nicolson, 1983.

Fisk, G.W., and D.J. West, "ESP Tests with Erotic Symbols," *Journal of the Society for Psychical Research*, Vol. 38, 1955.

——— "ESP and Mood. Report of a 'Mass' Experiment," *Journal of the Society for Psychical Research*, Vol. 38, 1956.

——— "Towards Accurate Predictions from ESP Data," *Journal of the Society for Psychical Research*, Vol. 39, 1957.

Foster, A. A., "ESP Tests with American Indian Children," *Journal of Parapsychology*, Vol. 7, 1943.

Freeman, J. A., "Sex Differences and Target Arrangement: High school Booklet Tests of Precognition," *Journal of Parapsychology*, Vol. 30, 1966.

——— "Sex, Target Arrangement, and Primary Mental Abilities," *Journal of Parapsychology*, Vol. 31, 1967.

——— "Sex Differences and Primary Mental Abilities in a Group Precognition Test," *Journal of Parapsychology*, Vol. 32, 1968.

Freeman, J. A., "Sex Differences in ESP Response as Shown by the Freeman Picture-Figure Test, *Journal of Parapsychology*, 1970.

Gardner, Martin, *How Not to Test a Psychic: Ten Years of Remarkable Experiments with Renowned Clairvoyant Pavel Stepanek*, Prometheus Books, 1989.

Goodfellow, L. D., "A Psychological Interpretation of the Results of the Zenith Radio Experiments in Telepathy," *Journal of Experimental Psychology*, Vol. 23, 1938.

Greville, T. N. E., "On Multiple Matching with One Variable Deck," *Annals of Mathematical Statistics*, 1944, Vol. 44.

Haight, J. Weiner, D. and Morrison, M. "Group testing for ESP : a novel approach to the combined use of individual and shared targets," *Research in Parapsychology, Abstracts and Papers from the Twenty-First Annual Convention of the Parapsychological Association*, 1978, pp. 96-98.

Hansel, C. E. M., *ESP and Parapsychology. A Critical Re-Evaluation*, Prometheus Books, 1980.

Herzberg, Alexander, "Methode und Ergebnisse des Berliner Rundfunkversuchs," *Zeitschrift für angewandte Psychologie,* XXXI (1928), 66-106.

Heseltine, G.L. and J.H. Kirk, "Examination of a Majority-Vote Technique," *Journal of Parapsychology*, Vol. 44, 1980.

Honorton, Charles, "Meta-Analysis of Psi Ganzfeld Research: A Response to Hyman," *Journal of Parapsychology*, Vol. 49, 1985.

——— and Diane C. Ferrari, " 'Future Telling': A Meta-Analysis of Forced-Choice Precognition Experiments, 1937-1987," *Journal of Parapsychology*, Vol 53, 1989.

Hyman, Ray, "The Ganzfeld Psi Experiment: A Critical Appraisal," *Journal of Parapsychology*, Vol. 49, 1985.

——— "Parapsychological Research: A Tutorial Review and Critical Appraisal," Invited Paper, *Proceedings of the IEEE*, Vol. 74, No. 6, 1986.

——— and Charles Honorton, "A Joint Communiqué: The Psi Ganzfeld Controversy," in Ganzfeld Debate Responses, above.

Inglis, Brian, *Natural and Supernatural. A History of the Paranormal*, Hodder and Stoughton, 1977.

——— *Science and Parascience. A History of the Paranormal, 1914-1939*, Hodder and Stoughton, 1984.

Jahn, Robert G, and Brenda J. Dunne, "On the Quantum Mechanics of Consciousness, with Application to Anomalous Phenomena," *Foundations of Physics*, Vol. 16, No. 8, August, 1986.

——— *Margins of Reality. The Role of Consciousness in the Physical World*, Harcourt Brace Jovanovich, 1987.

Jahn, R. G., Y. H. Dobyns, B. J. Dunne, "Count Population Profiles in Engineering Anomalies Experiments," Technical Note PEAR 91001, Princeton University School of Engineering and Applied Science, July, 1991.

Kanthamani, B. K. and K. R. Rao, Personality characteristics of ESP subjects, a *Journal of Parapsychology* series:
"I. Primary Personality Characteristics and ESP," Vol. 35, 1971, 189-207.
"II. The Combined Personality Measure (CPM) and ESP," Vol. 36, 1972, 56-70.
"III. Extraversion and ESP," Vol. 36, 1972, 198-212.
"IV. Neuroticism and ESP," Vol. 37, 1973 (a), 37-50.
"V. Graphic expansiveness and ESP," Vol. 37, 1973 (b), 119-129.

Keil, Jürgen, "How a Skeptic Misrepresents the Research with Stepanek: A Review of Martin Gardner's *How Not to Test a Psychic,*" *Journal of Parapsychology*, Vol. 54, June 1990, pp. 151-67.

Kennedy, J.E., "Redundancy in Psi Information, Implications for the Goal-Oriented Hypothesis and for the Application of Psi," *Journal of Parapsychology*. 43, 1979.

——— "The Capricious, Actively Evasive, Unsustainable Nature of Psi : A Summary and Hypotheses," *Journal of Parapsychology*, 67, 2003, 53-74.

McClenon, James, *Deviant Science. The Case of Parapsychology*, University of Pennsylvania Press, 1984.

Marks, David, and Richard Kammann, *The Psychology of the Psychic*, Prometheus Books, 1980.

May, Edwin C., Victor Rubel, and Loyd Auerbach, *ESP WARS: East and West: An Account of the Military Use of Psychic Espionage as Narrated by the Key Russian and American Players*, CreateSpace, 2014.

May, Edwin C., and Sonali Bhatt Marwaha, *Anomalous Cognition: Remote Viewing Research and Theory*, McFarland, 2014.

——— *Extrasensory Perception: Support, Skepticism, and Science*, Praeger, 2015

Michie, D. and D.J. West, "A Mass ESP Test using Television," *Journal of the Society for Psychical Research*, Vol. 39, 1957.

Milton, J., "Mass ESP: a meta-analysis of mass-media recruitment ESP studies," *Thirty Seventh Annual Convention of the Parapsychological Association*, 1994, pp. 284-292.

Musso, J.R. & Granero, M., "Group Gesp experiments tending to yield repeated positive results, Research in Parapsychology," *Abstracts and papers from the Twenty-Fourth Annual Convention of the Parapsychological Association*, The Scarecrow Press, 1981, pp. 100-103

Nelson, R. D., G. J. Bradish, Y. H. Dobyns, "Random Event Generator Qualification, Calibration, and Analysis," Technical Note PEAR 89001, Princeton University School of Engineering and Applied Science, April, 1989.

Nelson, R. D., and Y. H. Dobyns, "Analysis of Variance of REG Experiments: Operator Intention, Secondary Parameters, Database Structure," Technical Note PEAR 91004, Princeton University School of Engineering and Applied Science, December, 1991.

"Outline of CIA Project on ESP," 1952 memorandum retrieved under Freedom of Information Act, in Martin Ebon, *Psychic Warfare—Threat or Illusion*, McGraw-Hill, 1983.

Palmer, John A., Charles Honorton, and Jessica Utts, "Reply to the National Research Council Study on Parapsychology," Parapsychology Association, Inc, N.C., 1989.

"Parapsychology Debate and Peer Commentary," in *Behavioral and Brain Sciences*, Vol. 10, 1987, pp. 539-643.

Pratt, J. G., "Analysis of the Data from the Zenith Radio Experiments, September , 1937 to January, 1938. Typescript, 1938,

——— "The Variance for Multiple-Calling ESP Data," *Journal of Parapsychology*, Vol. 18, 1954.

——— "A decade of research with a selected ESP subject: an Overview and Re-appraisal of the work with Pavel Stepanek," *Proceedings of the American Society for Psychical Research*, Vol. 30, 1973.

——— and J.B. Rhine, Burke M. Smith, Charles E. Stuart and Joseph E. Greenwood, *ESP After Sixty Years*, Boston: Bruce Humphries, 1940.

Puthoff, H. E., "Calculator-assisted psi amplification," in *Research in Parapsychology, 1984*, ed. R. A. White and J. Solfvin, Scarecrow Press, 1985, pp. 48-51.

——— *et al*, "Calculator-assisted psi amplification II," in *Research in Parapsychology, 1985*, ed. D. H. Weiner and D.J. Radin, Scarecrow Press, 1986, pp. 73-6.

Radin, Dean "Enhancing Effects in Psi Experiments with Sequential Analysis: A Replication and Extension," *European Journal of Parapsychology*, Vol. 8, pp. 98-111, 1990-91.

"Report of a Workshop on Experimental Parapsychology," International Security and Commerce Program, Office of Technology Assessment, United States Congress, February 22, 1989.

Reswick, J. B., and L. Vodovnik, "Communication by Means of ESP," Engineering Design Center, Case Institute of Technology, August, 1965.

——— (with Vodovnik erroneously given as Vodonik), "Telepathy—Did It Happen?" *Analog,* November 1969, pp. 48-60.

Rhine, J. B., "The Precognition of Computer Numbers in a Public Test," *Journal of Parapsychology*, Vol. 26, 1962.

——— "Psi-Missing Re-Examined," *Journal of Parapsychology*, Vol. 33, 1969.

Rýzl, Milan, "A Model of Parapsychological Communication," *Journal of Parapsychology*, Vol. 30, 1966.

Schmeidler, Gertrude R., and R. A. McDonnell, *ESP and Personality Patterns*, Yale University Press, 1958.

Schwartz, Stephan A., *The Secret Vaults of Time*, Hampton Roads Publishing, updated 2005.

——— *The Alexandria Project,* Authors' Guild, 1983, updated 2001.

——— *Opening to the Infinite*, Neemoseen Media, 2007.

Scott, C., "An Appendix to 'The Repeated Guessing Technique'," *International Journal of Parapsychology*, Vol. 2, 1960.

Smith, Christopher Carson, Darrell Laham and Garret Moddel, "Stock Market Prediction Using Associative Remote Viewing by Inexperienced Remote Viewers," *Journal of Scientific Exploration*, Vol. 28, No. 1, pp. 7–16, 2014.

Taetszch, Robert, "Design of a Psi Communication System," *International Journal of Parapsychology*, Vol. 4, 1962.

Targ, Russell, *The Reality of ESP: A Physicist's Proof of Psychic Abilities,* Quest Books, 2012.

Targ, Russell, and Harold Puthoff, *Mind-Reach. Scientists Look at Psychic Ability*, Jonathan Cape, 1977.

Tart, Charles T., *Learning To Use Extrasensory Perception,* University of Chicago Press, 1976.

——— *PSI. Scientific Studies of the Psychic Realm*, E. D. Dutton, 1977.

Thouless, Robert H., "The Repeated-Guessing Technique," *International Journal of Parapsychology*, Vol. 2, No. 3, 1960.

——— *From Anecdote to Experiment in Psychical Research*, Routledge & Kegan Paul, 1972.

——— and Robert M. Brier, "The Stacking Effect and Methods of Correcting for It," *Journal of Parapsychology*, Vol. 34, 1970.

Turner, Nigel E., "Lottery Ticket Preferences as Indicated by the Variation in the Number of Winners," *J. Gambling Studies*, published online 3 January 2010:
DOI 10.1007/s10899-009-9171-7

Ullman, Montague, Stanley Krippner and Alan Vaughan, *Dream Telepathy: Experiments in Nocturnal Extrasensory Perception*, 1975, reprinted Hampton Roads, 2003.

Vaughan, Alan, *Patterns of Prophecy*, Turnstone, 1974.

Walach, Harald, "Mind-Matter Interactions—on the Rollercoaster from Data to Theory and Back again," Proceedings of the 10th Bial Foundations Symposium *Behind and Beyond the Brain*, 2014.

Wendell, John P., "More on Jahn's Statistics," *Skeptical Inquirer*, Vol. 16., No. 1, Fall, 1991, pp. 89-90.

Wolman, Benjamin B., ed, *Handbook of Parapsychology*, Van Nostrand Reinhold Company, 1977.

Woolley. V.J., "The Broadcasting Experiment in Mass-Telepathy," *Proceedings of the Society for Psychical Research*, Part 105, 1928.

Zilberman, Mark S., "Public Numerical Lotteries—An International Parapsychological Experiment Covering a Decade: A Data Analysis of French and Soviet Numerical Lotteries," *Journal of the Society for Psychical Research*, Vol 60 # 838 pp. 149-60, 1995.

About the Author

Damien Broderick holds an interdisciplinary PhD in the discourses of the sciences and literature, analyzing the semiotic strategies of the Two Cultures. He has published, edited and co-edited more than 60 books, ranging from cultural and literary theory to the future of technologies. His popular science book *The Spike* was the first study of the Technological Singularity, now a major topic. *The Last Mortal Generation* looked at the prospects of medical and engineering approaches to radical life extension, and *Year Million* reached forward to possible distant futures using the tools of both scientific rigor and disciplined imagination.

He has published a number of prize-winning science fiction novels, and received the 2005 Distinguished Scholarship Award from the International Association for the Fantastic in the Arts. A clear-eyed interest in paranormal phenomena (psi) led Broderick to re-investigate old studies that were abandoned too quickly, and to develop several important experiments of his own in the application of precognition (awareness of the future) to real-world tasks.

One of these, reported in *The Lotto Effect*, studied some 800 million guesses at lottery winning numbers. Another forecast horse race winners using a newspaper test, discussed in this book for the first time. His book on the vexed scientific status of parapsychology, *Outside the Gates of Science*, was followed by *Evidence for Psi*, co-edited with Ben Goertzel, PhD. *Knowing the Unknowable* is the first popular treatment of an overlooked approach to psi application, the use of redundancy ("repeated guessing") filtered by majority vote techniques.

Index

Surinam Turtle Press is the boutique press created by novelist Richard A. Lupoff, under the auspices of publisher Fender Tucker's **RAMBLE HOUSE**.

This book is available at Amazon, though if you order through Amazon you will be charged $20.00 plus shipping.

If you order directly from Fender Tucker at

fender@ramblehouse.com

he will give you a discount and free shipping.
(Shipping charges may apply for overseas orders.)

Made in the USA
Columbia, SC
05 November 2018